Polly Plum

Polly Plum

A FIRM AND EARNEST WOMAN'S ADVOCATE

Mary Ann Colclough
1836–1885

JENNY COLEMAN

OTAGO

This book is dedicated to my dear sister Andrea,
a firm and earnest woman's advocate.

Published by Otago University Press
Level 1, 398 Cumberland Street
Dunedin, New Zealand
university.press@otago.ac.nz
www.otago.ac.nz/press

First published 2017
Copyright © Jenny Coleman

The moral rights of the author have been asserted

ISBN 978-0-947522-47-6

Editor: Paula Wagemaker

Cover photograph: Mary Ann Colclough. Private Family Collection.

Printed in China by Asia Pacific Offset

Contents

ACKNOWLEDGEMENTS

I would like to extend a special thank you to Judy Malone (née Elphick) whose research first introduced me to 'Polly Plum' and who shares with me the respect for her feistiness, passion and commitment to the cause of women. Judy's enthusiastic encouragement through private correspondence early in this project is greatly appreciated. Special thanks are also extended to Mary Ann Colclough's great-granddaughter Sue McTaggart for introducing me to elderly relatives, for sharing material from private family collections, and for permission to reproduce photographs.

I am grateful for the financial assistance I have received through the Massey University Research Fund toward archival and newspaper-based research in London, Melbourne and Auckland, and for assistance from the School of Sociology, Social Policy and Social Work; the School of People, Environment and Planning; and the Pro Vice-Chancellor's Office in the College of Humanities and Social Sciences.

I would like to acknowledge the support I have received from the following institutions: Alexander Turnbull Library, Wellington; Archives New Zealand, Auckland and Christchurch branches; Auckland Research Centre, Auckland City Library; Baillieu Library, University of Melbourne; Documentary Research Centre, Canterbury Museum, Christchurch; Family Records Centre, London; Guildhall Library, City of London; Islington Local History Centre, London; Islington Museum, London; Massey University Library; Papers Past Collection, National Library of New Zealand; Public Record Office, London; Public Records Office, Melbourne; Queen's College Archives, Harley Street, London; State Library of Victoria, Melbourne; the British Library, Aldermanbury, London;

Victoria University of Wellington Library, Wellington; the Women's Library, London Metropolitan University.

I would also like to thank the following individuals for their assistance: academic colleagues at various Women Writing Away writing retreats at the Tauhara Centre in Acacia Bay; Miss Margaret Connell (principal, Queen's College, London); the late Anna Greening (archivist at Queen's College, London); and my brothers Peter and John for assistance in locating photographs. A very special thank you is extended to Rachel Scott (Otago University Press) for her enthusiasm in publishing this biography; to the various anonymous readers who provided engaged and constructive comments on earlier drafts; and to Paula Wagemaker whose close editing of the manuscript has really enhanced the work. My final thank you is to my partner and indefatigable research assistant, Mary Nettle, for her love and support.

Jenny Coleman
JANUARY 2017

INTRODUCTION

Polly Plum and the 'High and Holy' Cause of Women

'I am well known and everywhere known as a firm and earnest woman's advocate, and I am content and grateful to be so considered' – so declared Polly Plum in 1871. The woman behind the pseudonym was Mary Ann Colclough (pronounced 'Cokely'), described by a major Auckland newspaper in the early 1870s as 'the best abused woman in New Zealand of the present day'. At the height of her influence, Polly Plum was caricatured in poems, lampooned in plays and criticised in the columns of the daily newspapers for her unswerving advocacy for the cause of women. Although she was recognised by her contemporaries as an advanced social thinker, her contribution over the years to girls' education, women's rights and a range of social reforms was largely forgotten. By the centenary of women's suffrage in New Zealand in 1993, she was described as one of the few isolated early voices whose ideas, although read and discussed, 'did not prompt widespread agitation, sudden changes in the law or even a sustained debate on the position of women'.[1]

In many respects, Mary Ann Colclough was an isolated voice, but she was by no means a solitary voice. As part of an established international network, she was appointed in the early 1870s to the Ladies' Vigilant Society of England to act on their behalf by championing the cause of women. She also had contacts in America. Furthermore, like her contemporaries Mary Ann Müller in Nelson and Maria Rye who visited New Zealand in the early 1860s, and like the next generation of feminists headed by Kate Sheppard, Mary Ann Colclough was part of a reciprocal flow of information about the international women's movement which ensured that New Zealand was at the forefront of developments.[2]

Recorded in the 1966 *Encyclopaedia of New Zealand* as 'one of the earliest, and certainly among the most talented, feminist leaders in this country', it was not until the emergence of women's history in the 1970s that Mary Ann Colclough was rediscovered. At that time biographical detail was sketchy, but her actions and writings under the *nom de plume* Polly Plum have been acknowledged in histories of New Zealand feminism. Today, our more detailed knowledge of her life and activism warrants a reassessment of her contribution to the women's movement and to broader agendas for social reform. Her writings and activism may not have prompted widespread agitation for change in the ways associated with the massive suffrage petitions of the 'first wave' of feminism in the 1890s, or the large-scale protests and rallies of the 'second wave' of feminism in the 1970s, but her advocacy for women and her particular stamp of philanthropy did make a difference.[3]

More of a vanguard than a leader, Mary Ann Colclough has generally been depicted as a lone battler in the cause of women, but her legacy is clear. Two months after Mary Ann's death in 1885, Mrs Mary Clement Leavitt, a delegate from the Women's Christian Temperance Union in America, held a series of public gospel temperance meetings in Christchurch as part of her extensive New Zealand tour. Notably, one of the additional afternoon sessions she held for ladies was on the topic of 'organisation'. Mrs Leavitt's tour was a significant historical moment for the women's movement. She was constantly met with large and enthusiastic audiences highly receptive to the aims of promoting temperance, social reform and social purity through Christian values. In *Standing in the Sunshine: A history of New Zealand women since they won the vote*, Sandra Coney attributes the successful establishment of branches of the Women's Christian Temperance Union throughout the country to the fact that an awareness of women's rights already existed.

Mary Ann Colclough was instrumental in this process. Her advocacy of the cause of women was a key part of an earlier phase of the women's movement, one in which individual women such as Maria Rye in her work with female immigrants, Mary Ann Müller writing on the female franchise, and Learmonth Whyte Dalrymple endeavouring to establish higher education for girls, were working towards increasing public awareness of women's situation and making real changes in the daily lives of women and girls. Mary Ann Colclough's role in this early phase was even more significant. Through her writing and lecturing, which was reported in newspapers throughout the country, as well as through the practical assistance she provided to countless women and their families, she facilitated the development of what would now be recognised as a feminist consciousness.

The generation of feminists who campaigned for women's suffrage targeted a readership of like-minded women. Mary Ann Colclough preferred to engage directly with public opinion by presenting her arguments for women's rights in the columns of the daily newspapers. She produced lengthy polemics on women's employment, legal position and education, and on married women's property rights and political representation. She also engaged one to one with her readership and, importantly, her critics through the letters to the editor columns. This use of newspapers to convey her ideas lent immediacy to her analysis of women's position and stands in contrast to the more rehearsed arguments expounded by many of the leading temperance feminist writers who contributed articles to journals such as *The Prohibitionist* and *The White Ribbon* in the late 1880s and early 1890s. The reprinting of many of Mary Ann's articles and letters in the 'For the Ladies' columns of the *Weekly News* conferred a legitimate reading space for women in the privacy of their own homes.

In addition to engaging in newspaper journalism and correspondence, Mary Ann broke with accepted conventions and took her cause to the public platform in a deliberate attempt to influence people. In these ventures, her intelligent, fluent and eloquent manner stood her in good stead. Although she had more than her share of critics and detractors, her adherence to middle-class conventions of social respectability and her insistence that women's first and highest duty was to their roles as wives and mothers moderated her opponents' criticisms and lent a high degree of reasonableness to her message.

Mary Ann Colclough is also significant as one of New Zealand's earliest published female authors and newspaper journalists. Although some of her fictional work is no longer extant and articles paid for and published in English and American journals in the 1860s have proven untraceable, her 1866 novel *Alone in the World* is one of the earliest published in New Zealand by a female author. Her newspaper journalism for Auckland's *Daily Southern Cross* dating from the late 1860s also makes her one of the earliest paid female journalists in New Zealand.[4]

In addition to her international networks, Mary Ann Colclough was well connected to, and respected by, many influential high-ranking men within the churches, local and central government and the education and justice systems. She not only drew their attention to the inadequate conditions within the Auckland Lunatic Asylum and Mount Eden Gaol, but also, as did Mary Ann

Müller, constantly lobbied these influential men. A member of the Auckland Provincial Council took up her proposal that private facilities be established at the Auckland Lunatic Asylum, and many of the issues she raised in relation to the administration of the asylum were acted upon after completion of the 1872 inquiry into the Auckland Asylum.

Above all, Mary Ann Colclough led by example. Whether it was ensuring she was fully informed of her legal entitlements and negotiating these with school committees, employing young women as 'helps' rather than servants in the household, or accepting women in need into the safety of her own home, she continually challenged gendered and class-based social and economic hierarchies in favour of radical solutions. Her ability to challenge was particularly evident in her approach to philanthropy. Rather than follow the traditional model that tended to cement class-based divisions and rankings within society, Mary Ann drew attention to the causes of women's poverty and assisted women to become independent.

For as long as women have asserted themselves as individuals and demanded recognition of their rights and abilities, they have endured censure, criticism and often hostile abuse. The often-cited early English feminist Mary Wollstonecraft, for example, was dubbed a hyena in petticoats and a philosophical wanton. Mary Ann met with similar hostility. She was called an 'irrepressible busybody', reproached for disseminating pestilent and foolish notions and accused of finding a 'vent for [her] spleen in stirring up discontent in the bosoms of the fairer and more amiable' of her sex. Under her writing persona Polly Plum, she dismissed such hostility, joking that 'Plums' grow the better for pruning, and insisting that those who exist through the good opinion of society have to follow and cannot lead. She learned first-hand that forfeiting one's social status took courage.[5]

As a woman of neither means nor leisure, Mary Ann Colclough attributed her own chequered life to having placed her in a position to see the daily reality of the lives of many kinds of women. From an early age she had been aware of how unfairly society treats women, and as a young adult she began following the ideas and actions of the women's movements in England and America. It was reading John Stuart Mill's highly influential treatise *The Subjection of Women* that converted her whole-heartedly to the cause of women. She viewed herself as a missionary engaged in God's service by advocating on behalf of her fellow sisters.

Mary Ann's commitment was unequivocal. In addition to undertaking full-time work as a teacher, she wrote regularly for the *Daily Southern Cross* (Auckland) and was a voluminous correspondent to the letters to the editor columns. She presented public lectures, was active in the temperance cause, and was a regular visitor to the Auckland Lunatic Asylum and the Mount Eden Gaol. She often looked after young children whose mothers were either in prison or unable to care for them, and she used her own home to provide a receiving house for women on their release from prison until they found employment. With regard to politics, she said: 'It is perhaps needless to say that I belong to the liberal, and, as we believe, the progressive party.'[6]

I first encountered Mary Ann Colclough through the work of Judith Malone (née Elphick) when researching my doctorate in the early 1990s. While determined to write Mary Ann's biography someday, over the intervening 25 years I published a number of scholarly articles on her identity as an advocate of women's rights, her contribution as a female journalist, her role in the emergence of an organised women's movement in New Zealand, and her philanthropy in Auckland and Melbourne. As an academic trained in feminist studies, I was more used to questioning the assumptions and politics of feminist perspectives; learning to set that training aside to provide a readable account of Mary Ann's life has been a challenge. It has taken me many years to develop a sense of the private figure in what became a very public life. I recall the thrill of seeing her name on the head teachers' board at Tuakau School, albeit misspelt as 'Mrs Coakley' (suggesting it was provided from an oral rather than a written source). I also recall my sadness on first reading her death notice in a newspaper and finding out the circumstances of her passing. At the end of my doctoral studies, I went on what felt like a pilgrimage to the cemetery in Picton where she was buried, and experienced a sense of injustice to find neither a headstone nor a record of her plot number, although in fairness the latter is due to a fire in the cemetery records office a few years after her burial.

Unlike the situation with many biographical subjects, there are no significant archival sources or personal letters from which to piece together the details of Mary Ann Colclough's private life. She was connected with women such as Agnes Garrett and Isabella Tod, who were involved in the women's movement in England, but searches in relevant collections in the British Library and the Fawcett Women's Library in London revealed no surviving correspondence. Traces of her involvement with the American women's movement and writings published in an American journal likewise proved elusive. In an article published in 1936, Mary Ann's daughter Mary Louise Wilson referred to letters found in an old desk handwritten to her mother by Sir Julius Vogel, Sir George Higinbotham, Sir Robert Stout and Mr Alfred Deakin over 60 years earlier. Unfortunately, descendants do not know what became of these letters. The many letters Mary Ann received over the years acknowledging her philanthropic work have also not survived.

For the most part, I gleaned personal biographical details from Mary Ann's writings in New Zealand and Melbourne, as well as from newspaper and family sources. Family members recall earlier generations viewing Mary Ann as a meddler – as a woman interfering in a man's world. That she married an Irish remittance man who turned out to be a gambler was one thing, but her insistence on trumpeting the cause of women did her no favours in family eyes. It is possibly just as well that descendants were not aware that she was declared bankrupt in the mid-1870s. In a family with more than its share of accountants and bankers, this event would likely have been seen as her own inability to manage money rather than understood as the outcome of years of struggling financially, initially to compensate for her husband being an incompetent provider, but later as a widow with young children to support at a time when there were limited employment opportunities for women and no state benefits for widows.

Fortunately, rich newspaper sources have compensated for the paucity of private papers. Because Mary Ann was a regular columnist for the *Daily Southern Cross*, her articles engendered many responses from readers, and she was frequently the subject of newspaper editorials. For me, accessing those newspaper sources required many laborious hours in front of manual microfilm readers, but the advent of digitised newspaper collections over recent years has enabled a more thorough appreciation of the extent of her influence, both throughout New Zealand and in Australia. These enhanced newspaper sources provided me with a greater opportunity to capture Mary Ann's own thoughts and ideas, albeit written for a public audience. Where possible, I have deliberately privileged her words throughout the biography. Likewise, I have also tried to convey a sense of how her contemporaries responded to her ideas and actions through citations from correspondence to the newspapers. I have attempted to use notes sparingly, combining sources for direct quotations, archival sources and significant reference material in a single note at the end of a paragraph. Further contextual material is included in an extensive bibliography.

I have often wondered had Mary Ann and I been contemporaries whether we would have been political allies or perhaps even friends. Most certainly our shared commitment to women and to challenging social inequities would have seen us meet at many a political rally. I can imagine inching my way to the front of the hall after one of her lectures on 'The Subjection of Women', mustering courage to introduce myself and holding my voice steady to acknowledge and thank her for her bravery and strength in speaking out publicly. Perhaps with the courage engendered by anonymity, I would have felt compelled to write to the editor of the *Daily Southern Cross*, aligning myself with Mary Ann's views on girls' education and the rights of women. If Mary Ann were alive today, I think she would have been a stalwart feminist active in the Women's Studies Association and probably national president of the National Council of Women. Then again, she may have entered politics, been principal of the most prestigious girls' school in the country, edited her own feminist journal, become ordained as a minister, or, perhaps, she may even have become a professor in women's studies.

CHAPTER ONE

From Clerkenwell to Auckland

Late in the afternoon of 12 December 1857, Mary Ann Barnes, 21 years old, disembarked from the *Eastfield* at the port of Auckland. She was penniless and alone in the world. The anticipation she had held just over four months earlier, departing from London with her brother James to begin an independent life in the antipodes, had been replaced with a quiet desperation. After only 19 days at sea, 17-year-old James had died. The official cause of death was recorded as diarrhoea, but the circumstances leading to his death were surrounded with suspicion. To make matters worse, as the ship berthed in Auckland, Mary Ann discovered that the substantial sum of money she and James had saved for their new life was nowhere to be found. She had been led to believe the *Eastfield*'s captain had the money in safe keeping, but rumour had it that James, known to be a gambler of sorts, had squandered it during the passage.[1]

The voyage had started with promise. Under the steerage of Captain John Copland, the 412-ton (373 tonne) barque *Eastfield* had cleared St Katherine's Dock and received her 39 passengers at Gravesend. Bound for New Zealand, Mary Ann and James were travelling in the second cabin along with 15 other passengers. Conditions were not as spacious as those in the main cabin, but they were comfortable. The weather throughout the voyage – hot, with light variable winds – slowed the passage to the equator, so taking the ship 51 days to reach this destination. Another 65 days travelling around the Cape of Good Hope ensued before those aboard *Eastfield* sighted the southern point of Tasmania, and another four days passed before the ship anchored in Auckland harbour. Although the voyage was generally pleasant and agreeable for most on board, two other families experienced tragedy. Minian Redling, an infant travelling with his family in the steerage section, died on 29 September, and Mrs Susan Edmonstone, who had been ill throughout the passage, died on 4 October.[2]

Throughout the voyage, Captain Copland had been a paragon of consideration in attending to the needs of his passengers. In admiration for his ability as a captain, Mary Ann joined the other passengers in signing her name to a letter extending their thanks:

> *Auckland, New Zealand, Dec 12, 1857.*
>
> *Dear Sir, – We the undersigned passengers on board your ship, the Eastfield, from London to Auckland, in taking leave of you at the close of our prosperous voyage, beg to tender to you our united thanks for your uniform kindness and attention to us all, during the whole of the time we have been under your charge.*
>
> *We further desire to express to you our perfect satisfaction with all which has been done by you for us, during the passage, and we consider ourselves particularly fortunate in having been placed under the care of so trustworthy and able a man.*
>
> *We all join in wishing Mrs. Copland, yourself, and little daughter many years of happiness, and sincerely trust that you may have a speedy and prosperous voyage back to Old England.*[3]

The high esteem with which the passengers of the *Eastfield* held their captain quelled even a hint of suspicion that he had any involvement in the disappearance of Mary Ann and James's savings.

Born in the Parish of St James, Clerkenwell, in Middlesex, England, on 20 February 1836 and baptised on 16 March at Pentonville Chapel, Mary Ann Barnes was the first child of John Thomas Barnes and Suzanne de la Porquêt (known as Susan). Mary Ann's grandfather, John Barnes of Barnesbury Road, Barnesbury Square in London, had married the Comtesse de la Porquêt. Their son John, Mary Ann's father, married his mother's niece. By the time Mary Ann was just over five years old, she had three brothers, John, Thomas and James, and a baby sister, Louisa. Her mother had the assistance of two female servants, an elderly nurse, and extended family at close hand to the family's residence at 20 Penton Place. Paternal grandparents John and Sarah Barnes lived just a few doors down at number 27, and living one door along from them was Mary Ann's uncle Joseph, aunt Elizabeth and cousin Sarah, who was two years older than Mary Ann. Uncle Edward, Aunt Eliza and Mary Ann's cousins Eliza Ann and Lucy

Sarah lived a couple of blocks away at 54 Collier Street, while Uncle William and Aunt Frances also lived close by in the neighbourhood.[4]

Penton Place (now known as Penton Rise) could be described as respectable working middle class. Clerkenwell, a vibrant district and, in many respects, a microcosm of London's history, was associated throughout the eighteenth century with public and charitable institutions, including schools, hospitals and prisons. It was also a major centre for various trades. By the early decades of the nineteenth century, however, Clerkenwell had developed a rather mixed reputation due to its strong radical and intellectual tradition and industrial heritage – a background that would have a significant influence on Mary Ann's life.[5]

Before Clerkenwell became primarily a residential area, it was a fashionable resort for Londoners who enjoyed its spas, tea gardens and theatres. However, as with any district, Clerkenwell had its dark side. On Bowling Green Lane, just a mile or so from Mary Ann's home, stood Clerkenwell House of Detention, a facility that held prisoners awaiting trial. Across the way, in Coldbath Fields, Clerkenwell Gaol housed prisoners on short sentences. Increasing public drunkenness and loutish behaviour in what was still largely a rural area meant that patrons at the famous Sadler's Wells Theatre often needed to be escorted after dark to ensure their safe travel back to central London.

The opening years of the nineteenth century were a period of growth and expansion for the district. The first national census conducted in 1801 recorded the population of Clerkenwell as 23,000. A decade later, that number had risen to 31,000. The ending of the French wars of the latter decades of the eighteenth century led to a building boom that irrevocably changed the face of nearly every neighbourhood. For Mary Ann's grandfather, father and uncles working in the building trade, the boom meant relatively lucrative times.[6]

At the centre of the village was Clerkenwell Green, immortalised in Dickens' *Oliver Twist* as the site of the busy market where Fagin and the Artful Dodger initiated Oliver into the art of pick-pocketing. For years, streams of fattened animals had plodded their way down St John Street to the Green on Sunday nights ready for market day on Monday. By the late 1840s the Green was a favourite meeting place of radical groups such as the Chartists, many of whom were local workers in the printing trade. They actively campaigned for extending voting rights for men. Clerkenwell Green was also the scene of the famous demonstration in April 1848, the year renowned for its revolutions, when around 3000 protesters gathered as part of many groups mobilising for a mass rally intent on marching to parliament to petition for democratic reforms such as universal manhood suffrage and the secret ballot in elections.

Entertainment for the literary-minded was close at hand. During Mary Ann's childhood, adaptations of Dickens' *A Christmas Carol* and *The Old Curiosity Shop* featured at Sadler's Wells, and from the mid-1840s the theatre hosted a successful Shakespeare season. Literary connections abounded. Tom Paine was said to have written parts of *The Rights of Man* at the old Angel Inn on the corner of what is now Islington High Street and Pentonville Road, and at the Red Lion on St John Street. Early feminist writer Mary Wollstonecraft and her husband William Godwin as well as essayist Charles Lamb had temporary residence in Clerkenwell. It was also the birthplace of influential philosopher and politician John Stuart Mill, to whom Mary Ann would later attribute her conversion to the cause of women.[7]

An avid reader of Dickens, Mary Ann would have found her enjoyment of his works heightened by his many references to her local neighbourhood. Clerkenwell was the home of characters such as Jarvis Lorry, the clerk at Tellson's Bank in *A Tale of Two Cities*, Mr Pancks from *Little Dorritt*, and Mr Pickwick, who lodged on Goswell Road. Clerkenwell was also the location of the Golden Key, Gabriel Varden's locksmith shop in *Barnaby Rudge*. St Luke's Workhouse on the corner of City Road and Shepherdess Walk gained mention in *David Copperfield*.

From her own account, it would appear that Mary Ann had a heightened sense of what was happening around her. As an adult she recalled: 'I have never been more wretched at the greatest trials of life than I can well remember being at some of the troubles of my childhood.' Even though the causes were, from her adult eyes, trifles, they were the source of 'dread, sorrow, and disappointment' for Mary Ann the child. The actual events that led her to make this reflection are not known, and although her childhood was at a time when infant and maternal mortality rates were steadily declining, there were definitely sad times. When Mary Ann was 11 years of age, a violent thunderstorm resulted in widespread flooding of the Fleet River, which ran through Clerkenwell. The cellars in nearby Farringdon Street were flooded, and the road at King's Cross remained unpassable for several days. The tide of water carried away furniture, cattle and even three houses. In addition, Mary Ann's cousin Sophia died when just three and a half years old. Sixteen months later, Mary Ann's Aunt Frances died giving birth to her daughter Elizabeth, leaving Mary Ann's uncle William to raise the couple's five children on his own.[8]

In the autumn of 1848, when Mary Ann was 12, a cholera epidemic raged through the over-populated areas of Greater London. Authorities traced the outbreak to seaman John Harold, newly arrived from Germany, who died within a few hours of being seized with violent vomiting, diarrhoea and stomach pains. No one understood at the time that cholera is a water-borne disease and that a major source of the contagion was the Thames River. The epidemic and the commonly held belief that the disease was caused by breathing in air polluted with waste led to an atmosphere of constant fear for those living in and around the city with its heavily polluted waterways. Posters with remedies appeared on shop windows in every district. Fortunately for Mary Ann's family, the section of the Fleet River that ran through the now densely populated Clerkenwell had been covered. Although Clerkenwell had an average of eight people per household, the district's slightly higher elevation and its less polluted water supply from the New River, which was a tributary to the Thames, meant the district experienced relatively few deaths from cholera.

Although no records of Mary Ann's early education are extant, she described, in desultory terms, her early schooling as being firmly within the tradition that favoured rote learning, including columns upon columns of spelling. She was fortunate that her parents believed in the importance of a good education for girls. The census of 1851 listed all of Mary Ann's sisters (including Ellen, born in 1842, and Alice, born in 1846) as scholars. By this time the family had shifted just around the corner from their former home to Clarence Place. John Barnes' carpentry and building business was thriving to the extent that he was now employing 32 men and four boys, including Mary Ann's eldest brother John, who worked in an office position for the business.

One memory Mary Ann recalled from when she was, in her words, 'a little girl', related to her mother's friend who had a private school for young ladies near London. This friend had been born into a family of several generations of clergy, and the school catered almost exclusively for clergymen's daughters. As well as engaging in the traditional pursuit of knowledge with its focus on reading, writing and arithmetic that formed the basis of most school education, the young ladies of the school received instruction in every aspect of domestic work and home management, from cooking, sewing, washing, ironing and attending to their own wardrobe through to acquiring a basic knowledge of domestic medicine. The latter sometimes required the young women to accompany their teacher on errands of mercy, to attend to the sick and even assist with the dressing of wounds. There was rarely a vacancy in the school, a fact that Mary Ann saw as indicative of the good sense of the clergy of the Church of England. To her mind, the clergy, as a body, was obviously committed to providing a thorough education for their daughters.[9]

From the age of 15, Mary Ann attended the prestigious Queen's College in Harley Street, London, about two and a half miles (four kilometres) from the family home. Described as perhaps the best-conducted educational institute for females in England at the time, Queen's College had opened in 1848 as an offshoot of the Governesses' Benevolent Institution. Two prominent leaders of the Christian Socialist movement, Frederick Maurice and John Malcolm Ludlow, along with Charles Kingsley (better known as the author of *The Water Babies*), believed that the only way to improve the economic position of governesses was for them to receive superior education as teachers. In 1847, Maurice, previously professor of English history and literature at King's College, London, and now professor of theology, organised a series of 'Lectures for Ladies' by various King's professors. These attracted so much interest from pupils as well as the governesses that Maurice and his friends founded Queen's College. Queen Victoria was known to be a strong supporter of education for girls, and when one of her ladies-in-waiting, Miss Murray, aroused the sovereign's interest in the college, Victoria unhesitatingly granted permission for the use of her name. This nominal royal patronage went some way toward deflecting criticisms from those who considered a college for women both unladylike and a threat to social proprieties.[10]

Queen's College was located at 43–49 Harley Street in four adjoining four-storey terrace houses, which together presented a maze of over 100 rooms and 30 staircases. Two of the houses were in white stone and featured impressively ornate cast-iron balustrades. The staircases still carry the chatter and bustle of young women students to this day. Harley Street was, as it continues to be, an expensive upmarket area inhabited by the upper middle class. Over the years it has been home to a number of distinguished residents, including Horatio Nelson's widow Frances, the Duke of Wellington, the Victorian Liberal prime minister William Gladstone, and various admirals, dukes and literary figures. Florence Nightingale received her first training at a small hospital housed in what was then number 45. She later opened a hospital at number 90 Harley Street.

The college initially offered preparatory classes for girls between the ages of nine and 12, and evening lectures and music lessons for governesses already in stations but who were unable to attend during the day. Available records suggest that Mary Ann was in this latter category, attending evening lectures while working as a governess in a private home in the morning and afternoon. Because she was already engaged in tuition, she could attend the evening classes and sit the examinations without paying a fee. It is not clear how long she studied at Queen's College, but she attained a third-class English certificate.

The college admitted students of all denominations. However, because it was a strictly Church of England institution, its professors were, with only one or two exceptions, Church of England clergy seconded from nearby King's College. The Queen's College curriculum was expansive and included theology, moral, mental and natural philosophy, modern and ancient history, English literature, composition and grammar, reading, geography, arithmetic, mathematics, ancient and modern languages (including Latin, German, French and Italian), drawing, figure and landscape painting, vocal and instrumental music, and instruction in the art of teaching.[11]

The college also followed a non-competitive educational philosophy that rejected the usual systems of rewards and punishments. The primary teaching method involved professors delivering lectures and setting essays for correction, much like practice in a modern-day university. Essays were expected to contain original individual thought and not contain borrowed or unacknowledged ideas from others. Possibly with a view to preparing pupils for careers in journalism, the college also taught the art of paragraph writing. A later student of Queen's, reflecting on her long apprenticeship in mastering paragraphs, noted that the exercise was 'a most useful form of training, since a smart paragraphist, who must necessarily be versatile and range over almost every topic from theology and politics to the latest craze … acquires a facility which renders it as easy to write a leading article as a note upon any given subject'. Mary Ann certainly put this skill to excellent use in her early days as a journalist for Auckland's *Daily Southern Cross* when she wrote paragraphs on topics targeting a female readership such as music, novels and women writers, shopping and preparing a trousseau.[12]

The pupils at Queen's College were strictly supervised by Lady Visitors, whose ranks were made up of intellectually minded ladies of appropriate social standing. These women acted as chaperones in accordance with the etiquette of the day. College pupils could not sit and learn within the presence of a professor unless they were married or unless a single woman of advanced years was in attendance. In setting an example of social poise combined with an intelligent sense of responsibility toward the issues of the day, the Lady Visitors made clear to pupils that acquisition of this demeanour was an important part of the educational philosophy of Queen's College.

Although Mary Ann was to recall the dread and sorrow of her childhood, many of the events that occurred in London during the years she attended Queen's were full of excitement and spectacle. Thousands of people poured into the city every day on special excursion trains to see the magnificent Crystal Palace built in Hyde Park to house the 1851 Great Exhibition. Containing exhibits from all over the world, over the five months it was open the exhibition attracted six million people, about one third of the population of Britain at the time. A year after the Great Exhibition closed, King's Cross Station opened. Architecturally distinct with its laminated timber beam arches spanning 105 feet in width and 800 feet in length (32m x 243m), the new London terminus for the Great Northern Railway boasted two platforms and 14 tracks.

In March 1854 Britain entered the Crimean War, joining forces with the Ottoman Empire (Turkey), France and the Kingdom of Sardinia against Russia. With the advent of the telegraph, news from war correspondents kept the British public aware of developments on a daily level. For Mary Ann and others who had attended Queen's College, this war came to hold a particular significance because it was when Florence Nightingale, who had run the small private hospital a few doors down from Queen's College, came to prominence, caring for the troops and revolutionising nursing practice in the main British hospital at Scutari in the city of Constantinople.

It is clear from her later writings that Mary Ann was an alert and intelligent child with well-developed powers of observation and a sharp, analytical mind. Growing up at a time when social class was paramount in defining one's place and position in society, she, like all middle-class girls of the era, developed a keen sense of the importance of etiquette and social respectability. The childhood memories she referred to in her adult writings were undoubtedly selective and usually used to impress some moral lesson on her readership. But these writings also indicate that from an early age she developed an awareness of how social snobbery and the pressure to conform to social expectations could lead to very unfair and unfortunate circumstances.

As an adult, Mary Ann recalled the story of two families who lived in her neighbourhood when she was still a young girl. The first family was that of a gentleman employed in some official capacity who had three daughters, whom Mary Ann described as 'dashing', 'elegant' and 'highly accomplished'. After it became known that the father's income was the only money the family had, and although the daughters continued to have male admirers, they received no offers of marriage. When the father died, it was revealed that he was greatly in debt, and there was considerable condemnation of his want of economy and lack of thrift. Mary Ann never found out what became of his daughters.

The second family she recalled was that of the first gentleman's successor, and he also had three daughters. One of these young women worked as chief clerk in a telegraph office and another was a designer for a clothing factory. The third daughter was employed as the servant in her father's home. Mary Ann described the two ladies who travelled into London each day to work as 'unobtrusively and really gentle-women as any ladies I have ever known'. Their parents were comfortable and contented and had even managed to put some of their annual income of £150 away in savings.[13]

When commenting on the contrasting situations of these two families, Mary Ann observed that those who had condemned the first gentleman when his real financial circumstances become public after his death had also refused to leave their calling cards with the second family, believing it low and common for ladies to go out to work. Interestingly, she described the three daughters of the second gentleman's family as the first women's rights advocates she had ever met.

Mary Ann also knew a lawyer's family of five daughters who had all learned the art of writing legal documents. In the mornings and evenings, the daughters took turns in their writing room, which they called their office, to assist their father with his work. As befitted their social standing, they also 'went into society', paid and received calls and oversaw their father's household. Despite the father's concern that he might have to support his daughters, all but one of them married. Acquaintances such as these during Mary Ann's formative years contributed to her eventual strong views on the potential of women to engage in useful and productive activity alongside their duties as daughters, wives and mothers.

Mary Ann's experiences as a young adult also led her to develop a keen sense of how some aspects of social opinion on women's roles were simply unfair. On one occasion she visited a lady friend who had given birth the previous week to her fifth or sixth child. Intending to stay an hour or two, Mary Ann noticed how worn, worried and ill her friend looked. She had no energy or interest for the usual polite topics of conversation. After a while, the friend burst into tears, saying she wished she was stronger and able to be up and about, as her husband and the others in the household never managed very well when she was laid up. Mary Ann's friend rued the fact that only that morning her husband's toast was burnt, his eggs underdone and his drawer not settled in the manner he was used to, at which point, Mary Ann, despite her youth, felt highly indignant. She wanted to box the husband's ears for being so selfish as to worry his wife about his toast and eggs and to give no thought to her pain and weakness during and after giving birth.

Another person who made an impression on Mary Ann was the 'worthy old butcher' her mother used. People called him eccentric because of how he provided for his children. When his sons grew old enough to choose a trade, he gave them money to set up their own businesses. When each of his daughters married, he apportioned them a sum of money, confiding in Mary Ann's mother that it was sufficient 'to keep her and the young 'uns out of the workhouse'. Mary Ann remembered him saying that when his youngest son and daughter left home, he would spend what he had left on himself and his 'old woman'. Proud of his ability to give his children a better beginning in life than he had, he said he would rather strip himself of every penny to provide a good start for them than to have them wish their parents dead for the sake of what they might inherit. She recalled his words frequently expressed to her mother: 'No, ma'am: my sons know they've got all they're ever likely to get; and when the old woman and me take a little snug box at Hampstead or Highgate they can come out and see us free and pleasant.' In Mary Ann's view, if that was what society considered eccentric, she only wished such eccentricity were more common. As a mature adult, Mary Ann often drew, when writing, on the insights she gained through these early experiences of society's expectations of men and women.[14]

Only traces of the historical record about Mary Ann's early employment as a governess and teacher remain, but among those that have been found is an account of another event that had a profound influence on her. The incident happened when she was working as a teacher at Stratford in East London. While there, she heard that an old man who lived in nearby lodgings had beaten his wife to death because she would not give him their last 18 pence, which she had earned by selling watercress. She knew he would use it to buy alcohol. In his own defence, the husband declared that he was sorry he had killed her, but that she shouldn't have angered him when he was drunk. He added that any money she earned was legally his and complained that she always had the upper hand because she earned the money. He had warned her that one day she would refuse him too often and that day had come. The man's daughter, faint and in a wretched state, had been brought into the house in which Mary Ann was staying. The sight of the daughter on her knees, praying for vengeance and promising to go and see her own father hung for dragging her poor mother from decency to the lowest depths of poverty, brought a shudder to Mary Ann every time she recalled the scene. Formative experiences like this one facilitated Mary Ann's lifelong commitment to involvement in philanthropic and charity works. One of the earliest examples of this involvement was as a visitor to several asylums in London.

What led 21-year-old Mary Ann Barnes to decide to immigrate to New Zealand with her brother is not known. The most likely reason was that she, like many other young and educated middle-class women of her time, sought better prospects of employment and, perhaps, marriage. In many respects she was typical of the ever larger group of women in England at the time whom society most unflatteringly referred to as 'redundant women' – well-educated middle-class unmarried women, many of whom desired a life more independent than the narrow and confining options traditionally prescribed for them. The over-supply of governesses in England was a particular concern, and even as early as the late 1840s, various authorities were suggesting that such women should apply to the Governesses Benevolent Institution for financial assistance to emigrate. Colonial governments, private companies and philanthropic societies went to great effort and expense to encourage women to leave Britain and immigrate to North America, Australia and New Zealand. By the mid-1850s it was not unusual to read advertisements in *The Times* (London) for ladies interested in accompanying, as governesses or companions, families who were emigrating. Mary Ann may have placed such an advertisement herself or responded to one in the newspaper or posted via an emigration agency.

It is difficult to imagine what thoughts and impressions may have passed through Mary Ann Barnes's mind as she set foot on New Zealand soil for the first time. So much of what she saw would have been unfamiliar. With its dormant volcanic cones, lakes and lagoons, and the impressive Rangitoto Island rising out of the Waitemata Harbour like a quiet guardian over the city, Auckland was as different in geography to London as could be imagined. Instead of cobbled roads and winding alleys, there were wide, muddy, unpaved streets lined with wooden settler-style dwellings and unfamiliar trees, bush and scrub. Christmas was only two weeks away when Mary Ann arrived on the *Eastfield*, but instead of the accustomed chill of winter and the prospect of snow she encountered a temperate breeze, long sunny days and unpredictable downpours of warm rain.

Despite its relatively small size, Auckland was a city on the move. It still had no piped water supply or gas street lighting, but the population, by now just under 8000, was growing rapidly. As the seat of government, the city housed many government officials, while a steady stream of traders and merchants frequented the busy ports at Commercial Bay and Onehunga. Also in evidence were contingents of army officers, soldiers, artillerymen and engineers, stationed in Auckland to defend against possible Māori invasion by Waikato iwi. Beyond the city, the region was developing into the commercial heart of New Zealand. Market gardens lined the outskirts of the city, and the Waitakere Ranges to the northwest were being opened up by those intent on extracting logs and gum from the massive kauri forests on the ranges' slopes. A description of Auckland from the point of view of a 20-year-old accomplished governess in one of Mary Ann's later fictional works offers possible insight into Mary Ann's own first impressions of what was to become her new home:

> *I like the town, though it is directly opposed to all your previously conceived ideas. It is built on a series of hills and declivities (formed by the bays of a beautiful and picturesque harbor), that make walking rather a toil.*
>
> *The principle street is unique of its kind. It is the Cranbourne-street, Regent-street, Lombard-street, Borough, and even Ratcliffe Highway of the place, and the odd jumblings of buildings, from the superb to the squalid, may be imagined.*[15]

Although Auckland may have looked like a frontier settlement, it was not without its social and cultural amenities. No doubt Mary Ann would have been reassured by reading the local newspapers the *New Zealander* and the *Daily Southern Cross*. Interspersed with the many reminders that she was a very long way from Clerkenwell were the occasional comforting familiarities. Alongside advertisements for good working bullocks, ploughing contractors, farms for lease and rewards for stock who had strayed onto Grafton Road, were announcements of the reopening of various private educational establishments for girls in the new year. The *Cross* carried an advertisement posted by the Mechanics' Institute welcoming new arrivals and offering the privilege of two months' free use of its 'Reading Room', which carried an impressive array of national and overseas newspapers, including *The Times*, *Home News*, *London Illustrated News* and the Sydney and Melbourne *Heralds*, as well as periodicals such as *Leisure Hour*, *Chambers' Journal*, *Punch*, *Household Words* and the *Quarterly* and *Edinburgh Reviews*. Conveniently located on Auckland's High Street, just near the corner of Chancery Street and Courthouse Lane, the Mechanics' Institute, with its meeting room for lectures and concerts, was an important cultural hub. In the week of Mary Ann's arrival alone, it staged a public lecture on 'Mental Science;

its Relation to Education, Religion and Superstition' and hosted the Auckland Choral Society's performance of Handel's 'Messiah'.

Other entertainments were also on offer. The Young Men's Christian Association, for example, advertised an illustrated lecture by Dr Fischer on 'Life in Lesser Forms', while the Theatre Royal had on show the operatic drama 'Rob Roy Macgregor; Or, Auld Lang Syne!' and the screaming farce 'The Moustache Movement'. As Mary Ann soon realised, the arrival of a ship from England was greatly anticipated because it brought mail and news from the continent and elsewhere, as well as the latest fashions, books and all manner of commercial goods, from ladies' cashmere boots to Cumberland bacon and Wotherspoon's Confectionery.

The various social and intellectual entertainments held at the Mechanics' Institute along with its well-resourced reading room would have been a drawcard for an articulate, well-educated, refined and intelligent young woman such as Mary Ann. In turn, her sharp, inquiring mind, confident and composed manner, respect for, and observance of, social etiquette mixed with her heightened sense of social justice must have made her a welcome and refreshing addition to many social, educational and literary circles.

On 22 June 1858, six months after her arrival in Auckland, Mary Ann sat her Teachers' Examination under the supervision of the Auckland Education Board at the Mechanics' Institute Hall in High Street. The examination was designed to determine the qualifications, literary attainments and moral character of all teachers presenting to the board. Mary Ann sat examinations not only in the compulsory subjects but also for a Certificate of Merit in music and drawing. Of the 13 teachers examined by the board during that year, Mary Ann received the highest ranking and was awarded a first-class first-grade teaching certificate. When the board reconvened the day after her examination, its members approved, upon the recommendation of the special inspector, her appointment as assistant teacher in the Otahuhu Roman Catholic School, with the appointment effective immediately. Her testimonials of character were received in time for the next meeting of the board, which subsequently awarded Mary Ann her Certificate of Moral Character.[16]

The Roman Catholic School at Otahuhu was a reasonably large school by the standards of the day. With as many as 85 pupils attending, it was eligible for an assistant teacher paid by the board of education. Given Mary Ann's strong Church of England background, it is likely that she considered the position at the Roman Catholic School a convenient interim appointment. The character references she brought with her and her excellent educational qualifications and reputation as a teacher soon drew the attention of leading educationalists in Auckland. One such figure, the Reverend John Macky, who was to become a strong personal supporter of her efforts to provide comprehensive educational opportunities for girls, was probably instrumental in recommending her for a position at St Barnabas School in Parnell. After only two months at the Roman Catholic School, Mary Ann transferred to St Barnabas.

St Barnabas operated under the superintendence of the Reverend George Adam Kissling, a German Lutheran missionary who had served in West Africa before being ordained as an Anglican priest. He had also, with his wife Margaret, established a Māori girls' boarding school at Kohimarama, located to the east of Auckland. After the original buildings of this latter school burned down, Kissling reopened it in Parnell, today one of Auckland's oldest suburbs, under the name St Stephen's School for Native Girls. The school had an average attendance of 32 pupils; Mary Ann was the sole teacher.

Largely unregulated in Auckland province at the time, teaching was not a particularly secure profession, as Mary Ann was soon to find out. When she was in only her second full year of teaching, this characteristic of the profession in New Zealand became very evident. During July, August and September of that year, many schoolchildren throughout the province were ill. The extent of illness coupled with a severe winter meant school attendance was well down on the usual averages. As a result, school incomes were down, a circumstance that had a flow-on effect with respect to schools' ability to pay salaries and expenses. The smaller schools, such as St Barnabas, were generally hit the hardest, and at the end of September 1860 St Barnabas School formally ceased its connection with the Auckland Board of Education, although it continued to operate under the auspices of the Church of England.

It was around this time that Mary Ann met her future husband, Thomas Caesar Colclough. Thomas was the youngest son of a professional wealthy landowner from Galleenstown Castle, County Dublin, in Ireland. The Colclough family, whose estate was near Tintern Abbey, could proudly trace their heritage back to the 1300s. However, according to family sources, Thomas was a 'remittance man', which meant he received an annual income from his family in Ireland on the condition that he would never return to the family home. The specific circumstances that resulted in Thomas's family granting him a one-way ticket to the colonies are unknown, although his propensity for gambling was probably the reason. Thomas settled in Victoria, Australia, for some years and in 1849 purchased a substantial property of 105 acres (42.5 ha) in Toorak, Melbourne. A few years later he had a prefabricated house erected on the site, which he called 'Tintern' in memory of his childhood home. In time, he sold this property and went on to own and lease several modest residential properties in Commercial Road and Frederick Street, Melbourne. Despite these ventures, he was not a businessman at heart. By the time he arrived in New Zealand on the *Red Jacket* in May 1860, he no longer owned property in Melbourne.[17]

When, where and how Thomas and Mary Ann met is uncertain, but they very likely were introduced through members of mutual social circles. Mary Ann strongly believed that a woman was duty bound to marry, and even though Thomas was 30 years older than she, he was a handsome, well-presented gentleman settler. On paper, at least, he must have presented as a good prospect. Had Mary Ann known the full circumstances of her prospective husband's business endeavours and financial circumstances, the marriage would not have progressed. Innocent of his true colours, Mary Ann married Thomas on 9 May 1860 at St Peter's Anglican Church in Onehunga. Because Thomas was of the Catholic faith, he and Mary Ann undertook a second ceremony at the Catholic Church in Onehunga.[18]

In line with the custom of the day, Mary Ann, once married, ceased her employment at St Barnabas School. But it did not take long before Thomas showed his mettle as an incompetent provider. Mary Ann some years later described him, in the most respectful of terms, as 'not a bad, but a thoroughly unbusinesslike, unenergetic man [who] spent pounds and pounds of his wife's earnings in profitless, and even in ruinous speculations'. On another occasion she stated that all of her means, which under law were her husband's means, had been 'swallowed up by swindling Victorian speculations'.[19]

Mary Ann's upbringing had been financially secure. Two generations of her family had been employed in various aspects of the building trade, and the model she grew up with was of her grandfather, father and uncles all employed in honest hard work providing a secure and comfortable life for their families. Once aware that there was no prospect of her husband providing a reliable income, and with a child on the way, Mary Ann had no option but to take responsibility for earning the family income. In May 1862 she advertised the opening of her private school for young ladies. She had secured a large house with ample accommodation for boarders situated close to the Great South Road and within four miles of Otahuhu. Her classes would include English, music, singing, drawing, dancing and French.

Six months later, on 1 November 1862, Mary Ann gave birth to daughter Mary Louise (known as Lulu) in Papatoetoe. At such a momentous time in her life, Mary Ann must have found it especially difficult to be so far from her family. Although she engaged the services of a servant to assist with the domestic routines, caring for her baby, teaching full time, managing the boarding school and trying to keep Thomas's speculative behaviours in check must have been daunting and demanding. In those precious moments when she had time to reflect on her circumstances, she would have again felt alone in the world.

When Lulu was eight months old, Mary Ann fell pregnant a second time. Knowing she needed to reduce the demands on her time and energy, in July 1863 she found smaller premises for her Ladies' Collegiate School at Grangeville, about a mile past Otahuhu. To supplement her earnings beyond those provided by pupils attending day classes, she again took in a few pupils as boarders. William Caesar Sarsfield, Mary Ann's second child, was born on 26 January 1864. Now that she had two infants, the additional strain of running a private school took its toll, but the necessity of earning a regular income had to take precedence. Her good friend the Reverend John Macky, who was chair of the Auckland Board of Education at the time, ran a small school at West Tamaki with an average attendance of about 15 pupils. John Macky had considerable respect for Mary Ann and strongly supported her efforts in the field of girls' education. It is not known whether Mary Ann approached him or whether he, aware of her personal circumstances, offered the position, but in 1865 Mary Ann began teaching at West Tamaki School. Although she realised that teaching at West Tamaki would not be an easy prospect, she knew it would be simpler to organise care for her children around set hours of teaching than to continue running a private school in her own home and catering to borders.

During these early years of teaching, Mary Ann developed important networks with like-minded educationalists, including Henry Taylor, who was secretary to the board of education, and Reverend Samuel Edger, a Nonconformist minister and social reformer. Like John Macky, Taylor and Edger were very respectful of Mary Ann's acumen, judgement of character and commitment to education as a profession. She likewise respected their ability to judge character and sought their advice on various issues. In October 1865, for example, Mary Ann wrote to Henry Taylor seeking his opinion on the suitability of one of her pupils for the position of pupil-teacher. She had her reservations. The young girl had a speech impediment that became pronounced when she was under pressure, and Mary

Ann was not convinced she had sufficient passion for and commitment to the role. Henry Taylor shared her concerns, and his response provides an insight not only into how disabilities were perceived at the time but also into the perception that teaching was as much a vocation as it was a profession:

> *Education Office*
> *October 27 1865*
> *Dear Mrs Colclough*
>
> *If you ask for an expression of my private opinion upon the suitability of your pupil for the office of Teacher, I should pronounce her unfit 1st from the impediment of in her speech, which you represent to be augmented when under the influence of external annoyances or internal agitation and how frequently a teacher is subjected to these influences your own experiences can tell – 2ndly Because you represent her as about to engage in the work without feeling either interest or pleasure in her labours. I know of no profession where duties become so irksome than as that of a Teacher under such circumstances. For these two reasons I should advise you to dissuade her from embracing a profession, which from physical disabilities, and a lukewarmness, sure eventuates to increase into a repugnance, she can never hope to succeed in.*
>
> *Henry Taylor*[20]

Despite the demands on her time, Mary Ann was very active in literary circles, and she was encouraged in her own literary endeavours by individuals such as journalist and politician Julius Vogel, and the publisher and newspaper proprietor Henry Brett, both of whom became close personal supporters. For several years she had been writing short stories, and two of these, *The Half Caste Wife* and *Alone in the World*, were published in serialised form in Australian newspapers. No records could be found of the content or reception of *The Half Caste Wife*, but the praise that the second short story attracted encouraged Mary Ann to develop it into a full-length novel. Priced at two shillings and sixpence, *Alone in the World: A tale of New Zealand* was published by Mitchell and Seffern in Wyndham Street, Auckland, in May 1866. The green leather-bound book was beautifully produced with gilt-edged rice-paper pages, and the editor of the *Daily Southern Cross* rightfully commended the publishers for the quality of the printing. Unfortunately, the proof sheets were not sent to Mary Ann for correction before publication, and she wrote to the *Cross* to explain that any errors could not be attributed to her.

Of particular interest is the fact that the book did not include her name as author but instead had written on it 'By the Author of the Half-Caste Wife'. In similar vein, Mary Ann signed her letter regarding the proof sheets 'The Author of Alone in the World'. Because *The Half Caste Wife* was only ever published in serialised form in an Australian newspaper, the title would have been unfamiliar to a New Zealand readership. Authors of the period commonly listed other works they had written on the title pages of their books, but they generally did this alongside their actual name. Whether Mary Ann did not want her identity revealed or whether this was simply an oversight not detected because of the mix-up with checking the proofs cannot be known. The citing of 'authorship' may have been a deliberate attempt at anonymity on her part because aspects of the plot and characters in *Alone in the World* were undoubtedly inspired by Mary Ann's own life. But one's own life as a source of inspiration was (and is) not an unusual one, especially among first-time novelists. Whatever the case, any reason for anonymity appears to have passed a couple of years later when she wrote to the editor of the *New Zealand Herald* in which she identified herself as the author of the book, asked if anyone had a spare copy as hers had been misplaced, and then signed the letter with her name.[21]

The opening scene of *Alone in the World* presents 20-year-old Miss Annie Barrington sitting alone in a half-furnished schoolroom. Her simple, worn and faded attire suggests she has lost someone close and that she has not been left in good circumstances. It is soon revealed that both her parents have recently passed away and she is anxious to travel to New Zealand to try to locate her brother. Annie reads an advertisement in *The Times* for a lady governess for a family immigrating to New Zealand. Music, French and a thorough knowledge of English are required. The novel follows Annie's experiences as a governess, her circles of acquaintance and those of her employer, and her relationship and eventual marriage to successful farmer Mr Bernard Seaton. The twist in the plot is the sudden arrival of a friend whom Annie taught with in a private school in London. The friend tells Annie that her impetuous young husband abandoned her when she was carrying their second child. However, the friend advises, she then received a picture of Bernard with Annie, an occurrence that decided her to immediately sail for New Zealand to confront the couple and tell Annie that the man she thinks is her husband is actually her erstwhile friend's. After a great deal of mental anguish, the situation is resolved as a case of mistaken identity.

When reviewing *Alone in the World* shortly after it was published, the reviewer for *The Penny Journal* commended the author for presenting a 'very pleasing and well written story'. He noted that 'The interest throughout is well sustained, the dialogue is fairly managed, and natural, the characters are drawn from the author's point of view with skill, and the story throughout indicates the hand of an observant, fluent, rather cynical, but conscientious writer.' A description of the novel in the *Oxford History of New Zealand Literature in English* noted the work 'dilutes sensation material with Dickensian pathetic melodrama'. Both reviews are accurate.[22]

Typical of nineteenth-century English women's novels, *Alone in the World* is a commentary on social etiquette, manners and morality. Annie's story is interwoven with those of Mrs Willoughby Watkins, described as 'a lady of too much importance – at least in her own opinion', her eldest daughter, who 'has been taught to believe that vulgar display is an unerring sign of a lady', and Mrs De Costremonge, a social arbiter of style and breeding who has befriended Mrs Willoughby Watkins on the passage to New Zealand and who is subsequently exposed as being a grocer's wife, actress, and former lady's maid to the real Mrs De Costremonge in Devonshire. Annie's husband is also keeping a secret that threatens to undermine his social standing: his father was a convicted murderer, sentenced to death. When accused of bigamy, Bernard Seaton is at first prepared to leave Annie and provide ongoing financial support to her as well as to the wife and children he is accused of abandoning rather than face a public trial and have his parentage revealed. As Annie grapples with the prospect of having married a bigamist, she realises her only means of saving face is to accept support from an unassuming and honest working-class couple who will not divulge her dilemma.[23]

At times the detailed characterisation and social commentary of *Alone in the World* overtakes the plot, particularly in the early chapters. But the Dickensian-style characterisation and dialogue also prefigures the later more polemic critiques Mary Ann was to offer in her newspaper journalism on the follies of those who have aspirations beyond their social class. The closing scene of the novel describes Bernard looking lovingly on his wife and children as they play happily outside their pretty home while the summer sun slowly departs, and thanking God for the blessing of teaching him resignation to His will.

In contrast to the happy familial image at the close of *Alone in the World*, Mary Ann's life had more than its share of challenges, and her marriage continued to be far from easy. Her husband Thomas's general inactivity meant he did not enjoy good health, and it was Mary Ann's 'unremitting toil', as she described it, that kept the home furnished and the family fed. At times the family paid a high price for Thomas's speculative deals; creditors at the door were not an uncommon sight. One time when Willie was still a toddler, Thomas's debt collectors seized most of the household items, leaving Mary Ann sitting on the bare floor with the children. Despite this embarrassment, she remained stoic and loyal to Thomas.[24]

Reflecting on this episode some years later, she concluded that the fault lay clearly in social custom rather than in her husband. In a letter, she explained: 'I was the breadwinner, whilst he had all the breadwinner's powers and privileges, and such a position leads naturally to many troubles and complications.' Time after time Mary Ann had no option but to pick herself up and start again. Although she learned to live with the financial uncertainties, her situation was never easy.[25]

Mary Ann's graciousness in excusing her husband's failings was not tested for too many years. Having been generally unwell for a long period of time, Thomas was admitted to Auckland Public Hospital early in July 1867. Gangrene had developed in the upper part of his right foot, and as it slowly advanced the whole foot perished, obstructing the arteries in his leg, which had developed calcification. On 29 July, after 27 days in hospital, Thomas died while in a coma. At 31 years of age, Mary Ann was left a widow with two children under the age of five years to support. She had been the sole breadwinner throughout her marriage, but securing a regular and sufficient income was now more pressing than ever. Although widows did not have recourse to pensions or state support at this time, Mary Ann could take some consolation from the fact that she would have full control over her own earnings.[26]

Focusing on the positives, Mary Ann also counted herself as lucky to have employment. The Auckland Board of Education was struggling financially, and in his annual report John Macky described teachers as being in a 'precarious and insecure position'. Many parents could not afford school fees, and the erratic attendance of pupils had put undue pressure on the board's ability to meet teachers' full salaries. As a result, a number of teachers were 'labouring without prospect of remuneration'.[27]

One of her friends described Mary Ann at this time as a woman intent on 'keeping herself respectable and respected throughout' despite 'working against fearful odds'. After her husband's death, Mary Ann increasingly used her writing talents to secure much needed additional income. Having had several articles published and paid for in periodicals in England and in America, she turned her attention to the local press. An avid reader of periodicals from 'Home', she regularly read the London *Times* and the *Leisure Hour*. But it was an article titled

'Mercenary Marriages' that piqued her interest, and she decided to offer it to the editor of the *Weekly News* for publication.[28] In an accompanying letter to the editor she wrote:

> Dear Sir, – The appended scrap I have cut from The Ladies' Own Journal
> and Miscellany for May 30th, 1868.
>
> Do give it a place when scarcity of news gives you a spare column. It shows
> off so well the passions of some young men on matrimony. Well may
> the writer ask what they have to offer in exchange for their exorbitant
> demands. It is a comfort to know that they are not taken at their own
> absurd valuations, the market being quite over-stocked with these would-be
> benedicts. Even Auckland is not free from them, if we may judge from some
> of the conversations of the young men one meets in society; so do put it in
> the paper, and oblige
>
> Polly Plum[29]

Over the next few months, several short articles appeared in the *Cross* under the *nom de plume* Polly Plum, a name that, within a short while, would be well known throughout the households of the Auckland area and beyond. Mary Ann was poised to enter a new phase of her life as she embarked on a journalistic career that would bring with it the mixed blessings that inevitably accompany a controversial public profile.

CHAPTER TWO

Entering the Public Sphere

Encouraged by her good friend Julius Vogel, who had recently purchased the *Daily Southern Cross* newspaper, Mary Ann embraced the opportunity to embark on a journalistic career. It is testimony to her high standing in literary circles that she had the personal support of influential men such as Vogel, Charles Southwell, who was editor of the *Examiner*, and Henry Brett, publisher and newspaper proprietor. Charles Southwell can best be described as a free thinker, known for his radical views and his strong support for universal education. During the 1860s, Henry Brett gained recognition as an outstanding reporter while working for the *Cross* and the *New Zealand Herald*. Within a few years, he bought the Auckland *Evening Star* and became one of the most influential men in the newspaper business in the country.

For Mary Ann, Julius Vogel was a particularly significant supporter because he was sympathetic, as both a journalist and a politician, to the cause of women. In line with common practice at the time, newspapers owners not only wanted their papers to be a commercial success but also to use them as political platforms for their views. As proprietor of the *Cross*, Vogel was able to provide Mary Ann with the opportunity to exercise her writing talents, express her political views on the cause of women and earn some additional income in the process. A letter from an unnamed family friend in Geelong, Australia, written in late 1926 said that it was Vogel who suggested the pen name Polly Plum: 'Her name was "Mary", called "Polly", and someone saying she was a "plum". Mr Vogel – as he then was – said, "I have it, Polly Plum."' But a close friend from Thames maintained the *nom de plume* was 'sportingly given her by Southwell of the *Examiner*'. Mary Ann, however, said she had used the name on a series of articles she had contributed to an American journal and the sobriquet had stuck.[1]

Mary Ann's first steps into the public sphere of newspaper journalism were a mix of conservatism and outspoken commentary. Drawing on the journalism skills she'd learned as a young student at Queen's College, she wrote paragraphs and short articles of interest to women and girls giving advice on topics such as how to prepare a trousseau, what novels to read and hints on bringing up children. But there were also clear indications that Mary Ann was no shrinking violet preaching conformity to a passive readership. In a subject close to her own experience, she wrote of the formidable array of women who, for various reasons, had to procure paid work yet found themselves confined by social custom to ill-paid and over-crowded employments. In another piece, she bemoaned the expectation that all women should conform to a bland version of what she referred to as 'pattern womanhood'. After all, she argued, 'Nature has varied her works as much in womanhood as in other things', so why should women constantly try to follow a pattern and conform to an imposed ideal rather than find their own way of being in the world?[2]

In March 1869 Mary Ann turned her attention to the issue of religious education in schools, and what she said triggered a strong reaction from the reading public. A recent meeting of the Auckland Presbytery had discussed the clause in the Common Schools Act, passed by the Auckland Provincial Council, relating to secular education. The clause suggested that children's guardians could provide religious instruction if they considered it appropriate to do so. In a letter to the editor of the *Cross*, Mary Ann stated that it was always preferable for parents to provide religious instruction. Any parents, she said, who were willing to depute this responsibility to a stranger could not be very earnest about the matter. She had expressed a similar position in her novel *Alone in the World* when Annie's eldest charge displayed an extended unabashed tirade of lies and deceptions, placing the young governess in an extremely conflicted position:

> On the one hand, the mother was teaching her child every species of boasting and dissimulation; and on the other, as a servant of Christ, and a conscientious teacher, she would have to inculcate a pure love of truth – but how to eradicate the weeds? Oh! Parents, what a task do you impose when you expect a teacher to enforce precepts and principles which you yourselves wantonly disregard and outrage every day of your lives.[3]

But what caught readers' attention was Polly Plum's suggestion that all Romanists and Jews could unite in a common plan and that all Protestants could share combined Bible classes at schools, thereby removing the need for denominational schools. One correspondent, who considered Polly Plum 'generally very right in her remarks', thought that on this occasion she had made a 'blunder' in assuming parents would oversee teaching their children about sacred knowledge. Another, who described 'Polly' as a 'kindly and earnest lady', but who took umbrage at her referring to Roman Catholics as Romanists, thought she must be a very simple and inexperienced or a very ill-informed lady if she could persuade herself or attempt to convince others that the religious differences among Protestants were few and unimportant.[4]

In what soon became a hallmark of Mary Ann's newspaper journalism, she responded with a lengthy article in which she presented her arguments for religious instruction. She set out her arguments in a methodical and detailed fashion, a practice, she reminded readers, particular to women's nature. One of the points she stressed, and which showed her abiding concern with the employment conditions of teachers, was that in those districts where education was given over to denominational schools, few of those schools could afford the salaries that would secure good teachers.

Buoyed by the public responses to her writing, Mary Ann branched out over the following weeks into more controversial topics. She argued, for example, that men holding public office often abused their power and privilege, and that women who paid taxes and were responsible for their own debts deserved a say in politics. The struggles she faced on a daily basis as a widowed mother often fuelled her writing. She wrote of women who had to provide for their own and their family's livelihoods yet were constrained in this endeavour by the ignorant and damaging opinions of what constituted women's 'proper' sphere. She also wrote of the injustice and hypocrisy evident in two scenarios. The first featured a man or woman, poor and struggling, who owed the butcher or baker a few pounds and who was then blighted by righteous, indignant people willing to use that person's plight as an excuse to express hollow platitudes or pass harsh judgement. The second focused on men who, despite squandering hundreds of pounds, maintained a façade of financial respectability and so were excused and held up as great men.

By June 1869, articles by Polly Plum were a regular feature of the columns of the *Cross* as well as in the 'For the Ladies' columns of the Auckland *Weekly News*. But not all readers appreciated her views. One writer who carefully scanned all her 'effusions' and thought her writings were, for the most part, 'pithy and laconic', declared that she really had nothing new to say and was simply 'dishing up truisms in a new garb for our intelligent colonial public'. Far from taking offence, Mary Ann wrote back to say the writer had paid her a compliment by admitting he found it hard to prune or clip her productions. She then added that '"Plums" grow all the better for the use of the pruning-knife', and that she would soon give him a good day's gardening, as she was intending to publish a small volume of essays and had secured the highest patronage for it. After several weeks of banter through letters to the editor with this writer, who signed himself 'Jemmy Jenkins', Polly Plum drew the discussion to a close, asserting her credentials as a published author.[5] She wrote:

> *One of my weaknesses is a keen perception of the ludicrous, and it struck me as intensely funny that an unknown writer should address a lady, who had been some little time before the public, writing for the English and colonial press ... I am unwilling to accept the censorship of an unknown 'Jemmy Jenkins'! I aspire to be an author, and a fair criticism, conducted without prejudice of sex, I am willing to submit to. There is a very limited sphere for a writer here ... but I object to being dragged into a newspaper war with every unknown cavalier that chooses to take up the pen. [...] I hope Mr. Jenkins will see the propriety of retiring into private life – unless he is prepared to come before the public as a writer (not a letter writer). In that case I wish him success.[6]*

These strictures to Jemmy Jenkins are indicative of Mary Ann's sense of identity as a serious author and not simply as someone using the letters to the editor columns to engage in debate with her readership. There is also clear indication that Mary Ann's writing persona of Polly Plum was assuming a life of her own in the minds of readers. Diana Damson encapsulated the early badinage between Polly Plum and Jemmy Jenkins in a poem titled 'Cause Celebre – Polly Plum v. Jemmy Jenkins'. As well as capturing the attention of would-be poets, Polly Plum's 'effusions' were selling newspapers, and the editor of the *Cross* did not hesitate to cash in their public appeal by publishing another ditty penned by 'Fanny Fast' that framed the interchange within the old familiar line of the battle of the sexes.[7]

A few weeks later, a lengthy poem titled 'Colonial Fern Leaves' appeared in the *Cross*. It likened Polly Plum to the American journalist and novelist Fanny Fern, the pen name of Sarah Willis Parton (1811–1872). Fanny Fern offered satiric commentary on domestic subjects and was one of the most successful newspaper columnists of her day. Her regular column for the New York *Ledger*, for which she wrote exclusively for 16 years, paid the princely sum of £100 a week. Like Polly Plum, Fanny Fern wrote a mix of short pieces and longer articles using a range of writing styles. Sometimes Fanny wrote in the popular sentimentalist style, with little to distinguish her words from the many platitudes that filled the newspaper columns of the day. At other times, she used a satirical style to comment on current fads and fashions. However, on more taboo issues, such as prostitution, venereal disease, the sexual double standard and women's rights, she wrote in a forthright manner. In short, Fanny Fern and Polly Plum had much in common. Both took advantage of the medium of the newspaper to interpret social issues in the light of their personal convictions, most frequently highlighting the plight of the working girl, the suffering wife and the 'fallen' woman.[8]

Extracts from Fanny Fern's writings appeared regularly in the Auckland newspapers, and Polly Plum, aware of the comparisons drawn, was quick to acknowledge that she considered Fanny Fern's writings superior to her own. Typical of the situation endured by many of the women who, over the centuries, have publicly challenged the belief that men, by nature and God-given right, should dominate women, Fanny Fern was the target of ridicule and personal attacks. Critics dismissed her writing as full of 'un-femininely bitter wrath and spite' and as evidence that the writer was 'not sufficiently endowed with female delicacy'. Soon, Polly Plum was charged with similar characteristics.[9]

The author of 'Colonial Fern Leaves' signed himself John Smith, and it was apparent that Polly Plum's article titled 'A Good Husband', written several weeks earlier, had inspired Mr Smith's poem. In her article, Polly held up the late Prince Albert as a model husband: he always greeted his wife with a smile and a kind word, he was a wise and agreeable companion, he was entirely devoted to his family and their interest, and he assiduously avoided even the appearance of anything that may have caused his wife unease. Polly Plum then anticipated Messrs Smith, Brown and Jones bemoaning the likelihood that should they die tomorrow, their wives would not mourn for them as Queen Victoria had mourned for the Prince Consort. Mary Ann singled out the proverbial Mr John Smith and attributed a long list of husbands' failings to him. When 'John Smith' replied with 'Colonial Fern Leaves', Mary Ann was openly apologetic and replied with humility and good humour:

My Dear Mr. Smith, – If Polly is an Amazon she has yet sufficient justice in her composition to 'give in' to a Hercules when she meets with one, and she feels bound to own that you have defended yourself so cleverly and with so much good humour, that she would apologise for her article 'A Good Husband' (at least the part referring to yourself), except that she can't feel sorry for having written anything that has had power to call forth such an excellent reply. She can assure you that were even half the men so clever as yourself she would commission the Editor of the Cross *to present the 'lords of creation' with her articles to make 'pipe-lights' of.*

She is quite aware that Fanny Fern's articles are much better than 'hern,' and so are 'yourn' also, and with this attempt at the amende honourable she hopes she has soothed your outraged feelings.
POLLY PLUM[10]

Unlike some of her critics, Mary Ann was not one to engage in personalised criticism. She even wrote to the editor of the *Cross* to explain that while some readers inevitably would take her writings about the failings and follies of mankind personally, she never aimed her comments at any particular individual. Quick to admit that she, like everyone else, had her share of failings and peculiarities, she was quite aware that certain people saw her as a social pest and a public nuisance. Although she deemed some of what such people had to say as not very polite, she excused these criticisms on the basis that their authors needed to vent their feelings.

Every now and then a playful sense of humour came to the fore, and Polly would make light of the affected airs of some ladies. With tongue in cheek, she noted that anyone with pedigree could trace their families back to the Biblical flood, including the Plums. But this light-heartedness was set aside when she found out that someone had signed her name to what she described as 'silly advertisements':

It has come to my knowledge that some mean or malicious persons have taken the unwarrantable liberty of using the name of 'Polly Plum', in answering silly advertisements, and that it has been done more than once. Of course I feel annoyed; and, though no one who knows me would believe me capable of such a thing, those who do not may be deceived. I wish I could discover the names of these reprehensible practical jokers, and I would publicly expose them, as they justly deserve. I have not had occasion to answer an advertisement for years, and in every case I have always signed

my full and proper name, as the advertisements concerned me professionally,
and required testimonials, &c. No other advertisements have ever been
answered by the one and only lady who has really the right to sign herself,
POLLY PLUM[11]

The personal sense of injustice expressed in this disclaimer shows how strongly Mary Ann valued and protected her personal integrity and professional identity. Debate, criticism and even censure of her opinions were welcome; she even said that an author was not well used until they were well abused, but personal criticisms of and slurs on her private character were intolerable.

Evidence of Mary Ann having established herself as a talented, entertaining and provocative writer came toward the end of 1869 when the *Cross* commissioned her to write a series of longer articles on 'Social Topics'. Alongside her regular articles in the *Cross*, she was also using the letters to the editor column to correspond with readers on her more controversial topics. But despite the additional income that the longer articles brought her, her household budget continued to concern her. The Auckland Board of Education's financial difficulties had come to a head in February of that year when Mary Ann and 40 other teachers petitioned the provincial council for payment of their salaries, which had been outstanding for the March quarter of the previous year. Mary Ann's salary was in arrears of £12/10s at the time. She had always run a tight budget and managed her household as efficiently as possible, given her often limited means. From before her daughter Lulu's birth, there had been boarders to cater for, and while she continued to employ a domestic servant, this arrangement was not always satisfactory, as evident in her recounting of her experience with one newly employed young woman:

I once engaged a servant, and the morning after her arrival went into the
kitchen, as was my custom, to see what there was wanting and how things
were going on, and to prepare generally for dinner. 'Please give me your
orders, ma'am,' said the girl; 'I'm not used to missusses coming about my
kitchen.' 'My good girl,' said I, 'I have engaged you to assist in the work of this
house, under my superintendence, and with such help as I, in the intervals of
teaching, can give you. I assure you I work very hard for the money it costs
for housekeeping, and it is so very much my affair that it should not cost me
too much, that I could not leave the entire management of it even to my own
sister.'[12]

It was not uncommon at this time for domestic servants to display con-descending attitudes towards their employers. The 'servant problem', as it became known, was a recognised phenomenon in New Zealand and elsewhere, and was often the subject of considerable discussion. Part of the problem was that much of the emigration propaganda that specifically targeted single women for domestic service promised high wages, better working conditions, better chances for social improvement and fewer class distinctions in New Zealand. As one publication boasted, domestic servants in New Zealand 'are made rather companions than slaves'. One writer went as far as referring to the servant problem as 'the domestic affliction'. In his *Colonial Experiences*, Scottish lawyer and writer Alexander Bathgate lamented the fact that it was difficult to identify who was the housemaid and who was the family member in some households because the higher wages enabled servants to dress as well as their mistresses, and many had rejected the outward markers of hierarchy such as wearing caps. Bathgate recounted several examples of mistresses putting up with servants' audacious, indignant and impudent behaviour and displays of ignorance for fear if they dismissed their servants they might be left for weeks with no assistance.[13]

Mary Ann found working with young girls who had been spoilt by over-indulgence or who were unnecessarily harsh, particularly difficult. While she had no desire to assume commanding airs as the lady of the house, she had an equal objection to being bullied by ignorant and impertinent servants. She initially put such behaviour down to a lack of good training and supervision. However, after employing three incapable servants within four months when the children were still very small, she convinced her husband Thomas to try out a new plan: she would employ young, well-educated, respectable girls who would usually become needlewomen or nursery governesses and treat them as if they were part of the family.

Thomas was not at all confident Mary Ann's plan would succeed, but over the years Mary Ann proved him wrong. Convinced of the need to actively teach domestic work and household management, she assisted the young help with tasks such as writing a weekly list of supplies and noting down what was needed as they ran short of items during the week so as to avoid the constant expense of sending out for them. Some goods, such as meat, still had to be ordered on a daily basis, however, and delivered to the house. Experience soon showed that although the more respectable girls were rather sensitive, they were willing to work as long as they were not treated as inferior. Unlike their working-class counterparts, they were not impertinent, were amenable to instruction and were much more careful with the household expenditure. Mary Ann also engaged a charwoman or washerwoman for the 'rough work' of the house, and she hired a 'little girl' to take the babies out in the perambulator. All in all, her household arrangement suited the parties very well, and Mary Ann found it both successful and economical.

When the school year came to a close in 1869, Mary Ann decided to resign from West Tamaki School where she had been teaching for several years and to reopen her private day school at Lake Villa in Epsom. She advertised that a few boarding positions were available for the summer quarter, which started on 24 January. Her first-class teaching credentials and references of the highest respectability held her in good stead; by the start of the winter quarter at the beginning of July 1870, she was able to advertise that she had the patronage and support of most of Epsom's gentry.

The increased demands of running the day school and hosting boarders did little to curtail her writing. The opportunity to write longer opinion pieces saw her broach more contentious issues related to women's position in society. Having read the pamphlet 'An Appeal to the Men of New Zealand' on women, and the franchise written by 'Fémmina' and first published in 1869, she wrote in support of extending the franchise to women who were taxpayers and householders and who had to work for their living. Very few people knew that Fémmina was the *nom de plume* of women's rights advocate Mary Ann Müller. She wrote under a pen name because her husband Dr Stephen Lunn Müller held a prominent public office as the first resident magistrate for the district of Wairau and was not a supporter of women's rights. Fortunately, Mary Ann Müller had the support of her step-daughter's father-in-law Charles Elliott, who was editor of the *Nelson Examiner*, considered to be the most influential newspaper in New Zealand at that time. Elliott protected Mary Ann Müller's anonymity by receiving and forwarding her correspondence. He also secured publication of her articles in the *Nelson Examiner* as well as more widely in newspapers throughout the country.

Mary Ann Colclough agreed with Fémmina that it was unjust and a relic of barbarism to withhold the right to vote from women who lived by independent means. Several years earlier she had corresponded with Julius Vogel on the issue. In a 'somewhat jocular strain', Vogel had written to Mary Ann: 'When one thinks of some of our clever mothers, and our duffers of young brothers of 21, it seems just foolish that the former should have no say in the affairs of the nation, or of anybody in fact.' Mary Ann also agreed with Fémmina that the current law held women completely at the mercy of men. She had experienced first-hand how women were bound by laws that men made, faced the full share of penalties for breaking those laws, and yet were barred from having a voice in making the laws. She firmly believed that God had made man and woman different for a purpose, and she had no desire to see women occupy the position of men, but she was adamant that where women had to assume the duties and responsibilities of men they should be given fair play and not be confined to a limited range of occupations. To her mind, this position was a relatively moderate one to take; in fact, she made it very clear that she deliberately distanced herself from the more extreme advocates of women's rights.[14]

Mary Ann Müller had sent a copy of her pamphlet to John Stuart Mill, the English philosopher and politician who was known for his support for women's rights. Mill, impressed with the pamphlet, wrote a very encouraging letter in reply, enclosing a copy of his recently published work *The Subjection of Women*, today recognised by historians as perhaps the single most influential publication on what was referred to as the 'Woman Question' in the nineteenth century. In *The Subjection of Women*, Mill outlined his belief that many of the characteristics observed in women are not natural or innate but a consequence of women's social position. The title of his work encapsulated his main argument: under the current laws and customs, women, like slaves, were bound in a state of dependency and subjection. The New Zealand press reprinted extracts from his work, and these struck a chord with many social reformers. Reverend Samuel Edger was so impressed with Mill's 'deep truth and almost immeasurable importance as bearing on social reform' that he purchased as many copies as he could with the aim of lending them to anyone who wanted to read the full work.[15]

Reading Mill's work proved to be a significant step in Mary Ann's 'conversion', as she put it, to the cause of women. She chose the word 'conversion' quite deliberately and described the cause of women as a 'high and holy' cause of 'right and truth'. As she became more outspoken, her commitment became unequivocal. She even described herself as a missionary engaged in God's work, prepared, if necessary, to be a martyr in His service:

> *You will believe that I am true when I declare my honor as a Christian*
> *woman that dearly as I love my life, and many and close are the ties that*
> *bind me to it, I would this day, gladly and gratefully lay it down, if by doing*
> *so I would serve the great work which, next to my God, claims my highest*
> *service. No Missionary ever yet went amongst the heathen, who was ever*
> *more firmly convinced that he was doing God's service, and working to His*

honor and glory, than I am convinced that I am doing God's best work in the path I have chosen to follow. I fully believe, and am convinced, that neither I or [sic] my little ones will suffer in this enlightened nineteenth century, by my carrying out my earnest convictions of right; but even if it were otherwise, and I should be counted 'worthy to suffer', I hope and believe the strength will be given to say, 'Even so Father, for so it seemeth good in Thy sight, not my will but Thine be done.'[16]

Open as Mary Ann was to correspondence with those who were interested in the cause, readers of her articles soon began contacting her personally through the newspaper office with information related to women's activities and, in some cases, to request personal assistance. In March 1870 Mary Ann received several circulars produced by the North London Deaconess Institution, sent to her from a reader by way of the *Weekly News* office. Mary Ann was delighted to read of the institution's work and the practical steps its deaconesses were taking to assist the poor, provide religious instruction in schools and minister to those in hospitals, prisons and asylums. When describing her admiration for this order of women, she could easily have been describing her own philosophical stance. Not bound by vows or unconditional promises of the kind that informed the work of the deaconesses, Mary Ann set forth with true Christian conscientiousness to commit to high responsibilities and arduous duties. Her admiration for the Deaconess Institution led her to muse on the need for a publication devoted to the consideration of social topics and other matters of interest to people engaged in private humanitarian endeavours. While very grateful for the liberal access she had to the newspaper presses in Auckland, they were almost exclusively commercial ventures. What was needed, she suggested, was a well-conducted weekly paper to serve the purposes of those who had an interest in private philanthropic work.

Whether Mary Ann worked behind the scenes to bring this idea into fruition is not known, but in May 1870 E. Wayte's Booksellers and Stationers of Queen Street, Auckland, launched a monthly religious journal titled *The Christian Times*. Priced at sixpence per issue, the journal offered comment on leading topics of the day, religious news from New Zealand, Australia and England, book reviews and general correspondence. The journal received high praise for its 'freedom from sectarian narrow-mindedness, and the thoroughly readable nature of its contents' and for treating its subjects in a broad, liberal and cosmopolitan manner. The editor of the *Cross* considered *The Christian Times* an 'exceedingly creditable' publication and noted, 'Such well-timed remarks on public questions, conveyed through so excellent a medium, cannot fail to have a beneficial effect, and we think the proprietors of the periodical act wisely in choosing as their object not simply the dissemination of general religious truth, but in giving that truth a local application.' A feature of the first issue was the first chapter of a new fictional work by Mary Ann Colclough titled *Effie's Inheritance*, the remaining 21 chapters of which would be published over the next 12 months. Unfortunately, there are no known extant copies of *The Christian Times* so we cannot discern the content of *Effie's Inheritance*. However, given Mary Ann's personal experience and views on married women's property rights, and given the book's title, she very likely developed themes relating to the injustices of women's current legal position.[17]

It was at this time that a writer to the *Thames Advertiser* accused Polly Plum of plagiarism. An article attributed to Polly titled 'The Indisposition of Young Men to Marry' had appeared in the *Weekly News* a few weeks earlier, and a correspondent signing him or herself 'Veritas' alleged that a fuller version of the same article could be found in a work titled 'Sexology' by American author Mrs Elizabeth Osgood Goodrich Willard. Knowing nothing of the charge until a friend sent a clipping of the article to her, Mary Ann, in a lengthy reply to the editor, begged to assure him 'on the honour of a lady, that I never either saw or heard of the work referred to by "Veritas", nor has one with that heading appeared in the Cross'. Not only had she never heard of Mrs Willard or her work, but she also had never borrowed work from others. Anyone who knew Mary Ann personally knew that her time was fully occupied; she scarcely had time to write down her own thoughts let alone make her articles a business of study by looking up the works of others. Describing the charge of plagiarism as 'most monstrous' because it amounted to literary theft, which, to her mind, was morally as reprehensible as any other type of robbery, she had to assume it was a simple mistake on the part of the newspaper editor.[18]

Occasionally, something she read triggered a train of thought that led to an article. 'Lords of the Creation', an item published just two weeks earlier in the *Cross* and reprinted in the *Weekly News*, was a case in point. Mary Ann had recently read 'New America' by English historian and traveller Hepworth Dixon. One passage, about the Mormon practice of polygamy, struck a chord. Dixon had concluded that within Mormon society, 'Man is King, and woman has no rights. She has, in fact, no recognised place in creation, other than that of a servant and companion to her lord. Man is master, woman is slave.' Although Mary Ann did not name this work in 'Lords of the Creation', her opening comments acknowledged that she had found many new ideas and instructive and entertaining trains of thought while reading a very interesting work on America.[19]

'Lords of the Creation' was a hard-hitting piece on women's, particularly married women's, unfair place under current English and American law. Polly Plum wrote:

At the altar she completely sinks her identity – she places herself, her goods, her future almost absolutely at the disposal of another. When that other is completely one with herself – one in heart, one in thought, one in faith, one in life – the chain, though it exists, is never felt, never galls. But how often does it happen that the rosy garland of love and truth is not there to hide the fetters! And then how black, how bitter, how real the yoke is, none can know but those who feel it. What a risk there is in marriages! What a perilous step to take.[20]

In Mary Ann's view, the sexes were more or less equal, with each possessed of good qualities, but unfortunately too often wilfully blind to the good qualities of the other. Men's assumptions of their superiority were not borne out by their behaviour, and because they were their own judges, and very lenient judges when it came to their own failings, women who did not consent to being 'led by the nose' were judged as strong-minded. To make a difference, women had to be prepared to be disliked by many men, regarded with suspicion and only coldly admired at best. For many women, this form of judgement was too great a price to pay, and they remained silent, even though they felt the injustices deeply. However, separating the interests of the sexes was unnatural, impossible and absurd. The idea of men being the head of the household was a commendable idea *if* they proved a capable head; that many men were not was the reason why any law giving men absolute control over their wives and children was unjust.

For Mary Ann, acknowledging the influence of what one had been reading was perfectly acceptable, but for a reader who was also a writer a charge of plagiarism was very serious. Mary Ann's response again revealed her strong moral principles and the importance of her personal integrity and reputation. Several months passed before she was vindicated. For this she could thank a concerned citizen who took it upon himself to complete a detailed comparison of Mrs Willard's work and Polly Plum's article, after which he sent a lengthy letter to the *Cross* under the name 'Vincit Veritas'. It was no surprise that Mary Ann had never heard of Mrs Willard's work, as it was more likely to be found on shelves containing medical treatises than on the drawing-room table. Although Vincit Veritas identified several superficial similarities in the general concerns of the two works, he concluded that '"Polly Plum" in a great measure follows up the same line of argument as Mrs. Willard, in a more homely and practical manner; but, although she agrees with her to a great extent, she reasons her argument out in a very different style, and draws her conclusions more mildly.'[21]

Within just a few weeks the tables turned, and it was Mary Ann's turn to question whether her work was being plagiarised. A new local farce titled 'The Three P. Smiths' had been performed at the Parnell Hall. Several years earlier, at the request of friends, Mary Ann had written a farce for a private charade party. The piece, which centred on 'Three J. Smiths', provided great amusement at the time, and those who saw the performance encouraged Mary Ann to offer the play to a theatrical manager.

Mary Ann took up their suggestion and sent the script to a business acquaintance in Thames on the understanding that he would pay for the piece if he considered it of sufficient merit. Although this man eventually told Mary Ann that he thought the work not appropriate for the stage, he did not return the script. The subsequent appearance of 'The Three P. Smiths' therefore struck Mary Ann as more than coincidental, and she wrote to the editor of the *Cross* asking if any of the actors, management or audience would oblige her with a brief sketch of the play. She was more than willing to lend anything she had written if it was to support a charitable enterprise but decidedly objected to her work being used without her knowledge or permission or without even the grace of acknowledgement.

Ralph Levoi wrote immediately to the *Cross* to confirm that he was the author of 'The Three P. Smiths' and that it was an entirely original piece. He was happy for Polly Plum to peruse the manuscript but questioned why, when the play had been publicised for a full week before being produced, she had not availed herself of the opportunity to either contact the theatre or attend the production in person to satisfy her concerns.

The veiled hint of criticism in Ralph Levoi's response was indicative of a turning of public opinion against some of Polly Plum's writings, in particular those that presented harsh critiques of the marriage laws. Her article 'Woman and her master', published in May 1870, was particularly controversial. She wrote of women's reluctance to parade their matrimonial troubles in public, a situation that often meant they were prepared to submit to real martyrdom rather than go to a judicial court against the man they had sworn to love, honour and obey.

At the risk of being set down as a bore and a nuisance, she felt compelled to agitate to raise the sympathies of happy men and women 'to feel for those poor women whom the existing marriage law places in the sad position of almost absolute dependence on the will and caprice of a vicious tyrant, with no hope of release but death, or, what is to many the worse alternative, the Police Court'. Proposing a law that entitled wives to a fair share of their husband's means to support themselves and their children, she argued that such a law would hardly press on husbands who were ready and willing to support their families but would prove 'an inestimable boon to many a poor, suffering creature, who cannot obtain from a monster earning good wages even the sum necessary for food and shelter'.[22]

Those responding to her article through the press dismissed the article as not representing the opinions of women generally or even of many women. One correspondent to the *Cross* doubted that even 'one woman in every ten' shared Polly Plum's views, and he objected to the subject of women's rights being forced upon public attention. While prepared to concede that educating women to be fit intellectual companions to their husbands was a worthy cause, the writer claimed that inasmuch as change was needed in the marital relationship, 'it will be brought about silently and quietly, by the efforts of women, individually, to retain the affection of their husbands, far more surely than by any noisy demonstration or agitation'.[23]

Even the editor of the *Cross* made dismissive comments, claiming that nine tenths of what was written and published on women's rights was nonsense. Although he did not want to appear discourteous, he had no hesitation in stifling further discussion by refusing to publish readers' letters on the subject. He also reminded his readership of 'the practical good sense of the House of Commons, when thousands of the women of London petitioned, and sent a deputation to demand the release of their idol, John Lilburne – "Go home and wash your dishes," said Mr. Speaker Lenthall, in the name of the House; and we may add, by way of precedent, that the English women of that day had the good sense to act upon this most excellent advice'.[24]

Surprised and hurt by the editor's remarks, Mary Ann objected that he, as an intelligent and enlightened man and the editor of a newspaper, should allow his mind to be so 'warped by prejudice' as to set all women indiscriminately at the same level. He had misrepresented her mission, speaking of it as if she had made it the business of her life to revolutionise society. The comment 'Go and wash your dishes' was as sensible as if she had said to him 'Go and black your boots.'

Given that he had been ungenerous enough to side against her, she felt obliged to state explicitly what her mission was:

> *I merely write down my thoughts on things as you write your leading articles – because it pays me to do so. My mission is to provide for my little fatherless children, and if I confined my attention solely to washing my dishes they would not often want washing, as there would seldom be food to put on them, and by-and-by in all probability the dishes themselves would go …*
> *Were I to act as I do from mere vanity, and neglect my duty, there would be wisdom in what you say; but not only I, but many women are perforce in a position in which it is our bounden duty to use such talents as we have to the best advantage. We have to buy our dishes as well as wash them, as you have to do with your boots and their cleaning.*[25]

The editor hastily apologised and expressed his extreme regret that this esteemed contributor felt aggrieved. He was at pains to assure her that beyond the title that appeared above his note, he had not intended any reference to either her or her writings: 'We simply put an end to a controversy in which "Polly Plum" had taken no part, but in which her "mission" and her writing appeared to be misunderstood.'[26]

Possibly heartened by the editor's apology, Mary Ann wrote a lengthy letter to the *Cross* pointing out that there was no scriptural dictate for the monetary position of wives in England and America, and it was therefore good and fitting that this issue be discussed on this side of the world as well. She agreed that the right to 'maintenance money' might be an open question, but even so, it did not detract from the fact that men's rights over their wives' property was a relic of feudalism that should be done away with.[27]

The timing of the publication of 'Woman and her master' was significant because the Married Women's Property Bill was due to be presented to parliament. Of greater significance, perhaps, was the content of some of the debates relating to the Bill. This content clearly showed that several politicians were familiar with the arguments expressed by women's rights advocates and that the movement propounding such rights was growing locally. When introducing the Bill to the House of Representatives, Mr James Crowe Richmond acknowledged that it was likely that outside parliament the Bill would be 'misinterpreted and identified with the movement going on for many years in America, more recently in England, and which had lately given signs of life in some parts of this Colony, namely, the movement in favour of what were called "women's rights"'. He also stressed that the Bill was not intended to 'unsex woman' and place her in the same position as men.[28]

Mr Richmond's efforts to distance the proposed legislation from the movement for women's rights were telling. On the one hand, he assured his fellow members of parliament that he did not despise a movement 'in which some of the best educated and most endowed of their countrywomen were engaged'. On the other hand, he stated that 'the ludicrous extravagancies of the agitation as carried on elsewhere were patent to every one' but added that young movements were always liable to extremes and society would only assimilate that part of the movement that was good.[29]

The existing married women's property legislation provided protection orders over the property of a married woman's earnings in cases of desertion or misconduct. The Bill presented to parliament in June 1870 proposed that all married women reserve full control of all the property they possessed at the time of marriage, and of any property they acquired after marriage by gift, bequest or their own labour. By the time the Bill passed into law, its provisions were somewhat watered down, but they still represented an important incremental step in married women's property protection.[30]

Although her detractors were getting more vocal, Mary Ann still had some supporters who were prepared to publicly voice their respect for her personally and for the cause she advocated. Correspondent 'R.K.', for example, considered that Polly Plum had a 'manifest call to literary work; inasmuch as her style of composition is superior, the subjects on which she discourses are usually important, and the manner in which she treats them is vigorous and eminently judicious'. Licensing Justice Joseph Crispe, who was a frequent correspondent to the newspapers under the pen name 'Old Practical', was also a supporter of sorts. Although a rather controversial figure with a knack for getting offside with his contemporaries, he thought Polly Plum generally gave excellent and sound advice, and he felt proud to have such a forcible and common-sense female writer among the Auckland public.[31]

Many of Mary Ann's articles were still relatively conservative pieces unlikely to cause offence, and this aspect of her writing no doubt ensured that she generally had a reasonably receptive audience. Mary Ann continued to write frequently about girls' education, as did other contributors to the newspapers. For some years, a small but dedicated group in Otago had been lobbying the Otago Provincial Council for a girls' secondary school as a companion institution to Otago Boys' High School, which had opened in 1863. Foremost among these activists was Learmonth Whyte Dalrymple, a Scottish immigrant known for her discreet persistence and who was in constant contact with leading British educationalists. For six years she presented petitions, wrote letters and put constant pressure on the council, which eventually established an education commission to consider proposals from the local education board.

Having followed the progress of Mrs Dalrymple and her ladies' committee, Mary Ann, along with many supporters of girls' education across the country, was greatly heartened by the announcement that the Otago council intended to open the first public girls' secondary school in the new year. The Educational Society in Auckland had also been trying to establish high-class public secondary education for girls, although public opinion on the issue was divided. Some people were in favour of following the example set by the Otago council, but others thought there were already enough schools in Auckland and that simply offering some additional classes for girls would be sufficient.

The Auckland Board of Education grappled with these issues. In his annual report, Inspector of Schools Mr Richard O'Sullivan noted that although some of the 46 public schools in the Auckland area were being conducted in a satisfactory manner, many were in very unsuitable buildings and efficiency was not easily obtained. There was no problem attracting teachers at even low levels of salaries. However, because the education board did not have sufficient money to invest in teacher training schools, the inspector recommended that while the board should continue to try to establish schools with high standards of efficiency, it should also continue to fund those of lower grades, particularly in the remote and generally poorer districts of Auckland province. Schools, the inspector continued, needed to be established so that children could at least learn habits of order and neatness and acquire some elementary knowledge, even when their teachers were not well trained and the schoolrooms and resources not what they should be.

Mary Ann disagreed. She strongly maintained that inferior schools and inferior teachers often did more harm than good. Radical change was needed to ensure the provision of a thorough system of education, particularly for girls. A smattering of showy accomplishments and a barely elementary knowledge of English hardly constituted an education. Too many incompetent teachers, frequent and injudicious changing of schools and a lack of early home discipline were all adding, she argued, to the problem. Licensing teachers through an examination process, careful selection of schools on the part of parents to ensure they had superior teachers, and ensuring children were taught to be obedient, self-disciplined and respectful of others would go a long way towards remedying the situation. These arguments were certainly not hollow preaching on her part. She had petitioned leading members of central government as well as members of the Auckland Provincial Council on the issue of licensing teachers and fining unlicensed teachers who accepted fees from students, insisting that a bill be introduced to this effect.

Mary Ann's select ladies' school at Lake Villa was the largest in Epsom. Several prominent civic leaders visited the school, including Thomas Bannatyne Gillies, the recent Superintendent of Auckland, and Thomas William Croke, the recently appointed Catholic Bishop of Auckland. Although opposed to secular education, Bishop Croke was surprised and pleased when visiting Mary Ann's school to find a class doing a blackboard lesson on how to make bread. The annual break-up party and prize-giving for the school held just before Christmas attested to the success of Mary Ann's teaching methods. Having been educated at London's Queen's College in a system that gave sound practical knowledge in all branches of study followed by examinations, Mary Ann used this same system to great effect. Some of the young ladies who had been almost entirely ignorant of history at the commencement of the year now showed great proficiency in that subject, and similar improvements were evident in grammar and geography. In spelling and dictation, several of the elder pupils were rarely in error, even with difficult and unusual words. The school prizes were published in the newspaper, and Mary Ann took the opportunity to announce that she intended to engage a leading master to hold a viva voce examination the following year, for which extra prizes would be offered.

Successful as Mary Ann's teaching methods were, there were some who did not agree with publishing prize lists and examination results for girls, lest the young ladies in question forget their modesty. Writing from Mauku, a small settlement near Pukekohe, 'A Grandmother' said that she considered the practice unseemly, injurious and repugnant and had therefore been moved to write to the newspaper to protest it. Observing that some children had an intuitive aptitude for learning while for others it required immense effort, she thought that prizes given for a particular talent risked inflating the recipient with a false sense of superiority and could cause resentment in those less able. If prizes were to be awarded, they should be few and simple so as not to over-tax the hard earnings of the teachers, and they should only be awarded for general good conduct, punctuality of attendance and attention to study.[32]

Mary Ann responded to these criticisms with a lengthy article titled 'Examinations in ladies' schools'. She noted that while A Grandmother's views may have been generally held when that 'venerable old lady' was a girl, increased experience had proven how sadly useless and helpless women had become for want of a practical and thorough education:

> If 'Grandmamma' worked a sampler, and wasted many precious hours in minutely portraying impossible pink birds on some unknown variety of lavender-coloured trees, no doubt she felt very much elated at her triumph over some other young ladies not so learned in the mysteries of cross and satin stitch; and for my part I think it much better that girls should be elated over something more useful, and not a bit more injurious to their modesty, though no doubt the dear old lady who has provoked this essay does not agree with me as she looks at the framed wonders in ornithology and horticulture that cost her so many hours of hard work, and sighs to think of these degenerate days, when girls prefer to exalt over something more intellectual than a huge sampler.[33]

Prizes, Mary Ann admitted, were a great tax on a teacher's income, but until a better plan was devised, they were a necessary expense because they provided pupils with incentives to really exert themselves.

As she had pointed out many times, the underlying issue was the fact that there were very few respectable lucrative professions open to women. The unfairness of this state of affairs struck her again when she read that two women had recently been imprisoned in Mount Eden Gaol for debt. As usual, her immediate response was to write to the newspapers because, as she wrote elsewhere, 'the greatest social anomaly is to forbid women to vote, tie their hands with reference to a choice of employments, prate of their domestic sphere as the only proper one for women, curtail their sphere of usefulness so that it is almost impossible for a self-helpful woman to earn a decent living, and yet, whilst loading her with all these disqualifications, to make her as liable as any man to the pains and penalties of the law.'[34]

Mary Ann decided, however, not to put these thoughts into a newspaper article or letter, having concluded that the two women's misdemeanours must be cases of flagrant dishonesty and want of principle; perhaps each of these two women had wantonly and wilfully misappropriated money and never made an effort to repay it? But then she read an account from Mr Alfred Cadman, a member of the Auckland Provincial Council, whose attention had been called to the plight of one of the women. A poor widow with six children, she had been incarcerated for a debt of 12 shillings, which, with expenses of one shilling per day for maintenance and seven pence for food, now amounted to about 20 shillings. Appalled and angered by the injustice, Mary Ann asked:

> Tell me, 'Grandmother' from Mauku, who insists on extreme privacy and modesty in the education of girls, how those tender qualities would fit her for the law courts and Mt. Eden Gaol? Her lot – that poor mother now there incarcerated – is the lot of many, and may be the future lot of any girl – to strive, to work, to struggle, for fatherless children. Think of the thousands of widows left by the devastating war in Europe. Amongst us the evil may not be so apparent – the widows are not so many, but depend upon it there are cases of severe struggle and heavy responsibility in our very midst – women heartsick and weary with the effort to carry the load on their shoulders, too heavy for them because they are neither fitted by education nor by habit to bear it.[35]

Several months earlier, when writing under her pen name, she had presented the supposititious case of a small, healthy, intelligent and well-educated young woman left a widow with children dependent upon her, whose only real choice of occupation was to enter teaching. While the fictitious woman was well qualified for this profession and had an aptitude for it, her salary was not sufficient to cover her expenses of rent, food, paying for someone to care for the house and children, and all the other expenses that come with being a self-employed teacher and a lady. In posing the question, 'What can she do?' Polly Plum countered the most common response of 'Let her marry again' with the observation that even if the young woman felt inclined to do so, the opportunity could signal a change for the worse. Many men might see such a young lady as a possible source of income rather than a companion; even if this were not the case, she would face the painful struggle of having to reconcile the two duties of being a good parent to her children and being an obedient wife to a man on whom her children had no natural claim.[36]

The scenario clearly mirrored Mary Ann's personal circumstances and may account for why some regular correspondents, such as 'Old Practical', who knew Mary Ann personally and who often responded to such invitations to engage in discussion and debate, were silent on this occasion. However, this new case of a widow in gaol for debt was not supposititious but a case of genuine hardship. Mary Ann directly challenged readers, among them Old Practical, Jemmy

Jenkins and A Grandmother, when she wrote: 'On her [the widow's] behalf, and on behalf of others who are only so much better off than she is that they may have more gentle-hearted creditors to deal with, I ask again the question: What can she do?'[37]

Old Practical, who described himself as 'essentially a lover of womankind, and their devoted servant', took up the challenge and responded with a quick rundown of stock arguments for preserving the status quo: the law was not modelled on a code of gallantry, so women should face the same penalties as men if they broke the law; if there was to be universal equality between men and women, then this naturally meant that they must each be able to serve as soldiers, sailors, constables, policemen and the like; and finally, did not the Scripture forcibly describe the relative position of men and women?[38]

'Humble-Bee' found the incarceration of the widow very distressing, but took exception to those who placed the load of heavy responsibility on the shoulders of the heartsick and weary women Polly Plum referred to. Too many women lived with expectations beyond their husband's means, and therefore prevented their husbands from putting savings aside for future security. Instead, mothers should teach their daughters to assist in the household work and not put on superior airs. While Mary Ann did not disagree with the substance of Humble-Bee's remarks, having herself voiced similar views on the need for women to set aside artificial airs, she disputed his laying the blame at the feet of women, particularly poor dependent women. 'Prevailing erroneous views on respectability' certainly needed to be reformed because 'civilisation and refinement have created a class of women for whom there is no sphere of work'. However, she continued, there was a need for 'something easier of attainment than the entire revolutionising of the views of society' that Humble-Bee proposed. And while Old Practical may have intended to be a friend to the ladies, he was, at best, a mistaken one. Most of his arguments could be easily countered, especially his claim that 'The Bible obligations are all purely moral obligations, and have nothing to do with the legal question.'[39]

Mary Ann was not particularly interested in dragging the scriptures into the debate about women's rights, but because her opponents persistently claimed that what she advocated was contrary to scripture, she decided to tackle the issue head on. In what was to prove a provocative article titled 'The law and the Bible', she countered those who quoted the apostle Paul on wives' obedience to their husbands, pointing out that the Ten Commandments, which she considered infinitely superior in authority to the epistles, did not touch at all on the duties of wives to their husbands. However, when she questioned what right men had to set laws even in excess of apostolic injunctions in order to obtain additional marital power, it was too much for correspondent 'Ami', who charged her with breaking loose from orthodoxy by expounding a doctrine of discrimination.[40]

Mary Ann sincerely regretted giving the impression that she was saying anything contrary to the teachings of the Holy Scriptures and made it very clear that her war was with man's laws; she had no cavil with those of her God. When 'Amicus' entered the discussion to ask her what changes she thought the marriage laws needed, she welcomed him for agreeing with her without being 'contemptuous, discourteous, or illogical'. Tired of opponents who treated her as if she was a 'rabid revolutionist' who advocated social rebellion on the part of women, she expressed her frustration at the way many of her opponents persisted in either disregarding or misrepresenting all she had written about the responsibilities, duties and obligations of wives:

> *My sole objection to the laws as affecting the doctrine of wifely obedience is, that the jurisdiction presses very unfairly on the wives of men who are not governed by moral or religious obligations. Where both parties in the marriage contract are governed by the same moral and religious principles, I can see no reason why the wife should refuse implicit obedience in all things important. Of course she should obey; and if there were a difference of opinion, and she could not persuade him, she should yield to him, and, if she did not, she would find all good women against her.*[41]

As she was at pains to point out, the problem was that the laws gave men excessive power over their wives, children and property, and these laws were not in harmony with either the letter or the spirit of God's law. Interestingly, Mary Ann signed her letter in reply to Amicus 'Polly Plum, not "Mrs Plum"', which suggests that when she wrote under her *nom de plume*, she was writing as an independent woman.

The debates over women's rights and scripture continued for some time. 'E. Stephens', a scathing critic of what he described as the 'monomania which prevails in certain circles in reference to the rights of women', entered the fray by quoting numerous verses from the Old and New Testaments outlining women's divinely appointed rights. His letter was countered by Reverend Samuel Edger, who reminded the reading public that Mr Stephens strongly advocated capital punishment of prisoners. Happily, however, public opinion did not endorse his views on either issue. As a believer of the teachings of scripture, Reverend Edger objected to the practice of calling out isolated verses and claiming them as biblical authority for what amounted to ignorance and despotism. 'E. Earnest' also took Mr Stephens to task when he stated that while no true woman objected to the spirit of the texts he had quoted, women required that those who held them in such subjection should be trustworthy and principled and so worthy of respect. The editor of the *Cross* was even less obliging, particularly as Mr Stephens had engaged in a lengthy assault on the arguments proffered by John Stuart Mill without having read the work he had attacked. Deciding not to subject readers 'to follow the powerful ratiocinations of such a writer', the editor respectfully recommended that 'next time he essays to write about anything he should observe the preliminary of first seeing that he knows something about what he assails'.[42]

By her own admission, Mary Ann was fully occupied, and the pace of her activities increased as the year progressed. She was still contributing several lengthy articles each week to the *Cross* and engaging in debates through the letters to the editor columns on an almost daily basis. In the precious breaks when she was not teaching and her home was free of boarders, she often visited the women's department of the Mount Eden Gaol or the Auckland Lunatic Asylum. Little is known of the care or education arrangements for Lulu and Willie while their mother was keeping up her indefatigable schedule. Lulu would have been too young to attend her mother's private classes for girls, although presumably there were times when necessity required that one or other of the children sat in quietly at the back of the teaching room.

Mary Ann's evenings also tended to be full of engagements, meetings and community events. One notable event was a complimentary concert by Madame Moller, a well-respected performer who generously gave entertainments to aid a variety of benevolent charities. Organised by Madame Moller's musical friends and admirers, the concert saw the New City Hall in Queen Street crammed, and everyone attending the event considered it a great success. Happy to volunteer her services, Mary Ann, known among her closest circles for her singing and musical abilities, performed for the first time in front of a public audience. She must have been heartened by the long, deafening applause that met her when she took the stage. The reporter from the *New Zealand Herald* had no doubt that Mary Ann's appearance was the drawcard for many in the audience. Having been warmly applauded for her solo rendition of 'The Bridge', Mary Ann received a loud request for an encore.

Part of the reason for her enthusiastic reception was due to the advertisements for Madame Moller's concert, which identified Mary Ann as Polly Plum. In a sense, the concert was her dénouement. On the same day, another advertisement announced that Mrs Colclough ('Polly Plum') was to present a public lecture at the City Hall the following Tuesday on the topic of 'The Subjection of Woman'. Several weeks earlier, having had 'quite enough of *ad misericord am* appeals and eruptions of sentiment in newspaper columns', an anonymous writer had issued a challenge to all who advocated for 'women's rights' to stop hiding behind *nom de plumes* and anonymous letters and to show who they were and what they wanted through public meetings and open canvassing. Mary Ann read his challenge and under her pen name respectfully pointed out that while Auckland hosted women who both could and would take up the public platform for the cause of women, many of these women were 'self-helpful' with dependants. It was their dependence on the approval of that imaginary English character Mrs Grundy – the arbiter of social respectability – that held them back from any action fraught with the potential for ridicule and censure. However, in the following few days, some of the leading ladies of Auckland pledged Mary Ann their support if she agreed to follow the example of their American sisters and take to the public stage, which she did. For Mary Ann, this coming out on the public stage heralded a new chapter in her advocacy of the cause of women.[43]

CHAPTER THREE

A Modern Female Fanatic

By the time the doors to the New City Hall opened for Mary Ann's first public lecture at 7.30pm on Tuesday 26 June 1871, a large crowd had assembled. His Excellency the Governor and Lady Bowen had given their patronage, and while the reserved seats were filled with many of the prominent public men of Auckland, a noticeably large number of ladies were also present. For many in the audience, the novelty of a lady presenting a public lecture had been sufficient motivation to leave their homes on an inclement winter's night. In a piece announcing the lecture was to take place that evening, the editor of the Auckland *Evening Star* stated that although Polly Plum had her share of detractors, he was confident Mrs Colclough would be met with a chivalrous reception given her acknowledged ability and practical common sense.

Reverend Samuel Edger took the chair. In his introductory remarks, he noted that although the question of women's rights was in its infancy and the lady presenting before them was lecturing for the first time, he trusted the audience would excuse any nervousness and accord her a patient, quiet and thoughtful hearing. Mary Ann then took the stage in a calm and dignified manner and was met with a long round of applause. From the onset it was obvious that the gathered audience was receptive, although many in the crowded hall sat with bemused expressions in the expectation of something unconventional from a lady who, over the previous couple of years, had created somewhat of a sensation in the local press. After some initial signs of nervousness, Mary Ann gained confidence and, in the words of the reporter from the *Evening Star*, 'produced that sympathetic feeling between speaker and hearers which is the best and most pleasing stimulus to a lecturer'. Although Mary Ann continued to exhibit nervousness during her lecture, she spoke at times with great freedom and vivacity.[1]

Acknowledging that simply appearing on the public platform to present a lecture would doubtless offend some members of the audience, including personal friends, Mary Ann began by expressing her strong belief that what she was doing was right and that she would not be deterred from what she considered her duty. Heartened by spontaneous applause, she added that her conscience was at ease with this step she was taking, particularly as she was a self-dependent woman. A great deal had been said about the troubles of man's estate; now it was time for women to start enjoying some privileges.

Mary Ann began her lecture with an issue that had been the subject of recent debate in the newspapers, namely the question of women's right to vote at public elections. The question, she said, was not so much one of inclination but of fairness. It was no secret that drunken men played leading roles at many elections, thus presenting a bitter satire on man's boasted superiority. When she asked the audience, 'Would not a sober woman be better than a drunken man under such circumstance?' its members rallied with cries of 'Hear, hear.' If, she continued, granting women the right to vote mitigated such an evil, then she was heartily in support of women going to the polling booths.

Mary Ann then turned her attention to the main topic of the evening – women's subservience to men. She explained that she intended to divide her formal lecture into four parts, starting with the origin of the theory that woman is inferior to man and the basis on which that theory rested. Next, she would consider the evidence against this theory. During the third part of her lecture, she would elaborate on the effects of women's subjection, after which she would bring the lecture to a close by presenting her views on how women's subservient position could be remedied.

Those in the audience who had followed Mary Ann's writings in the newspapers would have encountered no real surprises in the arguments presented, but to hear Mary Ann in person, speaking in what one reporter described as a 'terse and telling' manner, found favour with the audience, and the lecture was punctuated with applause. Some of her comments, such as husbands not being fit for the position of sitting on a pedestal for their wives to worship, or the expectation for a wife to always have a ready smile for her husband no matter in what state or at what time he arrived home, met with supportive laughter. But her underlying message was very serious: the present marriage law was an insult to women, bad men should not have legal sanction to tyrannise their wives by means of their children, and wives should only obey all reasonable commands.

By all accounts, the lecture was a great success. The audience remained attentive from beginning to end and met Mary Ann's closing remarks with loud, sustained applause. Thanking those present, Mary Ann announced that she intended to lecture again in the near future on the issue of female education. A report in the Wellington *Evening Post* described her theory as 'sensibly and elaborately worked out' yet basically very straightforward and simple: 'By making women more self-dependent when single, and personally responsible when married, not only would a simple act of justice be done, but the sex would be benefitted [sic] in circumstances as well as intellectually and morally.' According to the reviewer for the Auckland *Evening Star*, Mary Ann discussed her subject 'with originality and great ability, praise and censure being distributed to the sexes with the utmost impartiality, and the truthfulness and point of the remarks elicited from time to time a genuine burst of applause and commendation. There was nothing either *outre* or revolutionary in the ideas enunciated, and Mrs. Colclough was the lady throughout.'[2]

The reviewer for the *Daily Southern Cross* was equally as complimentary and pointed out that 'No doubt some attended under the impression that there would be something ridiculous about a lady lecturing: if any did so, they would have been disappointed.' Mrs Colclough's enunciation was good and her manner pleasing, and although the fact that she spoke a little too rapidly for such a large audience detracted from the effectiveness of her address, experience would remedy this problem. Concluding that the lecture was one of the most interesting ever delivered in Auckland, the *Cross* reporter was sure that if Mrs Colclough chose to pursue this line, she would prove to be a very popular and successful lecturer.[3]

The review in the *New Zealand Herald* was more perfunctory and matter of fact, focusing only on providing a lengthy detailed description of the substance of the lecture rather than on the delivery and reception. This response was hardly surprising. The *Herald*, known to be considerably more conservative than its main competitor the *Cross*, had given only scant coverage to Polly Plum's views in the past, tending instead to reprint articles from international periodicals that expressed anti-women sentiments.[4]

Assuming the role of detached critic, the *Herald* also published a letter sent from the *Hawke's Bay Herald*, by a man who, having been in the habit of using Polly Plum's letters as opiates to help him go to sleep at night, decided, as a token of his gratitude to the benefactress of his regularly induced slumber, to attend the lecture. Leaving greatly disappointed at hearing nothing new, he encountered some days later a gentleman of his acquaintance. Knowing this man to be a good husband and an affectionate father, he was saddened to hear his life had been made a misery since 'the evil hour' in which he had taken his wife to hear Polly Plum speak. With tears in his eyes, the gentleman explained he did not know what had come over his wife Emma. They had always had a happy home life, but since attending Polly Plum's lecture his wife had sat, moped and cried for hours at a time saying she wanted her 'rights'. When the husband asked his wife what she meant by this, she either could not or would not reply, and the children had started to treat him as if he was some kind of monster who was killing their dear mother.[5]

Although grateful for the *New Zealand Herald*'s coverage of her lecture, Mary Ann was disappointed the newspaper had described it in such detail given that she intended to deliver the same lecture at the Academy of Music in Grahamstown (the northern end of present-day Thames) on the following Friday evening. She also considered the review to contain some important errors that she felt bound to correct because they conveyed sentiments at variance with her actual opinions:

> I am reported as saying that with me the matter of having a right to vote is a question of inclination and not of equity. What I did say was that it was a matter of equity and not of inclination. Then, again, Mr. [John Stuart] Mill does not advocate obedience in wives, and I do. In the last place, I said that I did not think that women in any great numbers would ever concern themselves about politics, but I think those who have proved good queens regent and self-helpful women demonstrate the capacity that is in women for government.[6]

For several days, the lecture was the talk of the town, and many rued not having been there to experience the event first-hand. Many ladies in Auckland apparently had been unable to attend because of the wet weather, and some of them urged Mary Ann to provide a repeat performance on their account. She obliged, although the audience this time was more select than numerous. A couple of days later she redelivered the lecture at Thames and received a hearty welcome from an audience whose numbers were fewer than anticipated. The paucity of the audience was attributed solely to the weather, however; it had rained all day, and the downpours became heavier as the evening progressed, to the extent that the streets presented an unusually bedraggled and uninviting prospect. But the rare entertainment of a lady lecturer encouraged enough to fill the dress circle and the boxes, thereby amounting to what could be described in theatre parlance as 'a house'. The Episcopalian minister Reverend Vicesimus Lush presided over the evening, and the great many ladies present showed a lively interest.

Although the Thames address was only Mary Ann's third appearance as a public lecturer, she was strong and confident in her presentation and thoroughly conversant with her topic. Her simple dignity of style, fluent enunciation and thorough conviction of the truth of her message impressed her audience; all those present, both women and men, applauded her frequently and loudly throughout her talk. The local Thames correspondent for the Auckland *Weekly News* commented in glowing terms: 'I feel assured that her labours in the new path of duty she feels called upon to tread will not be wanting in good effects, and also that she bids fair to become eminently popular as a lecturer. I have heard nothing but kind words spoken about her to-day (Saturday) by those who were present at Friday's very agreeable entertainment. One gentleman was even enthusiastic, and vowed that his whole family should hear her the next time she visited the Thames.'[7]

When the winter school vacation came to an end, Mary Ann reopened her School for Young Ladies at Epsom, and in the days and weeks following her first lectures she continued her busy routine of articles and letters to the editor under the name Polly Plum. For one letter writer to the *Evening Star*, presumably a medical doctor, Mary Ann's newspaper correspondence was blatant self-advertising. He wrote:

> *The letters which appear in the papers every day, signed by 'Polly Plum,' must be a splendid advertisement for that enterprising lady. She has certainly a great deal of 'go' about her, and sees this is greatly to her advantage to have a constant correspondence going on about her. And it is far more effective than a mere advertisement, for it is probably read, which her advertisements probably would not be. I think I must try and get up a little excitement about my medicine: kill a man or two with an overdose, and then fill the columns of the press with letters in defence.*[8]

This writer's sentiments were mild, however, in comparison with those expressed by the editor of the Wellington *Evening Post*. In a lengthy editorial, he denigrated Mary Ann Colclough for her exhibition on the public platform, which he considered 'both painful and disgusting':

> *This 'latest novelty,' in the way of sensational movements, has been*
> *introduced to the Auckland people by a Mrs. Colclough, who, under the*
> *nom de plume of 'Polly Plum', has, for a year or two past, penned an infinite*
> *amount of nonsense concerning the fair sex, through the columns of the*
> *Southern Cross. Finding that her lubrications in the Press did not seem to*
> *be productive of much effect, 'Polly' has at length abandoned the pen, and*
> *taken boldly to the 'stump' – in short, she has come forward as the platform*
> *denunciator of the wrongs of her sisterhood.*[9]

Convinced that Polly Plum would achieve little success 'in disseminating her pestilent and foolish doctrines, or in inoculating the women of New Zealand with the advanced opinions held by a noisy and insignificant portion of the sex in America', the *Post* editor relegated her to the 'special and peculiar' class of women, comprised of 'disappointed and ill-tempered old maids, who, never having had the chance of entering upon the connubial state, vow deadly vengeance upon the whole race of mankind, or married women who can't hit matters off with their yoke fellows in the bonds of Hymen, sometimes find a sort of vent for their spleen in stirring up discontent in the bosoms of the fairer and more amiable portion of the sex.' Erroneously assuming that 'Polly Plum' was 'a capital specimen of the intensely disagreeable type of female first mentioned', he claimed that her story was, to a certain extent, public property and one of disappointed hopes, and that her arguments were almost too absurd to excite anything but laughter.[10]

Aware that celebrity status always comes at a cost, Mary Ann was prepared for the likelihood that taking the bold step of becoming a public lecturer would attract increased criticism from her detractors. She responded to the *Post* editorial with a lengthy article titled 'What Women Want' in which she presented before the reader her heartfelt dedication to a cause from which 'no amount of contumely, insult, contempt, or ridicule, would make me swerve for one instant'. Mary Ann submitted the article, written under her *nom de plume*, to the editor of the *Herald*, who had reprinted extracts of the inflammatory editorial from the *Evening Post*.[11]

Had the *Evening Post* misrepresented only her opinions, Mary Ann might have been prepared to let the matter rest, but misrepresenting her private history in order to find mean personal motives for her advocacy of women was unacceptable. Her request to the Wellington editor to correct the statement met with an extraordinary reply: the writer had intended to represent her as a separated wife, and the representation of her as a disagreeable old maid was simply a printing error! With her respectability at stake, Mary Ann was determined to have the misrepresentation refuted to the Wellington public. The *Evening Post* refused to correct the statement, so she turned to its contemporary, the *Wellington Independent*, which obliged by prominently publishing her letter in its advertisements section.[12]

Undeterred, Mary Ann duly advertised that she would deliver her promised lecture on 'Female Education' on 31 July at the Auckland City Hall. Anxious not to miss out, a group of lady supporters from the North Shore chartered the ferry-steamer *Devonport* to enable their fellow North Shore residents to attend. In announcing the lecture, Mary Ann offered a special invitation to mothers and daughters. The editor of the *Cross* unhesitatingly added his recommendation, assuring readers that there was nothing that even the most fastidious would deem unladylike or unwomanly about her addresses, however contrary they might be to the ideas some had formed on women's duties and spheres. The editor of the *Evening Star* likewise reinforced Mary Ann's educational and intellectual credentials to speak knowledgably on the issue, anticipating that she would have something 'telling and racy' to say on the subject.[13]

On the evening of her 31 July lecture, unsettled weather again conspired against Mary Ann, leading her to muse that perhaps 'Jupiter Pluvious' was determined to prove himself a persistent foe of women's rights. The audience was not as large as expected, but the lecture was fairly attended by equal numbers of men and women. Notable among the gathering of well-known gentlemen in the audience were the Right Reverend Dr Cowie, Bishop of Auckland, and the Reverend Benjamin Thornton Dudley. Reverend Samuel Edger presided for the occasion. The warm and long applause that greeted Mary Ann echoed her reception at her first public lecture.

During her hour-long address, Mary Ann systematically outlined her views, most of which she had rehearsed many times in her newspaper articles. She also spoke of her intention, at the inducement of her supporters, to open a seminary for young ladies in Auckland. Mary Ann had first referred to this matter in an article titled 'Good Housewives', published in the *Cross* in May, and written after she had held discussions with several clergy and gentlemen about the scarcity and expense of servants in Auckland. She had in mind, she told these men, a scheme for providing a school for domestic instruction. She also said she would be prepared to act on her idea if sufficient support could be provided.[14]

Her scheme consisted of a large boarding- and day-school with a full complement of staff: a principal; a competent lady manager who would, by necessity, be a good teacher; a matron; a thorough cook and household manager;

a dressmaker who was an experienced needlewoman; and teachers, as in any ordinary school. During the morning of each school day, the school's complement of pupils would be broken up into detachments assigned to the kitchen, laundry or dressmaker, or to music or drawing teachers, or to some other branch of study that did not require the attendance of the whole school.[15]

Three hours each afternoon would be devoted to the usual school classes. Both boarders and day scholars would follow the same routine, but the boarders, under the superintendence of the matron, would also assist with breakfast and tea and attend to their own rooms. Because pupils would be trained in the areas of laundry washing, cooking, scrubbing and cleaning, and making and mending their own and their brothers' clothing, the usual expenses of boarding schools would be done away with, so keeping school fees at a moderate level. Moreover, because all pupils would share these tasks, the exertion of the hard work involved would provide them with a healthy and wholesome relaxation; much better, Mary Ann claimed, for the figure and constitution than hours of callisthenic exercises.

Two days after delivering her lecture on female education, Mary Ann wrote to the *Cross* about her scheme, indicating that it was something she had been working towards for a long time:

> *I have long waited to commence a school in Auckland for girls, founded on sound common-sense principles – a school where, without neglecting the so-called accomplishments, a thorough English education would be made the chief object, and, if possible, some amount of useful training secured. Want of means quite prevented my being able to undertake this work, earnestly as I desire to do so. Many friends advised me to try and raise subscriptions for this object, but I preferred earning the means to begging it; and therefore, making a strong effort to overcome all the dread of censure and sarcasm that I could not help feeling, I determined to try and lecture, praying earnestly to God to give me strength and courage to deal me through the ordeal. With such motives, you will see that the reasons that make me desire good audiences are not entirely personal, and that others will, I hope, be benefited as much as I shall by the success of my course of lectures. I think, perhaps, it will not be amiss to give these few particulars to the public. They can be vouched for by many clergymen and gentlemen, whose advice and assistance I asked before I began to lecture.[16]*

On the same day that Mary Ann delivered her lecture, the editor of the *Herald* dedicated his editorial to the issue of female education. Like many of his contemporaries, the editor considered female education a question of primary importance because it affected the social condition of the wider community. Current provisions for girls' education were, he agreed, not sufficient to adequately prepare them for their duties in the domestic sphere. Grounding in practical knowledge was needed alongside training in 'useful refinements', because this form of liberal education provided the means by which to elevate women's social and material position. However, he drew the line at the 'speculative and fanciful' view that claimed woman's proper position was one of equality with men. God had assigned woman to a 'quiescent and subjunctive' position. He contended that the question of women's rights was purely social, and that 'any attempt to give it political significance is proof of great ignorance, or bespeaks a love of notoriety which has overcome all regard for sound judgement and sober sense'.[17]

Others agreed. Respected Auckland-based educationalist Mrs Frances Shayle George supported the need for educational reform and proposed that a standard of female education be set. She considered the current educational system 'lamentably deficient' in providing the young girls of the colony with the necessary teaching and training 'to fit, or unfit them to be the future mothers of a great State, the Britain of the South Pacific'. Like the editor of the *Herald*, she maintained that 'a woman's sphere is not the world, nor to govern the world – but to purify it; to be the leading principle of good order, peace and refinement in man's sole remaining Paradise, his own Home'. Even the editor of the *Cross* argued that 'Disguise it as we may, the great aim of our education of girls is not to fit them for the independent exercise of those gifts which Nature has conferred on them, but for that state of dependence upon others which is set before them as the object of their hopes.'[18]

Mary Ann held a different view. The education currently provided for girls was severely deficient and needed a thorough overhaul. Why should a girl's education be confined to preparing her for future domestic responsibilities? The practical reality was that there were many instances of 'compulsory self-helpfulness': not all women would marry, some would be widowed, and some would find themselves married to idle incompetent men incapable of providing for their wives and families. Accordingly, it was 'perfectly ridiculous' to educate girls solely for domestic life. It was wrong to presume that man was naturally woman's protector or that men were better fitted for public activities and women best confined to the domestic sphere of influence. Of course a girl's education should be useful and thorough with a strong domestic element, but girls should still be able to choose their future.[19]

Taking an even more radical line, Mary Ann made explicit the links between the current education of girls, and women's legal position as wives. In her view, all the intelligence and learning of the present day had done very little for women as wives. It may have increased their mental status, but it had not ameliorated their condition. It had made them capable of thinking and acting reasonably, but their hands were still tied. Even if society did educate women like men but continued to treat them like children, Mary Ann cautioned they would rebel; the more women were educated, the less willing they would be to submit to their unequal position in law.

On the evening of 7 August 1871, Mary Ann presented her lecture on female education at the Academy of Music, Grahamstown, with Mr W. Lloyd presiding. Mary Ann's increasing confidence as a speaker was evident; her audience frequently applauded what she had to say, and at the end of her talk they proffered her a hearty vote of thanks. The reporter for the *Cross* commented that 'the ability and zeal of the lecturer in the cause she has espoused were abundantly manifested by the excellence of her discourse'. But despite the enthusiasm of those attending, Mary Ann's lecturing was proving to be a relatively unsuccessful means of raising funds for her proposed school, which she was now considering establishing in Thames rather than Auckland.[20]

From the earliest days of her newspaper journalism, Mary Ann and her views had triggered debate, but her increased profile as a public lecturer served as a catalyst for other women to write to the newspapers and engage in public discussion on the issues she raised. Not all agreed with her views, but some were emboldened to speak out publicly through the letters to the editor columns. Some even used pseudonyms inspired by Polly Plum's name. 'Janie Plum', for example, had not attended the first lecture on 'The Subjection of Woman' but had read the review in the *Herald*. The notion of a political woman was, she opined, a 'female monstrosity', and surely evils would ensue if women were granted the vote. Although she objected to all of Mary Ann's arguments, she stated her determination to attend the lecture on female education.[21]

'Maggie Plum' from Parnell, however, thought that whatever Polly Plum's masculine proclivities might be, she had a woman's share of vanity and more than average intellect and did not like to hide her light under a bushel. Maggie Plum felt a sense of affinity with Polly Plum because, as a poetess, she had often thought of printing her 'effusions', which she thought would be appreciated because they were 'racy and sparkling'. But Maggie Plum was practical as well as poetical and declared that if she were the superintendent, she would immediately order new docks, railroads across the whole countryside and attend to the water supply and drainage. Willing to forgo the pleasure of looking in the drapers' windows and to shop after six o'clock if the gentlemen would advocate closing the hotels at that hour, she would prefer that husbands and sweethearts worked until seven or eight o'clock in the evening than muddle away their wits at the bar.[22]

'Mother', who knew Mary Ann personally, had only heard her lecture on one occasion and was pleased, but not at all surprised, that everything she advanced was strictly in accordance with morality and Christianity. She wrote:

> *I have known that lady for many years; she has always borne a deservedly high character, and is most respected and liked where she is best known. She has imbibed the new views respecting women, and so have many of the most intelligent and excellent women in England. They have not been abused as Mrs. Colclough has been, and it is very little to the credit of the Auckland people that a respectable lady should be so much annoyed, only because she has become a convert to the new views held by so many worthy people. The whole of Mrs. Colclough's past history has been such that we may be sure she would not favour anything at variance with kindness and common sense.[23]*

There were signs, however, that Mary Ann's increased public profile and the growing number of attacks on her motives for advocating on behalf of women were starting to wear her down. In mid-August, compelled by what she described as 'a want … of kindness, moderation, and logic' in those who argued with her, she wrote to the *Herald* to reassert, as plainly as she could, why she was committed to the cause of women. It was iniquitous that in a Christian country, any person, whatever their sex, should be able to wrong and oppress others under the shelter of the law. 'I am a woman's advocate,' she explained, 'because I am convinced that women are placed in an unjust position by law, and because I have experienced, and do still experience, many of the evils that position entails on women.'[24]

Mary Ann's assurance that she was no Mrs Jellaby, the character from Charles Dickens' satiric novel *Bleak House* who espoused every imaginable worthy cause while neglecting her home and children, brought a response from letter writer 'Jellaby Pater', who sought a few short sentences 'without any of the circumlocution which characterises her letters' on what exactly she demanded as women's rights. He had patiently read everything she had published in the newspapers for the preceding six months, but because he was still, to use his words, 'in a state of blissful ignorance as to the nature of the so-called "rights" she claimed for women', he had set out the following questions:

1st. What rights are they which 'P.P.' desires for women? 2nd. Has not woman a perfectly legal right under the present law to protect her own property and secure it to herself by means of a marriage settlement? 3rd. On what does she ground her idea that women generally are dissatisfied with their present position? 4th. Setting aside the present agitators – Mill, Miss Nightingale, and others, – that 'P.P.' is so fond of quoting, can she state on her veracity that she knows six married ladies in Auckland who are dissatisfied with their present legal position? 5th. Can 'P.P.' bring to bear any text of Scripture which is violated by the present legal position of women?[25]

Polly Plum obliged with a private communication she sent to the editor of the *Herald*, asking him to forward her reply to Jellaby Pater. Responding to each of his questions in turn, she drew on her personal experience to illustrate the inequities in the current laws concerning married women's property rights. Although she took care to word discreetly what she had to say, she included some unflattering personal information about her late husband's financial speculations and the impact these had on her family's home life. Unfortunately, and to Mary Ann's dismay, the editor of the *Herald* published her responses and called a close to the correspondence. On seeing her private letter published, Mary Ann immediately wrote to the editor requesting that he publish her brief explanation clarifying that the letter had been intended as a private communication and, in justice to her late husband, making it clear that he had not wilfully wronged her in any way.[26]

Jellaby Pater was not alone in being a dedicated reader of Polly Plum's writings. The editor of the *Wanganui Herald* had read all the correspondence forwarded to him and occasionally reprinted extracts from her articles or news of her activities. He considered her an able contributor to the *Southern Cross* on the subject of women's right. He commended her considerable literary ability and great earnestness in the cause she espoused, but ventured that she had opened a hornets' nest with her public lectures. Nevertheless, he remained confident she would prove a match with any of her opponents, whom, he was sure, she could take on single-handedly.[27]

Auckland resident Francis Foscari was one hornet buzzing unpleasantly around Polly Plum's ears. Although he wrote tongue-in-cheek, Mary Ann found a great deal of sting in his cruel, sarcastic criticisms:

After much bragging and more parade of her assumed position as 'woman's advocate', 'Polly Plum' goes on to say, what in reality implies that, in the fierce and fiery prosecution of her self-imposed task, the 'flippant satire', the tart lampoon, the fierce invective, the coarse 'contumely', the gross 'insult', the cool 'contempt', the 'biting jest', and the jeering 'ridicule', though squirted at the boiling point from the porcupine quills of audacious masculine scoffers, will drop upon her as harmlessly as the showers of autumn on a buoyant water-fowl. This undoubtedly shows obstinate perseverance; but, like all others who persevere against fate, she will eventually be compelled to run for shelter.[28]

Just a few days after publication of Francis Foscari's invective, a light-hearted poetic lampoon of Polly Plum appeared in the satirical booklet *Rhymes without Reason*. It seemed that the public of Auckland were becoming weary of Polly Plum's 'noise' and 'twaddle', preferring instead to be entertained rather than informed. Aware that Mary Ann was now being constantly urged by members of the public to include singing and dancing in her lectures, the editor of the *Cross* believed that unless Mary Ann was prepared to amuse as well as instruct the public, her audiences, although comprised of highly select, intelligent and respectable people, would never be large. It was not that she was not an effective speaker; almost everyone who heard her agreed she was very effective and spoke common sense. Had she been in England or America, there was no doubt she would have commanded crowded houses. [29]

On 31 August 1871, a modest but highly respectable and appreciative audience assembled at the public hall in Otahuhu to hear Mary Ann's lecture on 'The Subjection of Woman'. She stood before them dressed in her usual simple black attire, as befitted her widowed status. Her long-time friend Reverend John Macky occupied the chair. In his opening remarks introducing the speaker, the reverend commented that he did not, as a rule, approve of ladies lecturing, but there were women with unusual abilities for whom exceptions needed to be made to enable them to enter those spheres usually reserved for men. Mrs Colclough, he declared, was one such exception. Praising her mental abilities and the special talent she had as a teacher of the young, he told the audience that had she not been present he would have spoken of her gentle and womanly traits of character. These traits, he went on, might not be apparent in the writer and lecturer, but they adorned her private life. Reiterating that Mary Ann was an exceptional case and that he did not want his role in these proceedings to be construed as a general support for ladies in any numbers appearing on the platform, Reverend Macky conceded that some wrongs very likely did warrant complaint and that the mind could easily become so familiarised with long-standing abuses that the evils of them went unnoticed.

Although largely repeating the content of her earlier lectures delivered at Auckland and Thames, Mary Ann took the opportunity to respond to some recent criticisms. Those that grated most were the charges of want of modesty, that she had tried to make women despise their marital duties and become less home-loving, and that she had made assertions that were subversive of Christian doctrine. She dismissed these claims by saying she felt confident that the people of Otahuhu knew her well enough to be assured that such accusations were not true.

In moving a vote of thanks to Mary Ann, Reverend Macky said he was particularly impressed not only with the moderate and reasonable nature of her views but also with her ability to advocate legal freedom for women while simultaneously demonstrating every grace and virtue that could possibly adorn the female character. He concluded that a greater drawback than opposition to the cause was women's apathy and the fact that those who were happy and honoured did not necessarily use this power for the benefit of their less fortunate sisters.

Reverend Macky's opening remarks at this lecture highlighted the blurring now evident between the public persona of Polly Plum and the private face of Mary Ann Colclough. Many now knew that Polly Plum and Mary Ann were one and the same. For example, in his diatribe against her published the previous week, Francis Foscari had said he thought he had managed 'to preserve intact the transparent veil separating "Polly Plum" from Mrs. Colclough', and increasingly Mary Ann was writing to the newspapers under her own name. In early October she ceased using her *nom de plume* altogether. Her final two letters under the name Polly Plum were a lengthy defence of women lecturing in public and an announcement that she no longer intended to debate the issues of women's rights through the columns of the newspapers.[30]

In her 'Plea for the Platform', Mary Ann wrote of the double standard of classing a lady's appearance on a platform to speak as a shameless action when it was perfectly acceptable for women to engage in public displays of singing and dancing. Cutting to the chase, she wrote:

> *The real grievance must be that there are men who object to women having brains or daring to use them. So long as the sex confine their public displays to singing vapid songs, or repeating words written for them, and learnt with parrot-like precision, we hear nothing of immodesty; but let a woman once think and be daring enough to give the world the benefit of her thoughts, and great is the indignation of many who can witness quite approvingly all sorts of nonsensical acting in charades, &c., by respectable girls on a platform.*[31]

Admitting she would have felt dreadfully grieved had she outraged propriety, she remained 'unconvinced and unabashed by the numerous anonymous strictures and more open objections' brought against her and therefore wrote to disarm those who tried to injure her, happy in the knowledge that the prejudiced class were not numerous enough to cause her alarm.

However, just under two weeks later, she wrote her final letter under her pen name, explaining that no one could be more tired than she of the controversy over women's rights or wrongs. The discussion had degenerated into tiresome reiteration, and every possible argument had been advanced on both sides. Unless something fresh could be brought into the discussion, it was unlikely that anyone on either side of the debate would change their views. Not that she intended to withdraw completely from newspaper correspondence; if she received any relevant news on what was happening in England, she would be certain to forward it through for publication. However, now that so many writers' letters had deteriorated into anonymous and personal abuse, Polly Plum was ready to put her pen down.[32]

CHAPTER FOUR

ﻭ

Widening the Sphere
of Philanthropy and
Social Reform

To those who knew Mary Ann Colclough personally, her decision to relinquish the persona of Polly Plum would have held little surprise. Not only had her articles and correspondence attracted more than their share of critics and personalised abuse, but her focus of attention had also shifted over the previous few months. Instead of continuing the debate on women's rights, Mary Ann was spending more and more of her time advocating on behalf of particular groups of women in need. The signature of Polly Plum may have disappeared from the newspaper columns but her letters continued under the signature 'Mary A. Colclough'.

During the winter of 1871, Mary Ann visited the Auckland Lunatic Asylum, and her time there created a deep and lasting impression on her. It pained her to see the patients roomed together, regardless of their level of mental illness or social position. While at the asylum, she spoke to the wife of a highly respectable man in Auckland. Of this encounter, she wrote: 'She was sensible enough to carry on a connected conversation and amuse herself with very nicely arranged patchwork; yet this lady was in the common room with gibbering idiots, and a maniac who was in a straight [sic] jacket – a tall ugly room with wooden benches – and she herself, except by the refinement of her manner, with nothing in her dress or surroundings to distinguish her from the Maori maniacs and pauper lunatics.'[1]

Mary Ann did not see the men's wards, but a brief glimpse into their dining hall confirmed that the men fared no better: 'They did not look a bit nicer in their dress and general appearance than the women; and though I know there were several gentlemen, and some not so very mad, amongst them, they were even a more sordid-looking set than the women – an indiscriminate crowd of almost sane and dancing mad, well-born gentlemen and pauper Maoris.'[2]

Her description of the effects of the inadequate conditions of the asylum on its patients was graphic: 'One week amongst those incurable epileptic patients, those frightful monuments of lost reason who sit for years immovably in the same position, those poor creatures who cry and scream and rave – one week of this would unseat the reason of a sane person with weak nerves. We may imagine the dreadful effects on the poor shaken mind gradually recovering its balance, and how it must tend to feed the excitement of a mind liable to be occasionally unsettled.'[3]

Certain that any attempt to cure patients was being severely compromised by the terrible sights the asylum inmates were surely conscious of during their sane intervals, Mary Ann was also struck with the marked difference between conditions in the Auckland asylum and conditions in the asylums she had visited in England. She observed that several of the asylums in England she was familiar with made provisions for women to have separate rooms, comfortable furniture and access to such things as books and music. Admittedly, these provisions relied on the ability of family members to pay for them, which meant that most of the women who experienced these comforts were from middle- or upper-class backgrounds. Mary Ann consequently thought that if the Auckland provincial government could not stretch its budget for poor and pauper patients, then at least those with the means should be able to secure some privacy and comforts and even a personal attendant.

Mary Ann also noted that even in the pauper asylums in England, patients could decorate their surroundings and amuse themselves with dressing up. Deprived of all ornaments and dressed in plain drab clothing, the female patients at the Auckland asylum had looked longingly at her dress and ribbons. Present when a patient was being admitted, Mary Ann had seen the patient's friends insist on removing all her ornaments and trinkets, including her wedding ring. Mary Ann did not blame the attendants or the friends of the patients for this situation. Over the years, she had found the asylum's attendants to be kind and attentive toward their charges, and they showed enormous gratitude whenever someone gave them patches of cloth or pictures and toys to help amuse their charges. The rules were set by the provincial council, and Mary Ann was adamant that the staff of the asylum should not be held answerable for the system they had to follow.

As winter gave way to spring in 1871, Mary Ann read of the melancholy death of a well-known Auckland resident, and this incident prompted her to write to the newspapers to raise public awareness of the need for urgent reform of the Auckland asylum. The newspaper report told her that a coroner's inquest had been held into the death of Mrs Susan Buckland, wife of William Buckland, the Member for the House of Representatives for Franklin. Mrs Buckland had been seriously ill for the previous seven months, suffering from 'great mental despondency'. Five weeks before her death, her doctor testified that he had examined her at her home and found her 'in a perfect state of melancholy and despair, wringing her hands, and throwing herself on the floor'. The doctor told the inquest his patient had confided to him that she felt she was of unsound mind and was fearful that her children might also be affected. On the morning of 4 September, Mrs Buckland's daughter found her mother lying on her bed amidst a pool of blood. Mrs Buckland had slit her own throat using a small pair of blunt nail scissors. Six years earlier when she had made an attempt on her life, her doctor had prescribed homeopathic medicines and advised that she should be kept under close supervision by her family rather than be removed to the asylum.[4]

For Mary Ann, families such as the Bucklands could hardly be blamed for choosing to care for their loved ones in the privacy and comfort of their own homes rather than send them to the lunatic asylum. Had there been access to some alternative facilities where money could secure some of the comforts of the middle class – perhaps even private rooms with a separate attendant, as she recommended in her letter to the *Daily Southern Cross* – the 'most delicately nurtured lady, the most refined gentleman' would not be reduced alike to 'share the un-pealed [sic] potato in the tin plate on the bare uncovered table'. Her comments did not fall on deaf ears. Two months later councillor Andrew Beveridge took up her idea and proposed to the provincial council that it build a cottage on the asylum grounds for the benefit of 'the better class of patients'.[5]

Mary Ann was not the only person raising concerns about the asylum. During the course of 1871, H. Hanson Turton, the inspector of asylums for the Auckland province, and Thomas Aickin, resident surgeon for the Auckland asylum, identified several problems with the administration of the asylum, and this led to an inquiry being conducted the following year. The conditions at the institution were part of a much wider unease about provisions for the poor and destitute and the difficulties experienced by society's outcasts in general in the Auckland province. In August 1871, just a short time before Mary Ann wrote her letter expressing her disquiet about the lunatic asylum, Bishop Cowie had organised an interdenominational conference of the ministers of Auckland at his residence. During the meeting, Reverend Samuel Edger proposed the appointment of a missionary to the Mount Eden Gaol, the Auckland Hospital and the Auckland Lunatic Asylum. The role could be supported, he suggested, through voluntary contributions. The ministers approved his proposal and agreed to set a salary of £150. They also decided that the person selected for the position would be someone who met the approval of at least two thirds of the ministers present.[6]

Several members of the public suggested Mrs Colclough as a worthy prospect for the position. 'C.B.', who considered that a woman would be more suitable, by nature, for the role than a man would, considered Mrs Colclough an appropriate candidate because she had 'a sensitive motherly heart that can understand how easy it is to fall'. Rather than endless sermonising, what was needed was 'the grasp of a hand, the silent tear', and whereas a female missionary would give herself, men would likely give 'dead dogma' and 'cut-and-dried creeds'. 'Hope' also thought that Mrs Colclough's 'warm woman's heart would win its way among the sick and fallen, and appeal with irresistible force to the better nature of the stalwart man'. Although 'Philanthropos' was at first surprised to read of Mrs Colclough's name being put forward, the more he thought about it, the more it seemed exactly the right thing. Writing to the *Cross* in support of Mary Ann's nomination, he said: 'Polly Plum may have her faults, but she is a woman of feeling, judgement, and experience; and I think her appointment would command the sympathy of the entire better part of the community of Auckland.'[7]

Insisting she was not fit for so great a responsibility, even though there was no doubt in her mind that she would like to be engaged in such a role, Mary Ann wrote to both the *Cross* and the *Herald* to explain why she could not accept the nomination. Stating that 'missionary labor is specially congenial to me', she revealed that had providence seen fit for her to be born a man, she would have entered the ministry. But the reality was she was not in a position to provide her services for free and did not consider herself a likely candidate against others when remuneration was at stake.[8]

Given that financial responsibilities may have prevented her from undertaking the position, she wrote two days later to the *Cross* to encourage the women of Auckland to take a lead from the ministers by banding together and raising a salary for a missionary and teacher for the female prisoners in Mount Eden Gaol. Through her earlier voluntary work in England and her contacts with women involved in the women's movement there, Mary Ann was familiar with the work of English prison reformers, Elizabeth Fry and Sarah Martin. In 1817 Elizabeth

Fry had established the Association for the Improvement of the Female Prisoners at Newgate Prison and had published an influential book on prison reform. Sarah Martin was almost single-handedly responsible for improvements in the living conditions at Yarmouth Gaol in Norfolk.

Inspired by these women, Mary Ann wrote several lengthy letters to the newspapers drawing attention to the need for reform in the women's section of the Mount Eden Gaol. In line with practice at the asylum, the gaol made no real effort to classify female prisoners. Young girls who had 'fallen' and were often serving a first offence, along with moral and decent married women who, usually through financial pressure, had pawned work that had been entrusted to them, were incarcerated with old and hardened offenders. Mary Ann suggested that visiting ladies could make friends of these 'decent' married women and seek their cooperation to help reclaim the younger girls. These women were not hardened, Mary Ann emphasised. In most cases, they were as chaste as the lady visitors and just as horrified at the vices some of the young girls had succumbed to. The long days of imprisonment gave them the opportunity to reflect on the folly of their conduct; what they needed was friends rather than judges to help them get back on their feet. If these classes of women could occupy the same cells as the young girls during the 13-hour period each day from five o'clock in the evening until six o'clock in the morning when they were locked up, they might, Mary Ann proposed, be able to help rehabilitate the younger girls.

Mary Ann was also aware that the upstairs section of the women's quarters of Mount Eden Gaol housed a good-sized, well-lit dormitory with a fireplace. This knowledge prompted her to offer another suggestion, which was to use the dormitory as a day school dedicated to teaching young girls how to read, write and sew. Unfortunately, the scarcity of domestic servants, engrossing home duties and, in cases such as hers, the necessity of engaging in paid work to provide for the needs of the home, meant a paucity of women who had the time to do this work. If the authorities agreed to the day school, then a salary would need to be raised in order to attract a respectable God-fearing woman able and willing to act as a missionary and teacher for these girls.

Mary Ann's suggestion prompted an editorial in the *Cross* on the plight of young women who were on the downward path toward a life of prostitution. The editor set forth a passionate challenge to the women of Auckland:

> *In a city where there are so many churches, and so many institutions intended to ameliorate humanity, is there not one to reach the hand of sorrowing sympathy and kindness to a falling or a fallen sister, and seek*

to lead her back to peace and life? Is this our vaunted charity that folds itself up in its own mantle of integrity, and passes by on the other side with averted eyes from the deepest of human wretchedness disguised in the hollow mockery of gaiety and gladness? Are there no women in this city of churches and benevolent institutions that can suppress in the cause of goodness the natural shrinking from defilement, and devote themselves to rescue at least the least degraded from a life of infamy? ... We feel confident that it requires but one lady with kind true womanly feeling to originate the movement, and plenty will be found to aid in this, one of the saddest, but eventually most gratifying spheres of benevolent effort.[9]

Assuring the editor that Auckland was home to many ladies who were deeply interested in the matter and who, despite their 'pure life and exalted position', would have no scruples about helping these poor girls if they only had the means to offer them a home, Mary Ann set out an equally passionate challenge to the men of Auckland:

The other sex, to whose fault the existence of this terrible class of the community must be charged, are those who have the means; and though they claim to be the protectors of woman, the boast must be considered an empty one in many cases, since it is a notorious fact that fallen women find it easier to make a living than honest ones do. I am sorry, truly sorry, to soil my pen with even so little on the subject as this, but what can ladies with very little means do against men with plenty? And, alas! it is too often men, with modest and good female relatives who would be thankful for the means to help the unfortunate, who refuse money to their sisters, mothers, and wives for charity, and yet spend large sums in vice.[10]

Among those prepared to do what they could with the limited means at their disposal was a lady of high standing who, while she did not want her name made public, was prepared to accept subscriptions through the office of the *Cross* toward the provision of a refuge for fallen women. Mary Ann was sure the lady's name alone would reassure subscribers that the effort was a truly charitable work and that the funds would be properly applied. Her letter drew an immediate response. 'Rescue', for example, pointed out in his letter to the *Cross* that in England this work was not generally confined to ladies, as ministers and Christian men also took an active role. He recommended that a committee be formed and subscription lists drawn up for the purpose of obtaining the £100 designated as the required amount.[11]

While commending any efforts to reclaim 'fallen' girls, another writer to the Cross drew attention to the inherent double standard and suggested a more radical approach:

> *Why are the girls to be pitied and then punished – and not far rather the men who help them to sin, but who yet go unblamed, unnoted, and who are even received in so-called society, because their deeds, being deeds of darkness, are hid from the light of day and veiled from the pure eyes of their wives and sisters? I do not exactly know the powers of the police, but could they not have authority to enter all inspected houses, any night, at any hour, take note of the men found there, and have these men brought up the next day to the Police Court? Perhaps some of them for very shame might cease to demoralise our city, in their cowardice dreading to bear the brand of infamy. To my mind, no moral punishment can be too severe for the base, cowardly fellow who for the gratification of his own selfish nature ruins a girl, never caring in the least what degradation falls upon her, so long as he goes free.*[12]

Mary Ann agreed, considering it 'frightful that the unfortunate girls are punished whilst those who make them what they are walk unblushingly in the light of day'. Having observed that such men were among those opposed to women's social position being raised and women taking part in shaping laws, she pointed out that unchecked male depravity was the chief enemy the friends of the fallen had to deal with. She remained convinced that sending the girls to prison, as the current law required, was not the answer and often did more harm than good: 'The women have congenial company, sufficient food, not too much work, and many of them would rather be there than not. I believe they just go the round – gaol, a drunken frolic, lock-up, and gaol again. They are permanent depraved pensioners on Government, and then they get ill from dissipation, and drift into the hospital, and, at last, end in the Refuge. These people never dream of keeping themselves; they are a regular social ulcer, a permanent charge on the State.'[13]

Mary Ann went on in her letter to advise that some of the women dragged their young children around with them through scenes of drunkenness and vice. Those children, often only two or three years old, were then locked up with their mothers and grew up surrounded by criminal influences instead of being placed in the Home for Destitute Children. Having been to Mount Eden Gaol many times, she could not help but feel sorry for these women. While others saw only rogues and vagabonds, Mary Ann saw clever needlewomen and capable domestic servants. The possibility that these younger women could be other than what they were presently was an added reason why they should be sent to a reformatory.

Efforts to reclaim the 'fallen' were certainly not without precedent in Auckland. As Reverend Benjamin Thornton Dudley, the vicar of St Sepulchre's, explained in a letter to the *Cross*, the Auckland Women's Home had opened some time back in Parnell but after struggling for nine months had to close temporarily. The idea of establishing a more appropriate facility had never been abandoned, and the ladies involved in this endeavour had been quietly collecting money. To date they had about £175 in hand and needed another £60 or £70 to enable them to secure a suitable site on which to build. Bishop Cowie had consented to take over the general supervision of the institution, and an experienced matron from Sydney said she was willing to take charge as soon as required. Many prominent public figures who were well qualified to offer an opinion on the project, such as the resident magistrate, the provincial surgeon, the dispensary surgeon and Captain Eyre, the governor of the gaol, had given their warm approval; the only immediate want was more money. Some interested parties desired that the home be extended so that it could also offer a reformatory, but others considered this development beyond the scope of public philanthropy and saw it instead as a government responsibility.[14]

Because she had not made the matter clear in her earlier letter, after publication of Reverend Dudley's letter Mary Ann hastened to confirm that it was the Auckland Women's Home she had in mind when she wrote to the *Cross* to encourage subscriptions for a further £100. She had identified two blocks of buildings conveniently situated some distance from town that would be appropriate and had also located some public houses that would make suitable premises for a reformatory. The structures she had her eye on included the old mission station at Kohimarama and several buildings previously used by St John's College. The St John's buildings were of sufficient size to allow for separate accommodation for young and old offenders. As with her earlier proposal for a practical day and boarding school where young girls could be instructed in all aspects of household management, Mary Ann envisaged that the committee charged with overseeing the enterprise would take in young female offenders for two or three years and provide them with training that would fit them for domestic service positions. If the institution also took in work such as washing and sewing, it could be self-supporting.[15]

With public support for the Auckland Women's Home rekindled, Mary Ann shifted her attention to the needs of discharged female prisoners. Early in October, a correspondent to the *Cross* had written of the urgent need for a prisoners' aid society 'to assist the penitent prisoners, male or female, when they leave the prison, with clothes – a little timely aid to avoid temptation and to obtain situations in the country, or out of the reach of their accomplices and haunts of ill fame'. Although Mary Ann was not opposed to such a society, her priorities were for the women who were doubly disadvantaged. As well as bearing the stigma of having served a prison sentence, these women had few avenues of legitimate work open to them simply because they were women. Women who had served their prison sentences, Mary Ann said, frequently approached her for money and clothes. Some of them were addicted to alcohol, and even if it were in her means to help them, giving them money or articles they could sell to buy alcohol would be unwise. However, many were skilled in needlework and could be employed as tailoresses. Understandably, shopkeepers were hesitant to provide these women with outwork for fear they would abscond and pawn the work.[16]

Mary Ann came up with a plan. What was needed was a bond of five or 10 shillings paid to the shopkeepers to secure outwork for the women. The bond could be raised through public donation. If the women then stole or pawned the work, as undoubtedly some would, they would not receive any further assistance. Given the scarcity of people willing to come to these women's aid, this stipulation alone might serve as an incentive not to betray the trust accorded to them. For those capable and willing to work, this small amount of assistance might be all that was required to put the women on the path to become self-supporting.[17]

It is testimony to Mary Ann's commitment as a women's advocate that, despite being under constant financial pressure herself, she tirelessly attempted to garner public support to assist those less fortunate. Not one to rest on her laurels, she placed the following advertisement in the *Cross* a week after setting out her plan and requesting donations from readers:

Notice

Any Female Prisoner Discharged from Mount Eden Gaol, who can bring a good character from the matron, will sign the pledge, and keep out of the streets, striving to amend, can, on satisfactory proof that she has complied with these demands, obtain a small amount of security, varying from five to ten shillings, such security to be given to shopkeepers who employ these women as needlewomen, or people who employ them in the laundry work. The amount of security will in no case exceed ten shillings, and that sum will only be guaranteed in promising cases. Assistance will be given in seeking for situations in the country districts, for women whose sole vice is drunkenness, and who desire to amend. All applications are to be made through the Gaol Matron or the Relieving Officer.

Mary A. Colclough[18]

In addition to taking on this new venture, Mary Ann was preparing, given the imminent commencement of the fourth quarter of the school term, to embark on a new venture in the educational arena. Despite her best efforts, she had not secured sufficient funds for a new school for girls. While not prepared to abandon the idea completely, she had decided instead to establish a series of daily 'Classes for Ladies'. She managed to secure use of the Provincial Council Chambers until the end of the school year, and advertised that she would hold classes on these premises. The classes would cater for 'Young Ladies who have been superficially and imperfectly instructed, and ladies desirous to qualify themselves to pass the Board of Education', and would take place between 10am and 2pm on week days. Prospective students could enrol either on a weekly or monthly basis, and classes would provide 'thoroughly sound and practical instruction in all branches of an English Education', including history, geography, arithmetic, composition, natural history, domestic management and mental training.[19]

Drawing readers' attention to Mary Ann's advertisement, the editor of the *New Zealand Herald* provided a warm endorsement: 'From Mrs. Colclough's large experience in teaching, and her popularity in the treatment of all subjects appertaining to female education, we have no doubt that her effort to establish ladies' classes in Auckland will be a success.' The editor of the *Cross* was equally complimentary: 'Mrs. Colclough has carried on a seminary for young ladies in the vicinity of Auckland for many years, and is very highly spoken of as a teacher. In extending her sphere, we trust she will receive an amount of support commensurate with her merit.'[20]

The week beginning Monday 16 October was a high-profile, demanding one for Mary Ann. She not only posted the advertisements for her two new ventures during the week but also gave a public lecture on the Friday evening in the rooms of the Young Men's Christian Association. Former Presbyterian minister and current editor of the *Auckland Star*, Mr George McCullough, known for taking a keen interest in all social questions, chaired the lecture. Mary Ann addressed the topic of 'Marriage' to an audience of about 150, of whom a large proportion were ladies. Reviews were mixed. The *Auckland Star* reviewer rated the lecture as 'very interesting and truthful' and thought Mrs Colclough had treated the subject 'with ability and great impartiality'. The reviewer for the *Cross* agreed, describing the lecture as 'an exceedingly interesting' one delivered by 'a very able, and a very earnest lecturer'. He elaborated: 'Mrs. Colclough has the advantage of possessing a very clear and distinct voice; of being able to clothe her subject in appropriate and frequently in eloquent language; and of convincing by fair argument those who listen to the enunciation of her opinions.' As he rightly observed, Mary Ann's opinions on marriage were not, in the language of the day, 'free' or 'advanced'. She held that marriage should be sanctioned and solemnised by the church, she 'was quite sensible of the heavy obligations which are involved in so momentous a subject', and she thought it 'better by far there should be no marriage than the utter mockery of a union where a man and a woman come together for life, who do not do so by the ties of mutual love and affection'. Her ideal of marriage was based on a very high standard, one the reviewer for the *Cross* feared was too ideal to be often realised in this life.[21]

But where the *Cross* reviewer offered 'a full meed of praise at the able manner in which the subject was treated', the reviewer for the *Herald* was unimpressed: Mrs Colclough had spent the hour telling men how bad they were, labouring repetitively over her topic, being inconsistent and, at times, contradictory, displaying an obvious disposition to sermonise and bitterness against what she viewed as sarcasm. Altogether, she had treated her subject in a very unsatisfactory manner. Most of those who attended the lecture, however, appeared not to share the *Herald* reviewer's opinion. The audience was attentive throughout, greeting Mary Ann's comments from time to time with sustained applause.[22]

The advertisements for the lecture and the review in the *Herald* were printed under the banner 'Young Men's Christian Association', a happenstance that concerned the honorary secretary of the YMCA because it suggested the association was sponsoring Mrs Colclough's lecture. As the secretary explained, had the Reverend Warlow Davies not been due to deliver a lecture for the YMCA the following week on the topic of marriage, this oversight might have passed without comment. However, anxious that readers not gain the impression that the YMCA was sponsoring two lectures espousing the same views, he felt obliged to write to the newspapers to correct any misconceptions. He advised in his letter – written shortly after Reverend Davies had delivered his lecture to a capacity crowd, the members of which lined every possible standing place, including the stairwells – that the topic might be the same, but the reverend's treatment of 'Love, Courtship and Marriage' and his views on women's rights could not differ more from the views Mrs Colclough offered. During his address, Reverend Davies felt bound to say that an infinite amount of rubbish had been spoken and written on the subject of marriage lately, and it was his opinion that girls should be trained with a view to becoming wives and mothers. Yes, women in overcrowded countries had to submit to great hardships, but it was not so in this colony, where women had their rights 'to the fullest extent'. In fact, he argued, it was the men who seemed to be placed at a disadvantage because the imbalance of sexes in the population meant that one out of every three men had to remain unmarried.[23]

Ill health prevented Mary Ann from participating in a panel discussion on 'Woman's Rights in a Teetotal Aspect' organised by the Total Abstinence Society the week after her lecture on marriage, but she recovered sufficiently the following week to deliver the first address in her new series of educational classes on 'Mental Training'. The 'beautiful and salubrious' classroom in the Provincial Council Chambers set an appropriate tone for the innovative approach to girls' higher education that she wished to offer. Modelled on the system she had experienced at Queen's College, her proposed system would combine classes with lectures and require pupils to take only a few subjects at a time and thereby thoroughly master them. She also intended to challenge the conventional methods of meaningless lessons based on parrot-like repetition.[24]

She wanted, she told her audience, to make every lesson a real study and a pleasure that the whole class could enjoy together. She had never used the well-known spelling books with her children or with any of her pupils, preferring instead the Nelson's school series that included only a few words of spelling at the beginning of each reading. However, she explained, 'in all other cases' pupils would 'learn to spell their reading lessons, and after a time to find out the meanings of the most difficult words by reference to the dictionary. This fixes it on their minds, as they usually have to write it, as well as look it out, in order to learn it'.[25] She continued:

> But my great agent in teaching spelling is dictation. As young ladies advance in proficiency I frequently change the work from which I give dictation: today, it is a work on geology or natural history, tomorrow it may be a catalogue of jewels, an inventory of furniture, a list of eminent authors, or a page from geography. Thus every kind of word becomes familiar, and if any error is made the mis-spelt word is written out several times with its meaning; and I can say from long experience that I find this method of teaching spelling more effectual than all the spelling-books that ever were written.[26]

Mary Ann's audience would have included some of her many supporters, keen to see her venture succeed and for it to become self-supporting. Known for excelling as a teacher of elocution, for example, she perhaps did not need to remind those present, as she did, that some of the highest authorities on education supported her approach. Noted educationalist Henry Worthington was one such person. He fully endorsed her views and teaching methods and looked forward to the day 'when we shall be told that Carpenter's Spelling Book and Magnall's [Mangnall's] Questions are relics of the past, and that we shall only be able to find copies of them stored away in a museum as objects of curiosity'.[27]

Determined to keep the classes within the reach of many, Mary Ann set her school's fee at what was considered at the time to be a very moderate level of half-a-crown per week, paid on either a weekly or monthly basis. Aware that properly establishing the classes could take some time and anxious not to be discouraged by early difficulties in securing pupils, Mary Ann decided to act on the advice of some of her gentlemen supporters and invite honorary members on a subscription of a minimum of a guinea a year. She also extended a warm invitation to all ladies with an interest in high-class education to attend her repeat of the first lecture on mental training so that they could experience at first-hand her teaching methods and content.

The schedule of educational classes did not curtail her advocacy for women in need. For some time she had offered her home to young women on their release from prison until a position could be found for them. Early in November she placed the following advertisement in the *Cross*: 'WANTED, on next Saturday, a Decent situation in the country for a woman at present in Mount Eden Gaol. She has served two short sentences in gaol for drink, but has now signed the pledge. – Apply to Mrs. Colclough, office of this paper.' Well aware of the difficulty women had gaining employment after their release from prison, let alone securing a position while still serving a sentence for an alcohol-related offence, Mary Ann could not be faulted for her untiring dedication to female prisoners. Although still convinced that a reformatory was needed as an alternative to prison for younger women, she cast her mind to other more immediate alternatives. Noticing that only a small number of older girls resided at the industrial school in Howe Street, which catered for children up to the age of 15, she wrote to the newspapers to suggest its facilities as an alternative venue for reforming young women.[28]

Set up under the Neglected and Criminal Children's Act 1867, the industrial schools were intended as both a temporary alternative to sending criminal children to prison and as a residential institution for the care and education of neglected children. The Auckland Industrial School had shifted from its original premises at Fort Britomart to the former Grammar School buildings in Howe Street six months earlier. This arrangement was supposedly an interim one until more permanent premises suitably located in a rural district could be secured, so that 'the children would be removed wholly from their former haunts and scenes of crime, and where they could be trained up to practical knowledge of agricultural operations'.[29]

To Mary Ann's eyes, the Howe Street industrial school offered a splendid building capable of holding many more young girls than it currently did, and it was definitely suitable for training them in domestic service. As she had argued on many occasions, sending homeless girls to the industrial school for a year or two made far more sense than sending them to Mount Eden Gaol, because the girls in the school had yet to form 'vicious associations' and were therefore likely to be more useful. Mary Ann strongly believed that gaol made girls unfit for service. A few of the stronger women who had been in gaol might have the opportunity to do laundry work and some of the older women and a few girls might be able to sew, but the only employment for most was to pick oakum, a tedious task involving unwinding rope so that the strands could be used for packing the joints of timbers in wooden ships. While girls were in the school, Mary Ann explained, they would have the opportunity to learn to wash, sew, read, write, make and mend, and become useful servants.[30]

Disappointed by the provincial council's failure to act, Mary Ann continued her letter crusade to the newspapers, all the time taking pains to highlight the scandalous conditions for female prisoners at Mount Eden Gaol. The four small rooms housed six inmates apiece, and the other two rooms set apart for female debtors were also full. The day room was woefully inadequate, and in an effort to compensate for this, the gaol authorities had set up an awning of sorts in the yard. However, during the day, the women picking oakum took over this space. Untried male prisoners and debtors, of whom there were 12 and two respectively at the time Mary Ann wrote her letter, were using the two larger yards as day exercise areas. The third and smaller of the yards was reserved for the female prisoners. What with the pickers, the large wash-house where women and girls did all the washing for the gaol, lunatic asylum, hospital and refuge, and the lines of drying washing, there was no room for exercise. Mary Ann described the scene:

When I was reading to the women the other day, under the awning, a bundle of blankets was brought in from the hospitals so disgusting and pestiferous I was glad to close my book and beat a retreat into the matron's quarters. Now just think of the condition of some twenty-five to thirty human creatures shut up amongst these infected clothes, with no other air to breathe for three or four days in the week than that impregnated with their pestilential odour, for the things are not got rid of from Monday morning till about Friday, when the last are dry.[31]

Mary Ann also acknowledged the 'much overworked and most inadequately paid' matron, who was on duty every day of the year, working from five o'clock in the morning to six o'clock in the evening over summer and from six in the morning to five in the evening over winter. She itemised the matron's duties:

She has to receive and search the prisoners, superintend the giving out of meals, and their work, weighing the oakum, and cutting out the clothing. She has to count all those immense piles of washing, quell disturbances, and keep order. The quantity of routine work where there are prisoners constantly received and discharged, the untiring vigilance to prevent breaches of the prison regulations amongst such a large number, may be guessed; and for all this duty the matron receives the munificent stipend of £80 per annum and finds herself in food. It is out of all reason that any woman could, in addition to all these multifarious duties, give the women and especially the young girls the constant supervision that is really necessary.[32]

Mary Ann was full of praise for the 'truly missionary and philanthropic spirit' of the matron, who had cordially assisted her in every way possible to carry on her voluntary work with the prisoners. It was almost as if, by helping them, Mary Ann was doing the matron a personal kindness. Questioning why the visiting justice, who received a payment of £50 per annum for his duties, had not seen fit to report the inadequacy of the conditions for female prisoners to the authorities, she urged all who had a spark of Christianity to draw this situation to the attention of the provincial council while it was still sitting. She knew that the visiting justice had called the government's urgent attention to this matter in his latest report because someone had sent her a copy of it. However, in the meantime, she had been alerted to the fact that the cells beneath the Supreme Court were not currently in use. She accordingly suggested that the debtors and untried prisoners could be transferred to these cells, so allowing the area available to the female prisoners to be extended. This development, she argued, could provide a convenient and relatively cheap means of separating the young girls from the older, hardened women:

It would be a boon to have them by themselves, and to have them for as long as the law allows, and to try and teach them something useful, instead of having them for ever picking oakum, an employment which is of no earthly use to them outside the gaol doors; and I should think a Committee could easily be formed to take charge of the girls, and their safe custody would be secured whilst they are in the precincts of the gaol. From what I know of the Governor of the Gaol, I feel quite sure no obstacle would be thrown in the way of the benevolent by the authorities, if there exists no legal obstacle to our teaching the girls to sew, to wash, to scrub, to iron, to cook.[33]

As 1871 drew to a close, it was clear that Mary Ann's public profile was undergoing a significant change. More often than not the outspoken and controversial campaigner for women's rights was taking back stage to the persistent activist for philanthropic social reform. This change was also evident in the newspapers, where more measured discussions of the valued and necessary contribution of women to the social and moral welfare of the community were slowly replacing the polarised debates on women's social and legal status – although for Mary Ann, these issues were interrelated. The Licensing Bill was still being debated, as was an Education Bill that had arisen in response to local demands and the growing movement for a national system of education.

A revised and enlarged Married Women's Property Bill was also under debate in the General Assembly. As Mary Ann had frequently pointed out, current legislation gave all the power and authority to husbands, with wives not even accorded a separate legal status. Because the husband had full financial and legal responsibility for his wife and children, wives were not entitled to property of their own, even if they had property and possessions before they married or earned money during the marriage. The lack of a separate legal status meant that a wife could not write a will unless she had prior written legal consent from her husband. If the wife left the marriage, she would lose her children as well as any entitlement to maintenance.

Mary Ann saw this tremendous and unfair legal jurisdiction over women, their children and their property as women's main complaint. The most fearful example of the errors of the present marriage laws could be seen in cases where women did not marry the men they lived with because their legal status as married women would prevent them from fulfilling their responsibilities for the home and children if their male partner was a drunkard or an incompetent provider. Describing this situation as 'iniquitous', Mary Ann went as far as asserting that the current marriage laws were being used as a shelter under which married women were oppressed. The laws offered no protection from any abuse of extreme authority exercised by men within a marriage, and, in effect, sanctioned such abuse. Another 13 years would pass before the Married Women's Property Act of 1884 gave married women rights to their own property. Meanwhile, many women continued to need encouragement, support and, above all, opportunities to be independent and self-supporting.[34]

CHAPTER FIVE

Without Means,
Without Encouragement and
Without Help

Although admired by the public, Mary Ann's practical work in support of female prisoners proved to be a source of irritation to the prison authorities. Early in 1872 'Samaritan' wrote to the *Daily Southern Cross* praising Mary Ann's good work. He had read an official report from the gaol authorities which showed quite clearly that Mrs Colclough's letter to the *Cross* several months earlier did not exaggerate the inadequate conditions female prisoners endured at Mount Eden Gaol. He had decided to write to the newspaper to say the public ought to be obliged to Mrs Colclough because she had devoted valuable time she could ill spare for work that was not very pleasant.[1]

The prison authorities were far from feeling any sense of obligation toward Mary Ann and had responded to her criticisms by barring her from further visits to the gaol on the pretext she had not followed proper protocol in airing her concerns. Undeterred, and not at all prepared to give in to institutional bullying, Mary Ann, as was her wont, took up her pen and wrote to the *Cross*:

> *Can you tell me if the authorities have power to forbid people visiting the Gaol giving publicity to the abuses that come under their notice? After my letter on the female department of the Gaol appeared in the* Cross, *I was informed by the governor of the Gaol that it was the rule that, if a visitor had any fault to find, he or she must first communicate with the authorities before writing to the press, or the privilege of visiting the Gaol would be withdrawn. I felt indignant at this, because I think it is interfering with the liberty of the visitor. The Gaol is a public institution, and the authorities ought to know of all existing abuses, and not need any information from*

*unofficial people; and if they know of them, and allow them to exist, as in
the case of the woman's [sic] department of the Gaol, the public ought to
know of it: it is a matter of general interest. Since then a further restriction
has been made that I should fix one or two days a week for visiting, and
keep to them, not visiting on other days. With respect to the first restriction,
I have seen the Superintendent, Mr. Gillies, who informs me that I was told
of the restraint imposed on visitors by his instructions. Of this last restriction
of fixing days for visiting, I was informed by the matron, by Captain Eyre's
order. I am animated by no personal spite in giving publicity to these
tiresome restraints; but write only because I feel that they are vexatious
and oppressive, and cramp my powers of usefulness. I shall be glad if you or
any of your readers can tell me if they can be enforced. – I am, &c., M.A.
COLCLOUGH*[2]

Oliver Sydney Ellis, who had served on the provincial council as a member
for City East, and who had a reputation for his anti-authoritarian views, seized
the opportunity to respond to Mary Ann's concerns with an outburst of unveiled
hostility toward the superintendent:

*To the Editor: – Sir, – I was astonished upon reading Mrs. Colclough's
letter in the* CROSS *to find that Mr. T. B. Gillies, as Superintendent of
this province, has instructed the authorities of the Mount Eden Gaol to
forbid visitors to let the public know the abuses that apparently exist in the
Gaol, unless they are first informed, under pain of his absolute mandate
issuing that they should not visit them, so that he, by practising a bit of
unwarrantable tyranny, debars those who are confined of the assistance of
those who freely, gratuitously, and for the well-being of their fellow-beings,
make an attempt to reform them. Again, Captain Eyre by order compels
visitors to name the days they intend to visit, which I suppose must mean
that everything shall be in order, so as to keep the public – although they pay
the cost – from learning what is wrong on other days. I am not surprised
at Mr. T. B. Gillies; it is like the man – the little monarch of our province.
Captain Eyre, no doubt as a servant, acts from instructions received from
head-quarters. Will the public endure such monstrous acts of the powers
that be without remonstrance? I trust not; it is by expressing opinions on
abuses of public institutions that we may expect a cure. The public ought to
be grateful to those who enter upon the work of charity which must, more or
less – purify the erring portion of this community, and also save the pockets
of the taxpayers. Trusting that these restrictions may at once be withdrawn,
and that free scope be given to those messengers of mercy, so that they may*

go on unfettered with their work for the reformation of those who have
unfortunately stepped from the path of rectitude. – Yours, &c., O.S. ELLIS,
Hepburn-street[3]

Oliver Ellis's response was not entirely motivated by bombast. As a property speculator who had faced bankruptcy on several occasions, he had a vested interest in ensuring savings to his own taxpayer's pocket. However, he may also have been influenced by his wife Ellen Elizabeth Ellis, who was a passionate campaigner against the abuses of alcohol. Writing under the pen name 'A Woman', she had contributed to the newspaper debates on women's rights. One of her letters attracted the attention of Mary Ann, who correctly surmised that the writer had seen someone near and dear suffer through the evils of drink. Oliver Ellis was a habitual drinker, and Ellen later provided a fictionalised account of the effects of his drinking in her novel *Everything Is Possible to Will*, published in 1882 and now considered to be one of the first overtly feminist novels published in New Zealand.[4]

Like Mary Ann, Ellen Ellis was passionately committed to doing whatever she could to lift the burden of her 'less fortunate sisters'. The two women had worked together for the Auckland Total Abstinence Society, and in January 1872 they were among the first four women elected to serve on the society's committee. Mary Ann had been due to present a lecture on 'Strong Drink and its Victims' under the patronage of the Total Abstinence Society on 29 December, but the date coincided with a special service at St Paul's Church at which members of the Choral Society would sing 'The Messiah'. Mary Ann postponed her lecture and re-advertised it for Monday evening, 8 January, in the YMCA Hall on Wellesley Street. In a departure from her usual format, her lecture, she advised, would be followed by a concert. On the night of the event, the concert portion saw Mary Ann delivering selected readings from Dickens' *Nicholas Nickleby* and performing a duet and solo. Several other performers provided singing entertainments.[5]

Unlike some of her earlier lectures, a very large audience was in attendance, perhaps influenced by the recent publicity in the newspapers about her being banned from visiting Mount Eden Gaol, or perhaps attracted by the inclusion of entertainment. Most of her lecture focused on her experiences of visiting the gaol and her conviction that at least 90 per cent of the inmates were there because of alcohol. Describing the cycle of poverty and neglect that often resulted from children having to spend their early years in gaol, which they came to see as their home, she argued that nothing less than restrictions on the number of public houses or even total abolition would be needed to effect real change. The reporter for the *New Zealand Herald* noted that there was no question as to her powers of observation, even if people did not always agree with her reasoning. The vivid pictures of the wretchedness and misery caused by drunkenness she presented were, in the words of the reporter from Thames, 'heartrending', and her animated narrative was met with frequent bursts of applause from a thoroughly appreciative audience.[6]

Mary Ann's choice of readings from *Nicholas Nickleby* at this lecture was deliberate. Having advertised her selection under the heading 'Squeers of the Do-the-boys Hall', she focused on Dickens' account of the maltreatment of children in boarding schools. Modelled on a real Yorkshire schoolmaster and Dickens' own observations, Mr Wackford Squeers was the gruff and violent charge of Dotheboys Hall, at which Nicholas Nickleby worked as a tutor. Charging an exorbitant price, Squeers and his wife took in neglected boys, usually those who were illegitimate or suffered from a deformity. While lining their own pockets, the Squeers maltreated the boys and were openly cruel. Dickens' mix of social commentary and tragi-comic humour lent itself well to Mary Ann's ability to present what was more a performance than a reading.

With the new school term not due to resume until the fourth week of January, Mary Ann used her extra time to attend local Police Court sessions. A notable case being heard at this time was that of a 12-year-old girl. She had been charged under the Criminal Children's Act with being in servitude at what was described as 'one of the most infamous stews in the city'. Her mother, depicted as 'a woman of bad repute', had placed her child with the occupants of the house. The young girl, identified only by the surname Rogers, was subsequently removed by two detectives and conveyed to the watch-house. In court, her mother argued strenuously for her daughter to be returned, claiming she had not been aware of the character of the dwelling to which she had sent her. She gave her word that the child would be properly looked after, either in her own home or in respectable service. The police, however, testified that the mother's word could not be relied upon and that she had long been leading 'an abandoned life'.[7]

Throughout the proceedings, the girl, crying bitterly, clung imploringly to her mother. Judge Thomas Beckham was of the opinion that the most charitable solution would be to send the girl to an asylum where she would be under 'wholesome restraint' and would benefit from the discipline of the institution. Speaking up on behalf of the girl and her welfare, Mary Ann stated that the priority must be to remove her from the bad example and influence of her mother. The judge agreed and ordered the girl to be sent to a reformatory for 12 months.[8]

Two weeks later, a young woman named Martha Cusins, described as 'of a better appearance than usually belongs to women leading a life of degradation', appeared on a charge of having no visible means of support. Inspector Thomas Broham, later considered one of the most important policemen of the nineteenth century in New Zealand, argued for the case to be withdrawn on the basis that the girl had never appeared before the courts, was contrite and had promised to amend her ways. Taking the stand in Martha's defence, Mary Ann offered to take the girl into her own home to ensure she gained a respectable position. She added that she was prepared to do the same for any girl in a similar situation who was willing to reform. Judge Beckham acceded to Mary Ann's request and discharged Martha with a warning that if she broke her promise of reformation, the police would have the power to detain her again.[9]

As Mary Ann and Martha left the court, a policeman followed them and directed Martha to go to a particular public-house where she was to ask a man named Tom for 11 shillings. The money was to be used to pay the fine of a girl who had been one of Martha's companions and who had been charged with drunkenness. Within minutes, Martha disappeared. As soon as her whereabouts were discovered, she was arrested and taken into custody. When an account of this incident appeared in the newspapers, Mary Ann wrote immediately to the *Cross* to correct some misinformation about the case:

> *I do not believe she meant to go with me, from what I have since heard, as some man was, it seems, prepared to take her away and keep her in hiding if she got away from me; but it was wrong of any member of the police force to facilitate her escape. It may have been, and probably was, done as an act of good nature to the other girl, but still the constable deserves a severe reprimand.[10]*

Mary Ann also reported the matter to Inspector Broham, and the policeman at fault received a salutary reprimand and warning for his actions.

Late in February, an editorial in the *Herald* focused on the unsatisfactory nature of female education, particularly in the Auckland province. The editor advocated the establishment of a public school for girls, similar to and affiliated with the Auckland Grammar School, 'where something more than a slovenly and showy superficiality may be attained, where sound and useful, and above all, thorough and systematic education may have a fair field with the mere smattering of accomplishments, which at present form the chief feature in middle class female education amongst us'. The editorial met with a response from Mrs Frances Shayle George, but it was her comment that 'the unblushing effrontery which produces female lecturers, and female advocates of polygamy, may perhaps, have learnt its first lessons of hardihood and audacity at a girls' public school' that drew a response from Mary Ann:[11]

> *To the Editor of the* HERALD
>
> *SIR, – Will you allow me, on behalf of all qualified lady teachers, to thank Mrs George for her excellent letter in this morning's* HERALD. *A great part of that letter deserves to be written in letters of gold, and I should cordially endorse every word if the beautiful theory of Mrs. George were universally true, and man's home were always his paradise, and each woman destined to be the guiding spirit of that haven of rest.*
>
> *Anyone who reads Mrs. George's letter will see that she and I widely differ in our opinions on many things; but I am not anxious to enter into any controversy, or to complain that Mrs. George uses very strong language in denouncing what she disapproves. That lady had a perfect right to object strongly to anything of which she disapproves; but, may I beg to take exception to female lecturers and female advocates of polygamy being classed together?*
>
> *A lady who thinks it allowable for a woman to lecture may be a Christian and a gentlewoman, as witness Mrs. Balfour, Miss Todd, and many others, who stand deservedly high in the estimation of their fellow-creatures, but a female polygamist can only be a creature too dreadful for a Christian to countenance, therefore it is scarcely fair to place them together.*
>
> *I am not, however, anxious to open a discussion which would be equally unpleasant and undignified for both Mrs. George and myself.*
>
> *We are both trying to do good, though in some points we differ as to the way of doing it; yet the world is large, there is room for all, and as a certificated teacher of my experience, I cannot but wish success to a lady who has such just views on educational matters as many of those advocated by Mrs. George.*
>
> *I wish most heartedly that the Inspector of Schools would visit and report on all private academies. There would then be some chance of qualified teachers getting a just recognition of their capability. – I am, &c.,*
>
> *Mary A. Colclough*
> *March 2, 1872*[12]

The letter is evidence of Mary Ann's generosity of spirit as well as her unwavering adherence to social etiquette. As an advocate for women, Mary Ann welcomed informed sharing of views on important social issues. She had a great deal of respect for Mrs George, which was not necessarily reciprocated to the same degree. Quietly drawing attention to her professional credentials, with formal teaching qualifications among the highest of any teacher in Auckland and with 15 years of local teaching experience, Mary Ann countered Mrs George's bias against private academies by agreeing whole-heartedly for their formal inspection on the same terms as for public schools. She had argued as much in many articles and letters to the press over the years. Mary Ann also countered Mrs George's conflation of women's rights with other so-called 'Yankee notions' of polygamy and Bloomerism.

This conflation represented a common misconception, recently expressed by the editor of the Wellington *Evening Post* in his invective against advocates of women's rights. As Mary Ann pointed out, many respectable women, such as Mrs Clara Balfour, had lectured on temperance and various women's issues in England from the early 1840s, while Miss Isabella Tod, a leading advocate for extending education to middle-class women to qualify them for proper employment, regularly spoke at public meetings on temperance, women's suffrage and married women's property rights. Constantly drawing attention to the views and activities of such women, and distancing these from the more radical elements of women's rights as expressed in some parts of America, was an important way in which Mary Ann introduced feminist ideas and garnered support for the cause of women.

With the half-quarter break drawing to a close, Mary Ann advertised vacancies at her own private academy for girls. The advertisements stated that she had excellent accommodation available for a limited number of boarders at her private residence in Nelson Street, which was only about five minutes' walk from the school. Meanwhile, she was continuing to try to find suitable employment for women following their discharge from prison. On 8 March she placed the following advertisement in the *Cross*: 'WANTED, a Situation for a Young Girl who has been in Gaol, but is honest and sober; a good Servant, but cannot wash. – Apply to Mrs. Colclough, Nelson-street.'[13]

Although it is not known how many women Mary Ann helped into employment, she received reports that some of these women worked well in the domestic service positions found for them. Mary Ann's agitation for prison reform was also yielding results. The yard accommodation for female prisoners had been doubled, and there were plans to make improvements in the interior of the female department. The *Cross* reported that the work of reclamation was still going on quietly and unostentatiously, while the work of the small group of kind-hearted ladies being coordinated by Mrs Colclough was making a big difference in individual cases.[14]

It was clear to all involved in this work, however, that until the government established a reformatory, improvements would be piecemeal. Inspector Broham was doing all within his powers to assist in this cause. The editor of the *Cross* acknowledged that in the absence of an institution in Auckland where young criminals and females could be sent and be improved without being degraded and hardened, the resident magistrate and the Police Court judges were too frequently being placed in very difficult positions. There was also general agreement that the urgent necessity for establishing a female gaol and reformatory separate from the stockade at Mount Eden was one that needed to engage the provincial council at its next sitting.[15]

Mary Ann had for many years publicly argued the need for respectable fields of employment to be more readily open to women. Her practical efforts to secure training for young women in the fields of domestic work were also motivated by the acute shortage of domestic servants both in Auckland and in the country as a whole. Although not restricted to New Zealand, the 'servant problem' was not simply the lack of a sufficient number of domestic servants, but also that increasing numbers of young women were not seeing domestic toil as desirable employment. A good general servant could expect to earn about 10 to 12 shillings a week in New Zealand in the early 1870s. While these sums were higher than the wages domestic servants could expect in Britain, the work hours in New Zealand were often longer and the tasks more demanding because middle-class households usually employed only one or two general servants or a general servant and a cook. There were also differences between the two countries in attitudes toward social hierarchy, a matter frequently commented on in the letters and diaries of British immigrants. New Zealand newspapers were also increasingly commenting on a growing audacity among servants who were refusing to perform tasks they saw as beneath them.[16]

As Mary Ann had observed, the comparatively high level of wages commanded by domestic servants in New Zealand at this time was something of a two-edged sword, particularly for semi-genteel girls because there were relatively fewer openings for their class of domestic service. Mary Ann's very busy life meant she depended on assistance in her private home to manage the household and provide care and oversight for Lulu and Willie. For many years now, she had employed educated young girls as a 'help' and treated them as friends of the family rather than as employees. Her approach had proven a great success, and her suggestion that others follow this example was picked up by the press in Nelson, Christchurch and Otago. The newspapers noted that 'Mrs Colclough strongly urges ladies capable of taking other views of their position than the mere pride of being "Missus", to follow her example, and save themselves much annoyance, while giving a helping hand to a class more perhaps in need of it than any other.'[17]

Mary Ann's actions drew the attention and scorn of the *Weekly News* columnist who wrote the topical opinion piece 'Under the Verandah'. The advertisement Mary Ann placed on 8 March seeking a position for the young girl who had been in gaol but could not wash was, he admitted, probably motivated by kind-hearted, sensible and intelligent ladies, but he found the endeavour neither sensible nor intelligent. How, he asked, could a servant be a good servant if they could not even wash clothes? Undeterred, Mary Ann placed an advertisement in the *Auckland Star* a couple of days later stating that three young girls were seeking situations. What became of the women who took up those positions is unknown, but on Mary Ann's recommendation a respectable local tradesman took the young woman who could not wash into his service.[18]

In mid-March the Auckland Ladies' Benevolent Society held its fifteenth annual meeting. During the previous year, the provincial government had handed over management of the Lying-in Hospital and Refuge to the society. The hospital was known locally as the Old Women's Home, even though the lying-in part of the official title meant that the hospital provided rooms for women who had recently given birth. The society's committee had been hesitant at first to take on this new role, knowing it would substantially increase demands on society members. However, with generous assistance from the government that included rations of tea, sugar and bread, use of government kitchens and washing provided by the gaol, they had managed to provide adequately for the 11 aged and infirm residents, all of whom were totally dependent, with several suffering from dementia. After some deliberation during the annual meeting, those present agreed to rename the institution the Benevolent Society's House for Old Women and to abolish the lying-in rooms.

Several days after the society published its report of the annual meeting, Mary Ann wrote to the *Cross* to commend the society for its good work and the 'exceeding long-suffering kindness of the ladies'. To her mind, the Old Women's

Home was the most valuable aspect of their work, and she could personally testify to 'the admirable order and cleanliness of the arrangements'. However, the home was not sufficient for the current daily needs of the city:

> *There are always a set of disreputable old persons whom the ladies naturally demur at receiving into their Home. Their habits are such as to render the charge of them no very easy or enviable task. Outdoor relief is equally unsuitable for these people. They spend the money given to them in drink, and sell their rations for drink, and are besides a continual pest and worry to the charitable, who do not like to turn them away homeless, helpless, and hungry, and yet know that to aid them is only to put additional sin in their power, for they will surely drink so long as the money given to them lasts. These wretched creatures – men and women – drift in and out of Mount Eden under the Vagrancy Act, and are a continual pest and charge on the country.*[19]

Appreciating full well that the Ladies' Benevolent Society catered for the repentant and that the women she was referring to were certainly not repentant, Mary Ann proposed that what was needed was an almshouse or a workhouse, along the lines of the establishments offered in England, which made residence in such places compulsory. Providing for women in such an institution would cost no more than what these women currently received in rations, and the expense of buildings and staff would amount to less than the amount lost through the women's frequent pilfering and convictions.

Although Mary Ann closely followed the work of the Ladies' Benevolent Society, she was not a member. She preferred to work independently or, as one writer to the newspaper described it, 'free from the trammels of official etiquette'. As time permitted, she would pursue a cause, propose a solution and try to garner support before moving on to her next project.[20]

On the evening of 20 March 1872, Mary Ann attended a crowded public meeting at the Theatre Royal organised by the Auckland Alliance for the Suppression of the Liquor Traffic. The mayor for Auckland presided over the meeting, and Mary Ann sat on the stage with members of the alliance, several members of the committee of the Total Abstinence Society, and other prominent citizens with an interest in the liquor traffic question. During the evening, some speakers argued for total abolition of the importing, manufacture and sale of spirits while others aired more lenient positions. Discussion was often noisy and at times somewhat confusing for those present, but most of them agreed that the very serious problems suffered in Auckland as a result of excessive alcohol consumption would not be remedied if the sale of liquor was suppressed in one district but permitted in another. After passionate addresses from several of the speakers, the resolution – 'That in the opinion of this meeting the history and results of all past regulations with regard to the liquor traffic abundantly prove that it is impossible to regulate its system, so essentially mischievous in its tendencies' – was carried unanimously.[21]

At one point in the discussion, someone in the house asked why Mrs Colclough did not go to Chancery Lane and reclaim the wretched people there. Standing to reply, she explained that she had visited that part of the city and what she encountered there had led to her decision to become an abstainer. The problem was there were just too many public houses. With so much competition, proprietors relied on men and women drinking to excess to ensure their businesses were profitable. Drunkenness, she insisted, had to be understood in a wider context. In all the time she had been a prison visitor, she had encountered perhaps no more than six female prisoners who could read.

Disagreeing with one of the earlier speakers who claimed that education did no good to the cause of temperance, she proposed another resolution: 'That this meeting approves the action of the Auckland Alliance in its efforts to prevent the granting of any new licenses to sell intoxicating liquors in the city of Auckland, and pledges itself to support the Alliance in its canvass of the city against the new licenses applied for.' She concluded her address by stating that the general government, the provincial council and the Auckland City Council were the organisations that needed to deal with the matter. Mary Ann's fellow Total Abstinence Society committee member, Mrs Waters, who was a strong advocate for women to be involved in religious works, seconded the resolution, which was carried.[22]

It was fitting that Mrs Waters seconded the resolution. The previous year she had been viewed as something of a novelty when she delivered a public address at a soirée held at the Mechanics' Institute by the Auckland Alliance. The soirée had been organised to celebrate the provincial council's adoption of the 'permissive principle', which, if passed, would mean the local authorities could refuse to issue licenses to sell intoxicating liquor.

After her address, Mary Ann moved a vote of thanks to Mr Creighton, the leader of the Temperance Reform Party in Auckland, for having initiated and carried a clause in the Licensing Bill allowing females to take part in voting on the granting of licenses. This motion was also passed, as was (unanimously) the final resolution: 'That this meeting deeply deplores the intemperance which prevails in the city, and regrets the increase of applications in the city, and requests that his Worship the Chairman will present a copy of the resolution to the licensing Justices.' Mr John Williamson, the local member for the House of Representatives, brought the proceedings to a conclusion by assuring those present that the liquor traffic question would be put before the next session of the government, and he was sure that any resolution put before it would be carried.[23]

Despite her best intentions, Mary Ann's personal brand of philanthropy often met with unanticipated results. Some members of the community had not welcomed the scheme she had set up in October the previous year, whereby women upon their discharge from Mount Eden Gaol could apply for a security for outwork. In particular contention was the fact that Mary Ann had also managed to secure some work for women still serving their sentences. This action on her part prompted a protest from respectable needlewomen in Auckland. Understandably, they considered it most unfair that they were now in competition with women with bad characters who were clothed, fed and housed at government expense, while they, as honest, hard-working citizens, unknown to the police and courts, had to support themselves.

Amidst this controversy, the *Cross* reported that a young woman whom Mary Ann had assisted into employment had subsequently stolen from her employer and been dismissed. Although not mentioning Mary Ann by name, the editor of the *Cross* referred to 'the sanguine expectations indulged in by some of our lady philanthropists' and concluded that while his view might appear harsh, he did not think 'these gaol women should be thrust upon families'. He then added:

> *The scum which floats on the surface of society, like the scum which rises to the top even of molten gold, requires skimming off and setting aside – the ash-pit for the one, the gaol or reformatory for the other. It is very good, so far as intention goes, for philanthropic ladies and gentlemen to attempt to conceal the moral scum which comes under their notice by mixing it with the good material of which respectable society is composed, but it will only float to the surface again after leaving behind it some of its impurity. Magistrates know this; the police know it; men and women of the world know it. They may regret it; but it is too apparent that there is but one remedy. These must be separated from the outer world just as those stricken with infectious diseases must be quarantined ... The sentences of the class of women we refer to should be longer, and the discipline severer. Moral*

*suasion will have but little effect; bread and water and plenty of hard labour
– not sewing or knitting – may have some. It is very romantic work the
making of penitents, but compelling them to work out their own redemption
will be found infinitely more practical, and the best method for bringing
about their reform.*[24]

Mary Ann was outraged at what she described as 'virtuous indignation' on
the part of the editor in his 'highly sensational and exceedingly cruel' editorial
comment. The employers of 'fallen' women were always made fully aware of the
circumstances of the women, and because of the risk, these women received a
relatively low wage.[25]

There was no doubt that the young woman within Mary Ann's employment
the editor referred to had been abused by the people who had raised her. This
was clearly evident from several broken fingers and the marks of many severe
blows about her head, face and arms. Her mental capacity was questionable. On
the one hand, she could easily be bribed and influenced, but on the other she had
the street-wise cunning that 'half-witted' people often relied upon. She had run
away from home, and on the promise of marriage had lived with a bushman for
three years. He had proven to be a drunken, worthless fellow, who eventually
left her penniless in Auckland while he absconded to the Thames. Up until her
subsequent arrest on the charge of having no visible means of support, she had
never, in her 24 years, been known to the police or convicted of any charge.

To Mary Ann's mind, the young woman was not a person who would generally
be considered a thief. Despite plenty of opportunities for theft during the period
she had resided in the Colclough household, she had never shown any signs of
temptation, even when money had been deliberately left on the kitchen mantel.
In the two months she had been in domestic service, the only items observed
missing were three Crimean shirts. The young woman had, of course, denied
taking them, and they were not found in her possession. However, even Mary
Ann agreed it was highly likely she had been induced into taking them, as she
knew she had communicated with at least one former prison acquaintance who
lived near the Colclough residence.

Adamant that the essential mistake was in unwisely and hastily consigning
the young woman to prison in the first place, Mary Ann challenged the editor of
the *Cross*: having requested that something should be done to help such women,
he was now condemning those who tried to help them. Mary Ann wrote urging
that talk be followed through with committed action:

To be sure, Government has granted £200 for reformatory purposes, and the Parnell ladies must have almost as much more: yet with all this talk no one is doing anything to stay the evil, if we except my humble efforts to do what little I can without means, without encouragement, and without help. It is a sad and awful thing that so it should be, and I shall be glad of your article, painful and discouraging as it has been to me, if it has the effect of rousing the so-called philanthropists to a sense of their great neglect. Some great and united effort is wanted. My attempts have been so simple and humble that no wonder they sometimes fail. Nevertheless, the experience I have gained has been worth something, and would be worth hearing. Some day, perhaps, I may give it to the world, and when I do there will be some grave disclosures as to the law and justice of our Auckland Police Court. This case I have given will I think go some way to prove the facility with which it is possible to make criminals.[26]

To do her best, 'without means, without encouragement, and without help' and then to be publicly criticised must have been extremely discouraging. Mary Ann had been keeping a close eye on the young woman in question but had to leave Auckland for a few days to present a public lecture in Coromandel, and it was during her absence that the woman had succumbed to the demands of her former prison-mate.

The success of her lecture would have been some compensation at least. The Theatre Royal in Coromandel was not the best venue in terms of lighting or ventilation, but it was the only hall available that was suitable for public addresses. The lecture drew a capacity crowd; all 100 seats were taken, and some latecomers had to be turned away. The evening was a great success, and Mary Ann was warmly invited to visit again as soon as the community had managed to build a more suitable venue for public lectures.

Returning to Auckland, Mary Ann reopened her school for the new term in the first week of April, leaving her less available for public engagements and community work over the following weeks. She did manage to find time to speak with the people who had raised the young woman lately dismissed from service for stealing, and she reported her conversation with them in the *Cross*. The people she spoke to denied having ill-treated the woman, insisting she had gained her injuries from falling from a window. They also confirmed that she was not a thief. Rather, being ignorant of the value of money or goods, she would not, unless incited to the act by people she had met in prison, have stolen anything apart from lollies, fruits and cakes, and those she would not have been able to resist.

Mary Ann added that because she was 'half-witted, cunning, and passionate, they found her utterly mismanageable, and concur with me in thinking that, if she again falls into the hands of the police, the proper place to send her to will be the Lunatic Asylum'.[27]

Another unanticipated effect of Mary Ann's court and prison work was that she developed a reputation among the criminal fraternity for being available for cases beyond the scope of her ability to assist. The most public instance of this was in relation to the case of Cyrus Haley, a speculator on the stock exchange who was convicted on multiple charges of arson. Among the buildings he damaged were the Auckland Choral Society Hall in Symonds Street, Aachard and Brown's Kerosene Store at Mechanics Bay, and the New Zealand Insurance Company's buildings in Queen Street. Haley also faced the more serious charge of shooting with intent to kill. After several appearances in the Police Court and the Supreme Court, he eventually confessed to all the charges against him and was sentenced to life imprisonment.

It was during the early stages of his trial on some of the lesser charges in February 1872 that he had contact with Mary Ann. Testifying two months later at the Supreme Court, Detective George Jeffrey related overhearing a conversation between Haley and his wife, where Haley said he was sorry his wife had engaged a solicitor to defend him, as he was sure he would be in prison for a very long time and she would need money for herself. Haley advised his wife to shift to a smaller home and not to rely on him for any assistance. He would arrange to speak with Mrs Colclough and seek her advice on whether his wife should remain in New Zealand or return to England. Mary Ann subsequently made a very brief visit to Haley in prison and advised him to send his wife back to England. Haley was very polite and apologised to Mrs Colclough for sending for her, saying from what he knew of her she would be only too glad to assist an unprotected female.

Despite Mary Ann's advice, Mrs Haley did not return to England, and the family shifted to Dunedin when Cyrus Haley was transferred to Dunedin prison. On one of the severest nights in the winter of June 1875, police found four of the couple's children in a house, all four in a deplorable condition. The children were charged as vagrants and sent to the Caversham Industrial School for six years. Their mother was issued with a bad character for drunkenness and sent to the refuge. Four months later, Haley was shot and killed as he tried to escape from a working gang. The inquest into his death confirmed that Haley was well known as a dangerous and vindictive man and that he had objected to his children being sent to the industrial school because of its association with criminality. He had said he would rather have killed them than have them sent there. He'd also said that if he successfully escaped from prison, he would kill his wife and then take his own life.

Mary Ann made no reference in public to her encounter with Haley and kept a very low public profile throughout his trial and for some weeks afterwards. Apart from writing to the *Cross* to recommend the novel *A Brave Lady* by English author Dinah Maria Craik ('Miss Mulock') 'to the thoughtful perusal of all who hold the doctrine that every good wife and mother willingly accepts the positions assigned to her by the marriage law', she passed an entire month without contributing anything to the newspapers, the first time for several years that this length of time had passed without a word from her.[28]

In early May she presented a public lecture at the YMCA rooms on 'Signs of the Times: Religious Agitations, Social Revolutions, the Revival of Superstition, Spiritualism, and Scepticism'. In his remarks introducing Mary Ann, Reverend Samuel Edger noted that although many an able lecturer might shrink from such an ambitious topic, he considered it undoubtedly the pre-eminent issue of the day. He disagreed with the widely held view that the present age was one of disbelief, preferring instead to think of it as an age remarkable for its earnestness. Many of the old forms of belief were being found insufficient for the wider views now entertained on religious subjects. He felt sure that the various agitations for progress would lead to truer and better forms of faith in the Christian world.

The reviewer for the *Cross* was particularly impressed with Mary Ann's delivery:

> *Mrs Colclough's lecture was a remarkable one in many respects. It went altogether beyond the ordinary scope of evening lectures. It reviewed with considerable minuteness the origin of the religious agitations in progress, and looked upon them not doubtingly but hopefully. They were the indications of a deep awakening, from which she anticipated the best results for the cause of the Christian religion. The social revolutions were also dealt with ably. She portrayed the evils resulting to a State when inordinate wealth and extreme poverty existed side by side. There was danger then to the social fabric, but she hoped that the revolutions in progress in Britain would not culminate in the decay of Britain's power, as had been the case with other ancient nations when they attained great wealth and indulged in luxuries. Under one division of her subject – revival of superstition – she recited many wonderful instances of what was called spiritualism.*[29]

The reviewer for the *Herald* was less generous, noting that the scope of the address was such that it left the lecturer free to digress 'into the exhibition of particular views with which Mrs Colclough had identified herself'. Paying her a compliment of sorts, he commented: 'Upon matters within the sphere of her personal observation, it cannot be denied that the lady manifests on every occasion excellent good sense. Her manner is generally favourable to the enforcement of her views, and is well adapted to give effect to kindly feeling, somewhat hazardous upon occasion, but nevertheless genuine and earnest.'[30]

Throughout her lecture, Mary Ann frequently referred to Catherine Ann Crow's collection of supernatural tales, *Night Side of Nature*. In what the *Herald* reviewer described as 'curious testimony', Mary Ann also named several spiritual manifestations she herself had seen and said that she was inclined to think the cause of these might ultimately be found in animal magnetism. The 'moderately large and respectable' audience obviously agreed that the lecture was both entertaining and instructive and showed their appreciation with spontaneous applause. As the lecture came to a close, Reverend Edger invited open discussion of the topic, but no-one took the opportunity to express their views. Given Mary Ann's strong commitment to the Christian faith, her interest in the supernatural suggests an inquiring mind and a willingness to engage with new ideas and theories. By now she was so well known in the Auckland province and her views so widely reported in newspapers that her name would have been a drawcard whatever the topic.[31]

A week after Mary Ann's lecture, 'Sketcher' wrote a relatively light-hearted piece musing on the 'wearying existence' of barmaids in his 'Portraits of the People' column for the *Auckland Star*. In the piece he made an unabashed taunt to Mary Ann:

> *We often think how heartless and wearisome a barmaid's life must be, and how ruinous to all the domestic virtues of woman-kind it must be – with all its gaiety and soulless twaddle, and gaudy exterior – a broken state … Barmaids appear to exist beyond the pale of philanthropy. Does the genial light-hearted Polly Plum ever look with a feeling of Christian pity towards the bottle-and-grog surrounded barmaids, who, despite the supposed demoralizing influence of frizzled hair and the paint, may be a hard-working girl, though naturally inclined to flirting; a little shrewd, and a little ignorant, but not half so silly as the young noodle of small fashion who spends his time and his notes lounging about the bar with a view to an ignoble conquest.*[32]

Taking the bait, Mary Ann sent in a riposte titled 'A Polly Plum Paper'. She opened with the assurance 'Polly Plum does feel for barmaids, and for all the other poor pretty girls whom the intense selfishness of mankind force into demoralising spheres and pursuits.'[33] Her reply was met, however, with a letter of protest from several local barmaids:

> *To the Editor of the* HERALD
>
> SIR, *We, on behalf of several of the young barmaids of Auckland, request 'Polly Plum' and 'Sketcher' of the Evening Star, to mind their own business. We are not half so badly off as they imagine.*
>
> MAUDE HENNESSY,
> BARBARA WITDON,
> OPHELIA MARLEL[34]

Given lines in Mary Ann's reply to Sketcher, such as 'Under the protection of the law these bachelors get all the golden honours of life, women being always discouraged, and in many cases entirely forbidden from earning their living in any honest and lucrative way', readers could be forgiven for wondering if 'A Polly Plum Paper' signalled the return of the feisty feminist writings of Polly Plum. The content of a letter Mary Ann wrote to the editor of the *Cross* several days after her response to Sketcher suggests she was at least toying with the idea of resurrecting her journalistic persona.

In her letter, which appeared in the *Cross* on 20 May, she set up a case for inclusion of a dedicated ladies column. For several years, the *Weekly News*, a subsidiary of the *Daily Southern Cross*, had included a dedicated ladies column. Published on Saturday mornings and priced at sixpence, the *Weekly News: A journal of commerce, agriculture, politics, literature, science and art* marketed itself as a journal rather than as a newspaper. It aimed to cater for a more literate, educated and leisured middle-class readership as well as for the literate working classes who sought to 'improve' themselves through participation in the print culture.

The 'Ladies Column' in the *Weekly News* had first appeared in June 1868. Usually about one full newspaper column in length, it consisted for the first few months of a mix of recipes, pieces on etiquette, and a variety of short items on royalty, society gossip and snippets. Passed off as satire, the content nonetheless often had an underlying tone quite derogatory towards women. Occasionally, pieces provided news of activities of women on the international stage, but these too were frequently reported in a satiric tone.

In August 1868 a letter sent by 'A Young Lady' under the caption 'The Crusade Against Women' led to a flurry of letters to the editor confirming that the demeaning tone of many of the articles published in the Ladies Column offended Auckland's female readership. Two weeks later, Mary Ann sent in a clipping of an article she had read in *The Ladies' Own Journal and Miscellany* that derided the young men of the day who appeared to be approaching marriage as a sacrifice for which they expected to be handsomely paid. The *Weekly News* responded by shifting the balance of offerings in the Ladies Column, which it renamed 'For the Ladies', and regularly reprinting Polly Plum's articles over the next few years. By 1872, although the content had not regressed to that of the early columns, most of it, with the exception of the odd letter to the editor reprinted from the *Cross*, was relatively conservative and dependent on overseas news.[35]

Published under the caption 'Ladies and Newspapers', Mary Ann's letter to the *Cross* of 20 May called for a more responsive and engaged column for ladies:

> *Columns and columns are written solely for the information of men and the matters in which they only are interested, and it would be churlish in the extreme to grudge to ladies an occasional column or half-column of news or information for their special benefit. Indeed, I think the ladies have some reason to complain that too seldom in these days of mining fever do editors consult their tastes in arranging their columns, and to say that, when they do it, they do it for 'amusement,' and not out of courtesy or consideration, is too bad, and adds insult to injury.*[36]

Noting that the general press in England and America paid much more attention to women's literary wants than New Zealand did, she stated that although the *Cross* in the past had been the most mindful of local newspapers of this need, it had been somewhat neglectful of the interests of its female readership of late, particularly those interests pertaining to the women's movements overseas and to works of charity and philanthropy. Mary Ann's request fell on deaf ears, and it would be nearly two decades before women had periodicals dedicated to these matters.

At this time Mary Ann was receiving almost daily requests from young women seeking work as servants in an effort to turn their lives around. Unfortunately, even though servants were in increasingly scarce supply, few people were willing to give these women a trial period of work. Not all the women who approached Mary Ann had served prison sentences, and two out of every three for whom she found positions proved their mettle and showed themselves equal in every way to the ordinary run of servants. Determined to continue running her servants' agency, and wishing to cater in particular for those country settlers who required domestic servants, Mary Ann made herself available between her educational classes each day at a quarter past noon at the YMCA rooms.

As part of an established international network of women's rights advocates, Mary Ann was in direct contact with some of the leaders of the women's movement in England. She sent and received letters and papers and acted as a recognised agent and advocate in New Zealand on issues related to women's rights. Foremost among her contacts were Isabella Tod, who wrote for the *Leisure Hour* and had published on issues related to the education of girls; Agnes Garrett, sister of the much celebrated Elizabeth Garrett-Anderson, the first woman in Britain to qualify as a medical doctor; and Millicent Garrett Fawcett, who was a leader of the English suffrage movement.

One of the issues Mary Ann and Isabella Tod shared correspondence on was the circumstances of vagrant girls. Of particular concern was the plight of young children whose mothers were confirmed drunkards. The annual meeting of the Auckland Home for Neglected Children had recently taken place, and although the turn-out was very small, the reports presented confirmed that the home was full to capacity and so prospering beyond its committee's expectations. However, the continued need for a penal reformatory was clearly evident.

On reading the lengthy newspaper account of the meeting, Reverend B. Thornton Dudley, who had been unable to attend it in person, wrote to suggest that rather than continue to turn children away from the home for want of room, children could be sent to the Orphan and Destitute Children's Home, which had accommodation for 100 youngsters. However, neither the home for neglected children nor the home for orphans would accept the children who were of concern to Mary Ann, and the gaol authorities had indicated that they would only continue to admit infants who were still being nursed by their mothers. The relieving officer objected to paying for children who were under four years of age, the orphans' home objected to taking the children because they had no legal power to hold them if their drunken mothers demanded them, and the courts would not commit children under the age of four.

The situation was one that had immediate relevance for Mary Ann. With the assistance of her neighbours, she had been looking after a young girl named Nellie in her own home. Nellie was a pretty little girl who was just over three years old. Her mother had tried every avenue to have Nellie admitted to either the orphans' home or the home for neglected children, but the child was not eligible on account of her age and the fact that both her parents were alive. When her mother had last been convicted in court, Mary Ann had appeared before the judge on Nellie's behalf, but the magistrate did not have the power to admit the child into care. With no other alternatives in place, and not prepared to leave the poor little girl to fend for herself on the streets, Mary Ann herself had been caring for Nellie.

Her fear that the child might be left to fend for herself was not unfounded. Only a week after Mary Ann wrote to the *Cross* about the need for some facility for the infant children of drunken parents, the newspapers reported that two children about two years of age had been found almost unclothed on a bare floor at nine o'clock in the evening in a small tumble-down shanty on Wyndham Street. Because it was mid-winter, and because they had been left by their parents since five o'clock that morning, the children were in a very frail state and near death. The police located their mother, who was drunk and in a state of semi-dress at a nearby public house. Her husband was found in a similar state in another public house. The parents had been on a drunken debauch for several weeks and had neglected the children completely.

Public debate regarding the licensing of liquor again flared up, and Mary Ann wrote to both the *Cross* and the *Herald* to reiterate her view that the number of licensed establishments should be reduced, and that those publicans who served known drunkards or allowed people to get drunk on their premises should be prosecuted. She had witnessed the cycle of drunkenness and its effects on women and innocent children too many times to leave the matter in the hands of those who profited from drink.[37]

In late June 1872, Mary Ann advertised a new series of six public lectures on a variety of topics to be held at the YMCA Hall. When advertising the series, the *Cross* wrote: 'We hope to see these lectures patronised, not only because we believe their merits will deserve it, but because they are for the benefit of a lady who has untiringly exerted herself in the cause of public benevolence.' Despite inclement weather, a reasonable audience attended the first lecture on the topic of 'Self Culture', chaired by Reverend Samuel Edger and accompanied with music from Madame Möller and several duets from Misses Kate and Lilian Edger. Opening with an explanation for her choice of topic, Mary Ann asserted her belief in the value of serious dedication to increasing one's knowledge and intellectual development as an adult. Schooling could only provide the most rudimentary elements of knowledge; often girls did not even receive that because too much of their schooling centred on the attainment of 'a smattering of entirely useless and showy accomplishments'.[38]

Because Mary Ann knew the Reverend Edger well, it's likely that she took a great personal interest in the educational achievements of the young Edger girls. Kate, then 15 years of age, had received her early schooling from her father, who had graduated from the University of London. It is not known whether she attended any of Mary Ann's private classes, but Kate's father used his contacts to enable her to study alongside the top classes of boys at Auckland College and Grammar School. Because the school was affiliated to the University of New Zealand, Kate was able to study toward a degree, and in July 1877 she attained the distinguished position of being the first woman in the British Empire to gain a bachelor of arts.

A few days after Mary Ann's new lecture series commenced, an editorial in the *Cross* drew attention to the scarcity of female domestic servants in the colony. The editor observed that as servants' wages increased, the efficiency of their work appeared to decrease. He reprinted an extract from the English *Saturday Review*, in which the writer commented that it was surprising the agitators for women's rights had not taken the issue of emigration more in hand, as this would have secured them more sympathy and cooperation from many men who otherwise were predisposed to laugh at them. The article exhorted those of the middle classes to look more to emigration than to educating their daughters, particularly those parents who could not be confident of leaving sufficient financial security to daughters who did not marry. The colonies were heralded as providing hope and opportunities for young single women of the middle classes to find a comfortable marriage.[39]

The writer of the *Saturday Review* extract also urged the government of New South Wales to request that 'an assortment of young women suitable to become wives of artisans and farmers' be sent out by the emigration commissioners in England. The author justified this recommendation on the basis that 'If a young man in a colony can keep himself, he can usually keep a wife; and the more children he has the better, since they are all likely to be able to live, and some of them to prosper, in a country in which they have been born and bred.' Maintaining that 'hard work and plenty in Australia is preferable to listless gentility and semi-pauperism in Pentonville', the writer added, 'We wish that the ladies who are so busy with Woman's Rights and the Contagious Diseases Act would devote a little of their time and energy to arranging for the supply to New South Wales of as many "eligible female emigrants" as that colony is willing to receive.'[40]

For Mary Ann, the editorial was akin to waving a red rag to a bull. She lost no time in expressing her disagreement with what she viewed as exporting women 'like herds of cattle to foreign lands to make marriages of the grossest materialism, marriages with complete strangers, with the coarsest and grossest motives for marrying, who want simply a woman to bear them children and cook their dinner'. One did not need to look to England to find an overabundance of semi-genteel girls who did not seem to marry. As was the situation in many of the English colonies, New Zealand was over-represented in this class: '… young girls, poor, struggling, scantily supported by embarrassed fathers, perhaps doing some little "genteel" work to supply their own clothing, but too often idle and useless.'[41]

There were plenty of eligible bachelors as well, but Mary Ann had observed an increasing trend, in Auckland at least, of these young men clubbing together in groups of four or five and keeping house and a housekeeper rather than marrying and thereby relieving some overburdened father of the support of his 'useless' daughter. Having kept a servants' agency of sorts for some time, she had been contacted on several occasions by young farmers working in isolated areas of the bush seeking wives, sometimes even approaching her for a selection of photographs from which to choose a wife. She seldom replied to such letters and always declined to offer any assistance: 'Feeling as I do, I should not dare assist to consign a sister-woman to the probable misery of a desecration of marriage.' The problem was not that there were insufficient numbers of young women already in New Zealand who could work as domestic servants or marry men working in the bush; rather, young women did not view these options as desirable ones. In Mary Ann's view, the notion that women would want to marry indiscriminately was largely the result of society not respecting women as capable, intelligent and competent individuals who could and should choose their own pathways in life.[42]

According to the editor of the *Auckland Star*, Mary Ann's response to the letters received from farmers seeking wives betrayed a naivety and lack of judgement of human character. A similar lack of judgement was attributed to her support for Martha Cusins, given that the girl had taken advantage of Mrs Colclough's generosity and good nature. The editor suggested the letters from supposed farmers could simply have been some wags having a quiet joke at her expense by writing with requests for wives. While there were some occasions when Mary Ann's earnestness overrode her judgement, it was, perhaps, more that her dedication to assisting women in need and her outspokenness were viewed as unwelcome interference.[43]

Some members of the public were under the erroneous belief that Mary Ann received payment for her work with female prisoners at Mount Eden Gaol. Since her first visit in June 1871, she had dedicated many hours to gaol visiting and for some time had used her own home as a receiving house for women on their discharge who had demonstrated a commitment to reforming their lives. Mary Ann would do whatever was in her means to ensure the women had sufficient clothing and whatever else might be needed to find them suitable employment. She used her own money but received a modest recompense from the provincial government and private charity for costs incurred. It was not the most practical of solutions, and because Mary Ann was teaching from 9.30am to 5.00pm five days a week, she could only commit herself to this work on a sporadic basis.[44]

This situation explained why Mary Ann continued to stress the need for the authorities to provide a receiving house, and urged ladies with more time and means than she had to take up the work. She outlined the many different ways interested women could volunteer their services, depending on their interests, time and means. Lady visitors to the gaol were always needed, not just to preach to the prisoners but to assist with helping these women learn to read and write and make plans for their lives after release. Assistance was also needed to encourage women to reconcile with their husbands. The children of prisoners, moreover, needed carers. And there was always a need for clothing.

Working closely with individual women had its rewards. One such case was that of Eliza Lestrange. Eliza had faced three charges of drunkenness in as many months, and had appeared again before the Police Court charged with being a habitual drunkard and breaking two panes of glass valued at two shillings. On corroboration from the police that Mrs Colclough had obtained a position for her in Waikato, Resident Magistrate Thomas Beckham discharged Eliza with a caution. Unfortunately, however, for every success, there were many disappointments. Almost without fail when Mary Ann tried to assist a female ex-prisoner to turn her life around, there would be others enticing the poor woman back into sin and misery. Mary Ann had encountered several cases where women had been literally dragged away and brutally beaten by their husbands for trying to live decent lives.

An example was the mother of little Nellie, the child Mary Ann had taken into her own home because she was not eligible for state care in either the orphans' home or the home for neglected children. Mary Ann had assisted in securing a position in domestic service for Nellie's mother on her release from prison, but her husband had pulled her away and beaten her so badly she had to be admitted to hospital. Visiting his wife in hospital, Nellie's father convinced her to give up the idea of domestic service and return to him. Mary Ann likened the woman to Nancy from Dickens' *Oliver Twist*, clinging all the while to Bill Sykes even though he abused her more and more. During the three months Nellie was in Mary Ann's care, she had a bad attack of inflammation of the lungs, brought on by the miserable conditions to which her wretched parents now dragged her back.

Soon after Nellie was again with her parents, her mother had the audacity to arrive on Mary Ann's doorstep demanding the few clothes and belongings Mary Ann had collected for the little girl. Convinced the mother's intentions were to sell these items for drink, Mary Ann sent her away empty handed and without her daughter, who stayed under Mary Ann's care. Little Nellie was dirty and bruised and had the type of cold that signalled the development of another attack of inflammation of the lungs. When Nellie's mother appeared at the door again that evening to take Nellie away, Mary Ann was so disgusted she could not bring herself to see her. She had grown to love little Nellie, whose screams as her mother tore her away from the house left Mary Ann bereft and distressed in knowing she was powerless to do anything about the situation. Her plaintive plea for 'Poor little beaten, sick, unhappy Nellie, as good a little child as ever was', was an indictment on the legal system that professed to protect children.[45]

The second of Mary Ann's evening lecture series took place in the YMCA Hall on Monday 12 August. The topic was English history. Once again, the Reverend Samuel Edger occupied the chair. The evening, advertised as a musical and literary entertainment, attracted a moderate audience. Mary Ann split her lecture into two parts so that it could be interspersed with songs, duets and musical accompaniments by a number of people including the ever popular Madame Winter and Kate Edger and her sisters. The Mount Eden School was the venue for the third lecture on the evening of 21 August. During her talk, 'Signs of the Times', Mary Ann addressed a range of issues that included religious agitation, social revolutions, and the revival of superstitions, spiritualism and scepticism.

Largely retired from newspaper journalism by this time, Mary Ann was still very aware of the opportunities the daily press held for influencing public opinion. In mid-August she wrote down her 'Thoughts on a Few Things' for the *Cross*. She reiterated many of her familiar views on the inadequacies of the current education system and the unworkable nature of sectarianism, particularly in country districts. For the first time, she conveyed her views on compulsory military training for boys. As a Christian, she considered warfare a deplorable evil and a great sin but conceded that defensive warfare was a sad necessity. Having seen the cadet movement introduced in schools, she considered, 'The doubtful good of knowing how to shoot and march in line is gravely counterbalanced by the evils of being out at night, learning to smoke and drink and swear, to be miniature "men", and despise parental control.'[46]

Returning to another of her former themes, she insisted that teachers, for the sake of children and for the profession, should be protected by certificates and licenses. She deplored the current situation in which more than two thirds of schools were presided over by untrained teachers who were not apt to teach either by education or personal suitability. As concerned as ever about the perennial problem of domestic servants and the growing numbers of respectable girls who could not find suitable employment, Mary Ann ended her 'thoughts' by arguing that, wherever possible, the mistress of the family should employ a companion instead of a servant so that semi-genteel girls could become gainfully employed and escape the confines of genteel poverty.[47]

Mary Ann's ongoing concern regarding opportunities for young middle-class women was matched by her commitment to securing appropriate employment for young women of the working classes. She typically advertised for country positions for them: 'WANTED, a Situation in the Country for a Girl aged 13, a good worker; wages not so much an object as a home where she will be taken care of – Apply, Mrs. Colclough, Y.M.C.A., Wellesley-street, Auckland.'[48]

For some time, Mary Ann had been considering reducing her commitments. She decided to return to the public school system and applied for a position at Tuakau School, about 36 miles (58km) south of Auckland. As news spread of her impending departure from Auckland, tributes to her philanthropic work poured in. As befitting someone of her standing in the community, a farewell entertainment was announced. The public tribute from the editor of the *Cross* provides an insight into how highly she and her philanthropic work were regarded:

MRS COLCLOUGH

A lady – Mrs. Colclough – long known in our midst for her philanthropic endeavours to ameliorate the condition and work a reform among women who have fallen, and who have been cast out beyond the pale of society, is, we regret to learn, about to leave Auckland, having accepted the charge of a school under the Central Board of Education. Mrs. Colclough has, we sincerely believe, been the instrument by which young girls leading depraved and impure lives have been made to see the errors of their ways, and who are now following honest pursuits. If this lady has not met with as much success in her untiring efforts at reforming unfortunate women as she had reasonably hoped and expected, it has been due to those counteracting influences which women publicly engaged in a work of this kind have invariably met with from those who, instead of lending their aid in furthering a good cause, have thrown temptations in the way to draw erring creatures back into the paths of vice and ruin. Mrs. Colclough has been the means of directing public attention to many abuses by making herself heard through the columns of the newspaper press; has visited at regular and frequent intervals our gaol, and other institutions; has been the means of obtaining for female prisoners better accommodation, and fitting employment whilst under durance; has been the guardian of many deserted or parentless children; has reformed the drunken husband, and established for him a new home with the wife who had long been compelled to forsake him. What this lady has done with the drunken man she has done with the drunken woman, and there are not a few who, formerly dissipated and debased, are now leading sober and orderly lives, solely due to her advice, help, and mediation. Whether anyone with a heart as brimful of kindliness, a lover of her fellow-creatures however low they may have fallen, and with as sound an understanding, as good tact, and as practical a way of setting to work on her self-imposed task, will step out from the ranks of our matrons to supply this lady-philanthropist's place we do not know; but some such an one is greatly needed if the good work which Mrs. Colclough began is to be continued.[49]

Mr Broham, the inspector from the armed constabulary, likewise commended Mary Ann's personal qualities and untiring work in the cause of women in a personal letter. Expressing his sincere regret that she was leaving Auckland, where she had been the means of doing so much good in her endeavours 'to reform a class of creatures whom most persons only think of with horror and aversion', he trusted that in her new sphere she would still be able to afford such women the warm degree of interest she had always shown them. Confessing to having experienced great pleasure in finding a woman with sufficient faith in the goodness of human nature to believe in the reformation of 'these poor girls', and acknowledging the energetic way she had worked in their cause, he regretted her departure even more, as he feared 'there is no other lady in the place who can bring so many suitable qualities to bear upon what appears to me one of the most important matters that can engage the attention of any great reformer'.[50]

Although not one to court personal praise, Mary Ann must have taken pride in receiving public acknowledgement of her efforts as a woman's advocate, especially given her many years of enduring often personalised criticism in the newspapers. Being somewhat of a cause célèbre with a very high public profile for about five years had taken a toll on her personal life. On one occasion her daughter Lulu, then close to 10 years old, received a letter in the mail obviously intended for her mother:

> *To Miss Colclough. – Dear Miss, – Having heard of your disinterested efforts to make the unfortunates of Auckland abandon their course of life, and seek a more creditable course of life, and also of your having succeeded in many cases in bringing them to a sense of their folly, and trying to become respectable members of society, and good and honourable wives for working men, you will, I am sure, not think me presumptuous or foolish for writing a few lines to you with regard to myself. The case is this: I am a working man, earning good wages, and quite able to keep a wife; am a bachelor; age, 26; have not been long in the colony; have no friends or relations; have a comfortable home, in which myself and two more single men reside. I am working for good employers, well known in the province, can give a good reference, and lastly want a wife that will make me comfortable, and not squander or waste what I most certainly work hard for. If you can aid me in my endeavours to get such a one, I shall not look to what her former life may have been, but trust that her future life may be better; and, if it is, she will never have any cause to complain. Please, Miss, excuse my writing to you, and if you reply to this I will give you more particulars next time, – I am, with thanks, your obedient servant, A. D.*
>
> *P.S.: I should prefer one who can milk, as we have some cows.*[51]

Considering herself in a position neither to advise nor assist the writer, Mary Ann forwarded the letter to the *Cross* so that if any female reader aspired to the hand of this accommodating bachelor, she could obtain the address directly from the editor.

Proposal letters from bachelors aside, there were many everyday ways in which Mary Ann's commitment to the cause of women affected Lulu and Willie as they were growing up. Unlike many of their friends' mothers, their mother was generally not home during week days because she was busy earning the family income. During weekends, evenings and school holidays, she visited Mount Eden Gaol or the lunatic asylum, attended and spoke at public meetings, delivered public lectures and attended court sessions. Even when she was at home, she spent many hours writing articles for the *Cross*, penning an endless stream of letters to the newspapers, her friends and contacts both locally and in England, and using whatever means she could to find gainful employment for women who requested her assistance. Lulu and Willie also experienced the unpredictability of who would actually be staying in their home at any given time. During the winter of 1872 little Nellie had lived with them for three months, and then there were the women who would arrive on the doorstep, perhaps having been beaten and left destitute by their husbands, and now seeking Mary Ann's assistance.

Mary Ann's schedule of activities was exhausting and increasingly undermined her physical health. She had always preferred living in the country, and this, along with her desire to limit the demands on her time and energy, influenced her decision to take up the teaching position in the small rural settlement of Tuakau.

Knowing she was leaving Auckland, Mary Ann felt more able to express her disappointment at the lack of assistance she had received in some quarters for her work. This was certainly the case with the Temperance Society. She had felt personally slighted at the society's last annual meeting when members did not nominate her for a position on the committee. She therefore decided she would not now accept a nomination should one be offered. She said as much in a letter to the society, and also expressed her concern that 'the essential spirit of unity was altogether wanting in their organisation'. The society considered her letter during its September meeting, after which its secretary wrote to Mary Ann conveying the society's thanks for her past labours in the cause of temperance and assuring her that the lack of nomination had been unintentional.[52]

After 15 years of living in the Auckland province, Mary Ann must have spent her last weeks in the city working through the many arrangements that a move entails and finding opportunities to say goodbye to her personal friends. Importantly, there was also the matter of attending to the ongoing education of her private pupils. To this end, Mary Ann secured the services of Mrs Kaye Wright, who had recently arrived in Auckland. Mrs Wright, an accomplished musician, had been a pupil of eminent London master, Charles Glover. Mary Ann's imminent departure also meant her public lecture series came to an abrupt end. Those who had subscribed to the whole series, which, in addition to those talks already delivered, was to have included lectures on social reformers, ancient history, the women of history, and society in all ages, were either reimbursed or could, on application, exchange any unused tickets for entry to her farewell entertainment.

Although usually the preserve of public figures such as retiring ministers or theatrical performers, public farewells were a recognised means by which a community could pay its respects to those who had made a significant contribution to the life of that society. Extensively advertised in all of the Auckland newspapers, complete with details of the full programme, Mary Ann's public farewell promised to be a memorable event. On the morning of the farewell, the editor of the *Cross* wrote: 'Mrs Colclough has a substantial claim upon the good wishes and assistance of all classes in Auckland, and when an opportunity such as tonight's entertainment is afforded for combining a duty with a pleasure it should not be neglected. We hope to see a very large audience.'[53]

The audience that gathered in the Choral Hall was not as large as anticipated; nevertheless, the evening was a great success. According to the reviewer for the *Herald*, the entertainment, which consisted of vocal and instrumental music and various readings followed by a brief extempore address by Mary Ann, was one of the best he had ever attended in Auckland. The programme was extensive:

Part I

Trio, Pianoforte, Violin, Violincello (Mozart) – Miss Edger, Mr Hemus, Mr Frank Edger
Glee, 'Swiftly from the Mountain's Brow' – Glee Singers
Song, 'By the Sad Sea Waves' – Madame Winter
Fantasia, 'Lucrezia Borgia' – Mrs Kaye Wright
Song, 'Sing, Sweet Birds' – Mrs Kaynes
Reading, (Dickens) – Mrs Colclough
Song, 'Good-bye at the Door' – Mr Brookes
Duet, 'Harps Angelical' – Miss Edger and Mr Winter

Part II

Fantasia on Irish Airs – Madame Winter
Song, 'Come, oh Sleep', Violincello accompaniment – Miss Edger
Glee, 'I see them on their Winding Way' – Glee Singers
Song, 'Come into the Garden, Maud' – Mr Winter
Vocal Valse, Arditi – Madame Möller
Duet, 'Sainted Mother' (Maritana) – Madame Winter and Miss Edger
Song, 'Come back to Erin' – Mrs Rayner
Duet, 'The Sailor Sighs' – Mr and Madame Winter
Farewell, Mrs Colclough[54]

Nearly every song was met with calls for an encore, and the audience particularly enjoyed the duets and pieces with musical accompaniment. Taking the stage for her farewell, Mary Ann offered, instead of a formal speech, a few heartfelt words of thanks to those present and to the three or four gentlemen whom she deliberately did not name who had provided her with funds when she had needed them for her various ventures.

To some of her Auckland contemporaries, Mary Ann Colclough was an irrepressible busybody who offered support to the undeserving and actively sought female misery. Her particular 'stamp' of philanthropy certainly had more than its share of critics. It must therefore have been heartening for her to have her many philanthropic contributions, particularly those directed at women and children, acknowledged so publicly on her departure from the Auckland province.

Characteristically, Mary Ann encouraged the women present at her farewell to take up the causes she had worked for, convinced that they too would meet with friends who were kindly disposed to assist in whatever ways they could. She acknowledged she was leaving Auckland with some regrets – her work for women's rights was not finished, but she reiterated her sincere belief that there would come a day when women would be eligible to fill any office in church and state. She again urged the serious need for a reformatory for youth and a refuge for fallen women. However, on a personal level, what grieved her most was leaving the many good and kind friends who had supported her over the last 15 years.[55]

ڡ

CHAPTER SIX

ᡕᠣᡃ

Controversies and
Public Humiliation

Mary Ann and the children's arrival at Tuakau in late September 1872 was something of a red letter day for the local community. The district had been transformed from a bush-clad wilderness to a region of extensive green paddocks, grazing cattle and comfortable dwellings with tended gardens and the gradual influx of wealthier residents had fuelled demand not only for better roads and bridges but also for a well-qualified school teacher of high standing. Two years had passed since a school committee was first established, and during that time there had been several temporary teachers. Now that they had finally secured a permanent and extremely well-qualified teacher, hopes were running high for the successful growth of the school.

As occurred in many rural areas, classes had initially been held in a makeshift schoolroom. Considerable lobbying of the Central (Auckland) Board of Education meant that by the beginning of the 1872 school year, the community could boast a dedicated schoolroom well supplied with maps and books. The board had allocated money for the construction of a teacher's house, but in the interim there was a comfortable cottage with about two acres (8000 sq. m)of land available near the school.

Mary Ann immediately involved herself in the community. She led the singing at the local Presbyterian meetings and, with the assistance of the Sunday School Union, established a Sunday school in the schoolhouse. Being involved in a smaller community meant Mary Ann had more time to attend to international contacts. Encouraged by the recent letters and papers she had received from England, she was eager to organise a lecture tour in the South Island during the Christmas vacation.

The relative infrequency of mail deliveries was one of the most immediate changes Mary Ann noticed in shifting from the city to a small rural community. Receiving post only twice a week, she missed being able to keep up with news of the day, and although she had resolved to be a silent observer on local issues, she wrote a lengthy letter to the *Daily Southern Cross* within a few weeks of leaving Auckland. The letter was prompted by the case, reported in the Auckland *Weekly News*, of 16-year-old William Moore, who had appeared before the courts in Auckland charged with no visible means of support. The young man had a badly injured hand, which prevented him from being employed. Mary Ann was concerned that by the time he served his three-month prison sentence, his hand would be gangrenous and therefore need amputating. That disability, the taint of a prison record and the likelihood that the only ones to befriend him would be criminals were too much for her to contemplate. She even thought of sending the newspaper account of the case to her friends in England as an indication of the types of missions that were needed in this Britain of the South.

Unfortunately for Mary Ann, by the time she read of William Moore's plight, the news was several weeks old, and the account she had read in the *Weekly News* was inaccurate. A more accurate rendition was that when Moore, a stout-set young man of apparently weak intellect, appeared before the court with his arm suspended in a sling, the judge, concerned that the lad's arm might be gangrenous, remanded Moore so that a medical officer could examine him. Moore was subsequently declared to be of perfectly sound mind, but the medical officer confirmed that his arm needed serious attention. On that basis, the judge ordered Moore to serve a three-month sentence without hard labour so that he could receive appropriate medical care.

Over the next few weeks, several people wrote to the newspaper to correct Mary Ann's misrepresentation of the case, and gradually more facts about it came to light. For several months, Moore had supported himself by doing odd jobs around the neighbourhood. A local 'do-gooder' managed to find him employment in a flax mill at Waiuku, which is where he seriously injured his hand. The mill sent him to the provincial hospital for medical care, but he absconded from it before he had finished his treatment. However, his arm had healed a great deal by then, and there was no chance of gangrene setting in.

Moore returned to living on the streets in Auckland but was found by the police, who charged him with having no visible means of support. In prison, he had been kept apart from the other prisoners, his only associates being two small boys who were employed for part of the day breaking stones, and who spent the rest of the day attending school. All things considered, a better solution could hardly have been found for Moore. Even though Mary Ann had not had the full facts of the case, her concern for this young man and her insistence that something needed to be done in cases such as his further testifies to her heartfelt concern for the less fortunate and her conviction that society had an obligation to them.

Rather than be distracted by the criticisms of her detractors who accused her of writing publicly on subjects without any real acquaintance with their facts, Mary Ann focused on settling into her new community. The Boxing Day races at the race-ground on Hill's farm at Mauku attracted residents from the surrounding districts of Waiuku, Patumahoe and Tuakau and gave Mary Ann a welcome opportunity to catch up with friends. The race committee organised a soirée, and under the management of Sergeant Major Mowbray, the stage was set for an evening to remember.

From the side-lights entwined with roses and passion flowers to the beautiful arch of flowers over the platform, the Volunteer Hall was tastefully decorated with everything the bush or flower garden could produce. Major Lusk had donated a piano, and a standard adorned the platform announcing 'Welcome to Mauku'. After ample justice had been done to the refreshments, the highlight of the evening for the 50 or so gathered was undoubtedly the mock argument on women's rights by Polly Plum and her long-time sparring partner, 'Old Practical'. An amateur concert followed before the hall was opened for several hours of dancing, during which Mary Ann took her turn at the piano. All in all, it was a great evening's entertainment, and it also served the purpose of raising some funds for the new schoolhouse.

For reasons unknown, Mary Ann's intended trip south to lecture in Dunedin did not eventuate. Finding she had more time at her disposal during the Christmas school holidays than anticipated, she had opportunity to reflect on the differences between running her own private school and teaching in a state school. The Auckland Provincial Council had recently passed a new Education Act that provided free, secular and compulsory education for children between the ages of seven and 14. Many in her local community disapproved of the Act's content and called a public meeting to discuss it. According to one person attending, the meeting was 'the largest and most influential ... ever held in the schoolroom'. Immediately afterwards, the Tuakau school committee wrote to the board of education condemning the new Education Act and expressing their intention to oppose it in every way possible.[1]

Mary Ann, however, took a different view and expressed a cautious support for some of the changes. One issue that had always been of personal concern was the need to ensure financial security for teachers, and to this end she was a strong advocate for the establishment of a teachers' association. Throughout her long career as an educationalist, she had experienced and observed many of the inadequacies of educational legislation. Nowhere were these more evident than in rural areas, where government and local school committees shared the payment of teachers' salaries. Mary Ann was fully informed of her entitlements, and she always stipulated these when applying for positions. But she knew of teachers, some personal acquaintances or friends, who had not been paid what they were due and had been forced to manufacture receipts up to the correct amount to qualify for the government grant. There were also many hidden demands on teachers' income, such as school prizes, which teachers had to pay for from their own salaries. She pointed out that the legislation had not addressed issues such as these.[2]

One significant improvement in the new Education Act was the strengthening of teachers' positions in relation to school committees. Although Mary Ann had been teaching at Tuakau for only a few months, she had already seen how important these new provisions were. In early February 1873 she wrote to Mr O'Sullivan, the inspector of schools, to request that the schoolhouse be relocated closer to the teacher's residence. The teacher's house, surrounded by clumps of bush, sat on a rise above the railway line and afforded an extensive view over the Hapuakohe Range. Mary Ann had struck up a friendly relationship with some of the local workers on the railway line, and the foreman of works was the first to testify to her popularity and the respect she had earned through her 'active benevolence in the bush'. However, for Mary Ann, as picturesque as the setting was, the unsealed roads meant that after rain she had to plod through three quarters of a mile of thick clay to reach the schoolhouse. In winter, as she was to find out, the roads often became impassable for weeks at a time.[3]

Her request, which the board of education subsequently turned down, sparked animosity in the community. Some of its members felt that despite Mary Ann's excellent credentials, her services should not be bought at the expense of the whole district, particularly as there were many well-educated men and women who would be prepared to accept these conditions. While Mary Ann considered it wrong and unconstitutional for the teacher of a district or, indeed, any single individual, to try to override the wishes of the majority of that district, the matter of the schoolhouse's location was a personal one. She therefore felt justified in writing to the inspector of schools to ask if the school and schoolhouse could be located together on the school reserve.

Although Mary Ann had not realised Mr O'Sullivan was required to table her letter with the board of education, she was pleased, retrospectively, that he did so. Given the controversy her request generated in the community, she felt obliged to outline her position as clearly as possible and, typically, chose to do so by writing to the *Cross* in Auckland. The main problem, she wrote, was that the school committee had not informed her of the distance between the schoolhouse and the school and the state of the roads that separated the two buildings. Had she known these details, which she believed had been deliberately kept from her, she would never have accepted the offer of the position because it would have been physically impossible for her to perform her duties. She considered that school committees should be liable for compensation for any losses incurred 'when teachers are deluded long distances at heavy expense by a suppression of important facts':

> It is a serious matter to take a household a long distance and break up a home to be called on to perform impossibilities, or leave in a month or two. Therefore I have a very urgent interest in Tuakau school matters, quite sufficient to warrant some degree of interference in them; and I think it is for the interest of the district itself, as well as for the teacher's interests, that house and school should be together. If the road were a good metal road, the obstacle would be a comparatively trifling one; but as it is, the settlers will certainly during the winter months have much lost time, even if they had a strong man as teacher, and any female would find it impossible to teach for weeks together. It is not of so much importance for the children to live a short distance from school. They are more active on their feet than grown people, and are not besides forced to be at school as a teacher is. I regard it as a great mistake to have the teacher's house and the school separate, and believe that ultimately the reserve will be better than the present site. It is higher, much nearer the proposed railway-station – which will be sure to collect a little centre – and much more convenient for the Harrisville and out-settlers. Besides, it belongs to the Board of Education, and has a neat house on it, whereas the school is held at present in a wretched old building. There is some talk of taking the school much further from Tuakau; but that would be a great injustice, and I do not believe the Board will do it. I am, &c.,
>
> MARY A. COLCLOUGH[4]

It was hard to dispute her logic or miss her clear message that, under the circumstances, it would not be possible for her to remain in her current position and fulfil her duties. Despite signalling that her time in Tuakau was likely to be brief, she continued to engage in community activities. With the help of a Mr Mason, who was visiting the district under the auspices of the Bible Society, she organised a very successful soirée to raise funds for the new Sunday school. Nearly 100 people turned up, but because the schoolhouse could barely hold 50, a good many people had to wait outside while food was served in parties. The cramped facilities only served to highlight the need for a large public building, either a new schoolhouse or use of a Volunteer Hall. Several of the local women donated trays of food, and Mary Ann's donation was warmly referred to as 'the school tray' because the children and their parents had contributed to it.

After the tables were cleared, Mr Thomas Walker was called to the chair. Mr Mason, a great favourite in the district, then gave an earnest speech, thanking those present for the cordial welcome he had received in the few months he'd been visiting. He congratulated everyone involved in setting up the Sunday school. Mary Ann now took the floor and presented an abridged version of her lecture on 'The Subjection of Woman', which was met with enthusiastic applause. Several speeches and votes of thanks followed, and the evening closed with a hymn and a prayer.

The timing of the establishment of the Sunday school was fortuitous, as the old controversies concerning religious instruction in schools had resurfaced in relation to the new Education Act. Although education was to be secular, there was provision in the Act for school committees to decide, by majority vote, what religious education would be provided. Mary Ann had spoken out publicly on this issue many times over the years and did so once again:

> To the Editor. Sir, – If we force the Bible on everyone – on Roman Catholics who do not approve of our version, on Jews who object to the New Testament, and on Secularists, Deists, and, last of all, spiritualists, who do not believe the Bible at all, or look on it as a very ill-written and incomplete transcript of real history – are we not really denominationalists? As to its being left to the majority of the school committee to decide as to whether or not the Bible should be read, I would ask Mr Crispe or Mr McDonald, if they were living in a district where the majority were Roman Catholics, who would choose the Douay version, whether they would like their children to read it? The truth is, any attempt to teach religion in public schools is an attempt to force our views on others; and, as all should be fairly considered

in return for a tax that all must pay, I hope that strictly secular instruction
during school hours will in all fairness be upheld in State schools; and I am,
I hope, a good Protestant, and love the Bible for all that. Indeed it is from the
Bible that I have learnt toleration, for it teaches me, 'to do unto others as I
would they should do unto me'; and as I should object to Roman Catholics,
Jews, spiritualists, &c, forcing their views or standards of faith on my
children, so I equally object to forcing mine on theirs. I remain, &c.,

MARY A. COLCLOUGH[5]

Her letter attracted several responses, but because the authors of them were anonymous opponents, as a matter of principle she did not respond.

While she still enjoyed the support of many in the community of Tuakau, her relations with the school committee were becoming increasingly untenable, and she began turning her attention to securing employment elsewhere. In the meantime, the school committee granted her several days of leave so she could prepare for a lecture tour in the Waikato district on the topic of 'Woman's Rights and Men's Wrongs Toward Them'.

The first two of her lectures, held at Alexandra (later named Pirongia, to avoid confusion with the town of the same name in the South Island) and Hamilton, received barely a mention in the newspapers. A modest audience of about 50 turned up for her lecture at the school room in Ngaruawahia two evenings later. This third lecture was a significant occasion for Mary Ann, as it was the first time she had ever attempted a viva voce lecture, delivered entirely without notes. When referring to this aspect of her lecture in her introductory remarks, Mary Ann explained that she had recently been appointed a member of the Ladies' Vigilance Society of England and was honoured to act on their behalf by writing and lecturing on the objects of the society as frequently as possible in New Zealand.[6]

Mary Ann's experience and confidence as a public speaker held her in good stead. The *Cross*'s correspondent at Alexandra reported that she delivered 'a very excellent and temperate address'. He considered that with the exception of her claim that women should be entitled to the franchise, there appeared very little anyone present felt inclined to cavil at in her address, which lasted about an hour and a half. The reviewer for the *Waikato Times* was particularly impressed, saying 'she is undoubtedly one of the most fluent and accurate speakers we have listened to in the colonies' and that she was 'strong living evidence of the mental capacity of woman'.[7]

Several days later, as he had promised, the editor of the *Waikato Times* devoted a lengthy editorial to engaging with the detail of the arguments Mary Ann presented at her lecture. For the most part, his responses were a lesson in conservatism. He thought that giving women equality with their husbands would be 'disastrous in the extreme'. The majority of women, he pronounced, were not even fit to have authority over their children and still less over their domestic servants. Husbands would be driven to their clubs or the public bars, and wives would likely abandon their children to a nursemaid in order to attend some political meeting or lecture.[8]

On the issue of opening up all professions and employments to women, he was slightly more generous, so long as she remained single; the moment she married, her place was at home to watch over and nurture her offspring. Granted, not all women would have the opportunity to marry, and they should be prepared to support themselves if absolutely necessary. However, more contact with the outside world would only serve to decrease their attractiveness to men. As for the education of women, of course women should be better educated, if only because they have the responsibility for forming the minds of the next generation. In short: 'So long as woman remains a woman both by nature and in manner she will have the respect of all *men*. If she respects herself in her natural position she will always, as now, be respected except by the lowest of mankind ... Woman's power is her weakness, her tenderness, and her ability to love deeply.'[9]

Acknowledging the 'warm-hearted kindness and generous hospitality' she had received during her visit to the Waikato, and how gratified she had been at the excellent, respectable and attentive audiences at all three venues, Mary Ann showed a very generous spirit to the editor of the *Waikato Times* in a letter she wrote to him, albeit before his editorial appeared in it: 'I am aware that on the subject matter of those lectures, "Woman's Rights" so-called, I differ with you in opinion; but as I believe we both desire the same result – the good and well being of mankind, and are willing to give each other credit, at least for worthy motives, we can agree to differ, and I therefore desire to thank you for fair notices and personal courtesy.'[10]

Overall, the lecture tour was an enjoyable and satisfying one for Mary Ann. Her only regret was that she had not had sufficient time to visit her many kind friends in Cambridge. During her stay in the region, she had been convinced to apply for a teaching position at Ngaruawahia, and while the possibility of returning on a permanent basis may have had some influence on the generosity of her comments, she genuinely held that she would recall the tour as 'one of the "bright times" of life'.[11]

A few days later, after Mary Ann had found time to read the editorial in the *Waikato Times*, she wrote a lengthy reply countering each of the arguments expressed. In the meantime, however, her views on female emigration were creating a storm of controversy in England. She had taken umbrage with the fact that the New Zealand government was offering every possible inducement to persuade single women to emigrate to New Zealand without fairly stating the reality of the situation in the colony. This, in her view, was 'a cruel injustice'.[12]

First, there was not, as had been claimed, a want of single females in New Zealand, but a need for domestic servants. In a letter sent directly to the London *Times*, she elaborated: 'We have hundreds of half-educated, semi-genteel girls, who prefer earning a mere pittance by their needle, or in some so-called genteel occupation, to getting good wages as servants. Indeed, in a small way, we suffer from the home difficulty – no want of single women, but a great want of useful ones, willing and able to become domestic servants.' Her second point was that men did not marry more readily in the colonies than in England; in fact, the same disinclination to undertake the expense and respectability of a wife and family was as evident in New Zealand as it was in England. And, third, with a few rare exceptions, there was not much wealth in New Zealand.[13]

Accordingly, should semi-genteel girls decide to migrate to New Zealand, they would likely find themselves in an even worse position than in England. There were fewer openings for their class in New Zealand, and although strong, hard-working servants could easily get a good place with good wages, they would have to work harder and for longer hours because there were fewer servants employed per household and more manual labour was required. Mary Ann also presented a very graphic and unflattering image of what life in a typical domestic home was like:

> *The homes, even of the town dwellers, are very often comfortless abodes to English eyes; and in the out-districts the shanties, which too often do duty as homes to the labouring classes, are truly wretched – rough, unlined, wooden tenements of one or two rooms, with the daylight showing plainly through many a chink, with a big open wooden chimney, as large almost as the room itself. We may imagine the misery of such a home in winter; but few English people can imagine the utter wretchedness of such a home in summer, when that insect pest, the mosquito, penetrates through the cracks of the wretched dwelling and renders night hideous.*[14]

To those in New Zealand familiar with her views, the sentiments expressed in this letter would have come as no surprise. Mary Anne was an unknown name to the readers of the *Times*, but that did not prevent the content of her letter causing the stir it did. By the early 1870s, emigration agents for Canada, Australia and New Zealand were competing with one another to persuade certain groups of people to emigrate. Agricultural labourers and single women, especially those suitable for domestic service, were particular targets, and emigration agencies worked hard to protect the image of New Zealand as a desirable destination, actively marketing Arcadian images of the country as the 'Britain of the South Seas'.

Having lived in New Zealand for five years, Harriet Herbert held a much brighter view than Mary Ann of the prospects for working people who wished to immigrate to New Zealand. She wrote to correct what she considered to be Mary Ann's somewhat exaggerated and misleading picture of daily life in the colony. Major General R.S. Beatson, however, told *Times* readers he had spent some years in Auckland and could vouch personally for the accuracy of Mrs Colclough's letter. He considered her advice sound, and although he had not met her personally, they had mutual friends to whom she had been long and well known. He had therefore decided to write to the *Times* so that he could confidently affirm her as an appropriate authority on the subject of female emigration.[15]

By the time reports arrived from England confirming that Mary Anne's letter had 'excited some attention', the Auckland newspapers were ready to capitalise on the news. The editor of the *Herald* wrote that Mrs Colclough was quite capable of expressing her views on women's rights 'in terms never to be mistaken'. However, it 'would be hard to point out any intelligent well-educated colonial lady, who, like Mrs Colclough, has been so earnest and altogether mistaken in her advocacy of matters feminine'.[16]

The following week, the *Herald* received a copy of the letter as it had appeared in the *Times*. Although convinced the letter had been 'calculated to have a very mischievous effect', the editor of the *Herald* had no hesitation in reprinting it in full. Expressing his apology for feeling 'compelled to pass strictures upon a lady whose intentions are of the purest, but whose powers of observation are at the best very limited, and too often inaccurate', he took exception to the supposed numbers of 'half-educated semi-genteel girls' referred to by Mrs Colclough and proceeded to quibble with many of the claims she had made. Denigrating her judgement of the female population of the whole colony on the basis of 'an entirely Queen-street point of view', he reminded her that 'Queen-street' was not Auckland, and Auckland was still only a very small portion of the colony. What seemed to be at the heart of the issue, however, was that 'In the province where this lady's views are known, and accepted for what they are worth, she can do no harm; but her peculiarities obtaining publicity in the columns of the leading London journal, is a more serious matter.'[17]

Mary Ann took exception to the charge of conveying a 'Queen Street point of view'. Of her nearly 16 years of residence in the province of Auckland, she had spent over 11 years in country districts, during which time she had experienced ample opportunity to observe the types of settlers' dwellings she described. She took some pleasure in informing the *Herald* that she had a newspaper clipping from the *Auckland Star* commenting on a letter on female emigration she had sent to the *Cross* 12 months earlier that gave her credit for her common sense and for stating 'homely truths' – a clipping she had determined to send along with other related papers to Mr Bright, the honourable member for Manchester.[18]

Not prepared to let Mary Ann have the last word, the *Herald* editor reprinted the letter from Miss Herbert, noting that while Mrs Colclough may have lived in New Zealand for three times as long as Miss Herbert, she had spent that time in only one province whereas Miss Herbert had resided in all parts of the colony. He then added:

> *Mrs Colclough appears under the impression that because she has kept*
> *a girls' school in the colony, she therefore knows all about the social and*
> *domestic characteristics of our women. The inference is about as wrong*
> *as to assume that because a lady having a piano in a drawing room [sic],*
> *she is able to play on it with the ability of a Miss Goddard. Anyone at*
> *all acquainted with the colony, who has read the letters of the two ladies*
> *addressed to the* Times, *will not find much difficulty in pronouncing who*
> *has taken a more observant view of the subject they treat on.*[19]

The editor of the Wellington *Evening Post* decided to enter the fray and, in a scathing editorial, denigrated Mary Ann's actions. He accused her of pestering the various newspapers with the offer of her so-called literary services before turning to the public stage as a 'peripatetic lecturer' in the vein of Yankee proponents of women's rights. This career turn was, in his view, an utter failure, and it had led her to retreat into the affectionate bosom of her family. Although he stopped short of accusing her of wilful misrepresentation in her letter to the *Times*, he, like the editor of the *Herald*, considered the letter a calculated attempt to do the colony considerable harm. The editor of the *Otago Daily Times* took an even harsher view, saying it was a pity that the law of libel could not be amended so that the authorities could mete out punishment to anyone libelling a community.[20] After claiming that Mrs Colclough had painted an 'absolutely untruthful' picture of the life the average domestic servant would encounter in New Zealand, he presented an observation from an Otago perspective:

> [W]e know that her account is of a kind that people would feel inclined to laugh at, were it not that they know that its publication in the Times *might injure the Colony as a field for this class of immigrants. The mere refutation in an official manner of a libel of this nature through the same channel cannot possibly undo the mischief which this silly scribbler has perpetrated; and, as we said before, it is to be regretted that some wholesome chastening could not be provided by law to meet such cases.*[21]

Alongside general deprecation of Mary Ann, the editor of the *Evening Post* commented that he had recently observed a number of mysteriously worded paragraphs which appeared to suggest that several educational districts were vying for Mrs Colclough's services. This, at least, would appear to be true. In mid-June, Mary Ann had informed the Tuakau school committee that she had applied for the position at Ngaruawahia School. She had many influential friends at Ngaruawahia, and word quickly spread that she would soon be leaving Tuakau. The local newspaper correspondent acknowledged that she would be genuinely missed, as she had many warm friends at Tuakau. However, popular as she was, and through no fault of her own, she was hardly the right person in the right place. Not informing her of the conditions she was coming to had been a serious mistake, and so it would be most unfair of the school committee to request her resignation. She would surely be much more in her element at Ngaruawahia, 'where social qualities and educational abilities are of more importance than a talent for wading ankle-deep in slush'.[22]

A letter written to the *Thames Star* the following year stated that Mary Ann had been appointed to the position at Ngaruawahia subject to the approval of the board of education and that she had signalled to the Tuakau school committee her intention to resign at the end of July. But the committee from Kauaeranga School in the Thames was very keen to appoint her to the position of headmistress and had contacted her on several occasions. Not knowing that Kauaeranga was the Māori name for Shortland, Mary Ann had overlooked the advertisement. However, according to the writer of the letter, who positioned himself or herself as one of Mary Ann's friends, 'in an evil hour the unfortunate lady acceded to the repeated requests of the Kauaeranga Committee', and at the end of July she accepted the position on an annual salary of £200.[23]

Located at the southern end of the Coromandel Peninsula, 'the Thames', which the provincial government had declared a goldfield in 1867, consisted of a cluster of neighbouring townships that included Shortland and Grahamstown. Unlike other goldfields, the Thames was a quartz field, which meant longer-term yields and a more permanent population. As a result, the population of the Thames differed from a typical goldfield settlement; it was not dominated by single men, and by the time Mary Ann took up her position at Kauaeranga School, women made up almost half of the local population. As small towns had become established in the region, many opportunities had arisen for businesses and the usual services to develop, and a good number of the women in the area not only owned and leased properties but also ran a variety of ventures alongside the more usual occupations for women such as working in accommodation, domestic service and teaching.

The demand for education was particularly strong in the Thames, given the many families migrating to its goldfields. When Mary Ann arrived in August 1873, the district already had seven schools with large average attendances. Kauaeranga itself boasted two schools. The boys' school, run by the headmaster Mr Ritchie and his assistant teacher, Mr Gribble, was held in the Volunteer Hall and had an average attendance of 150 pupils. The girls' school was held in the old Presbyterian Church on the corner of Sandes and Richmond streets. Over the previous term, the girls' school had experienced an average attendance of 250 pupils, making it one of the largest girls' schools in Auckland Province. However, a severe outbreak of whooping cough had taken hold in recent weeks, and by the time Mary Ann took up her position as headmistress, average attendance had dropped to about 150. Although Mary Ann had the support of Miss Boon as an assistant teacher, as well as two senior pupils, Miss Lovatt and Miss Keven, who were responsible for teaching junior classes under the pupil-teacher system, her new position was still a very demanding one. In November, the school committee appointed a third pupil-teacher, Miss Wells.

Mary Ann soon made her mark as the new headmistress. Within only a few weeks of taking up her position at Kauaeranga, the Thames correspondent to the *Cross* reported that Mrs Colclough had won 'golden opinions' from all sides: 'The children are much attached to her, and their parents and the school committee are entirely satisfied with her system of scholastic rule.' Living just around the corner in Rolleston Street, Mary Ann no longer had the frustrations she'd experienced at Tuakau in terms of negotiating the muddy roads. But Kauaeranga School had its own problems, foremost of which was the inadequacy of the school buildings. During one week in February that year, 320 children had crammed into the school, with more having to be sent home due to lack of space. This excessive overcrowding had been drawn to the attention of the Auckland Board of Education by the school committee, which leased the building and land from the Presbyterian Church. The site was considered the most suitable in the district for a school and was easily large enough to house a school six times as big as the current building. However, because the board had insufficient funds to purchase the building and land outright, it left authorities in the local Kauaeranga educational district to find an interim solution to the problem.[24]

Mary Ann's popularity with the pupils and their parents helped her cope with several periods of ill-health over the ensuing months, but the cause of these bouts of illness is not known. She was still relatively young, in her mid-thirties, although photographs show that she was significantly overweight. Family sources suggest that she suffered from 'dropsy' (oedema) which manifests as swelling due to water retention, and that she may have had a heart condition. She was also facing serious financial difficulties. Her shift from Tuakau to the Thames had meant a number of additional expenses, and she owed money to several creditors. To make matters worse, her first monthly salary from the board of education proved to be only a fraction of what she was entitled to. A few months before Mary Ann took up her appointment at Kauaeranga, the Auckland Board of Education had introduced new pay scales for all teachers holding board-accredited certificates. As with the method used to determine the number of teachers for each school, pay scales were determined by average pupil attendance, and then there were separate rates for head teachers and for town and country schools. The significant drop in pupil attendance at the girls' school had also influenced the actual amount of pay Mary Ann could expect to receive. Her only option was to approach her creditors directly and appeal for some lenience with her repayments.

To this end, on 21 August she visited Joseph Saunders, a draper in Shortland, to request a two-month deferment of payments on her debt of just over £11. Saunders was familiar with the pressures and demands of being a breadwinner. About 10 years earlier, he had met with an accident that meant he could no longer follow his trade. With the few pounds saved from his hard-won earnings, he had set up a small store at the Thames, and through hard work and careful attention to his business dealings managed to support his large family. Impressed

*Mary Ann Colclough
with her children, Lulu
and Willie, 1865.*

Private family collection

Mary Ann Colclough with a class (school and date unknown).

Private family collection

i

Mary Louise (Lulu) Colclough, n.d.

Standish and Preece photograph, Canterbury Museum, 19xx.2.5265

William Caesar Sarsfield Colclough, n.d.

Grand and Dunlop photograph, Canterbury Museum, 19xx.2.5266

Mary Ann Colclough, n.d. Private family collection

Thomas Caesar Colclough, n.d. Canterbury Museum

MARRIED

On Thursday, the 9th instant, at Onehunga, THOMAS CÆSAR, youngest son of the late THOMAS COLCLOUGH, Esq., of Galleenstown Castle, county Dublin, Ireland, to MARY ANN, eldest daughter of JOHN THOMAS BARNES, Esq , of Pentonville, London.

Newspaper notice of the marriage of Thomas Caesar Colclough and Mary Ann Barnes, Daily Southern Cross, *14 May 1861, p. 2.* National Library of New Zealand Papers Past website

Advertisement for Mary Ann's 'Establishment for Young Ladies', Daily Southern Cross, 9 May 1862, p. 6.

National Library of New Zealand Papers Past website

Advertisement for Alone in the World, *Penny Journal 1, no. 2, 12 May 1866, p. 16. Alexander Turnbull Library*

THE GOVERNOR AND LADY BOWEN have graciously signified their willingness to patronise
MRS. COLCLOUGH'S LECTURE,
At the CITY HALL, THIS (MONDAY) EVENING, June 26.
Subject :- ·The Subjection of Woman.
Doors open at half-past 7, to commence at 8.
Admission 2s. ; Reserved Seats, 3s.

NOTICE.

Any Female Prisoner Discharged from Mount Eden Gaol, who can bring a good character from the matron, will sign the pledge, and keep out of the streets, striving to amend, can, on satisfactory proof that she has complied with these demands, obtain a small amount of security, varying from five to ten shillings, such security to be given to shopkeepers who employ these women as needlewomen, or people who employ them in the laundry work. The amount of security will in no case exceed ten shillings, and that sum will only be guaranteed in promising cases. Assistance will be given in seeking for situations in the country districts, for women whose sole vice is drunkenness, and who desire to amend All applications are to be made through the Gaol Matron or the Relieving Officer.
MARY A. COLCLOUGH.

PROVINCIAL COUNCIL CHAMBERS.

CLASSES FOR LADIES,
BY
MRS. COLCLOUGH,
DAILY, FROM TEN TILL TWO,
Commencing on next MONDAY, 23rd instant.

Ladies can enter by the week or month.

The course will comprise lectures on History, Geography, Grammar, Arithmetic, Composition, Natural History, Domestic Management. and Mental Training, with thoroughly sound practical instruction in all the branches of an English Education.

Young Ladies who have been superficially and imperfectly instructed, and Ladies desirous to qualify themselves to pass the Board of Education, will find this an excellent opportunity.

Application can be made To-day to Mrs. COLCLOUGH at the Council Chambers, between the hours of 2 an 1 4 p.m., or any day next week at the same hours.

Top: Advertisement for Mary Ann's first public lecture, to be attended by the Governor and his wife, Auckland Star, *26 June 1871, p. 1.*
National Library of New Zealand Papers Past website

Middle: Advertisement for Mary Ann's scheme for discharged female prisoners, Daily Southern Cross, *19 October 1871, p.1.*
National Library of New Zealand Papers Past website

Left: Advertisement for Classes for Ladies, New Zealand Herald, *21 October 1871, p. 1.*
National Library of New Zealand Papers Past website

CHORAL HALL.

MRS. COLCLOUGH'S

FAREWELL ENTERTAINMENT

ON

THURSDAY, SEPTEMBER 26, 1872.

PROGRAMME.

PART I.

Trio, Pianoforte, Violin, and Violincello (Mozart) – Miss Edger, Mr. Hemus, and Mr. F. Edger
Glee, "Swiftly from the Mountain's Brow"—Glee Singers
Song, "By the Sad Sea Waves"—Madame Winter
Fantasia, "Lucrezia Borgia"—Mrs. Kaye Wright
Song, "Sing, Sweet Birds"—Mrs. Raynes
Reading (Dickens)—Mrs. Colclough
Song, "Good-bye at the Door"—Mr. Brookes
Duet, "Harps Angelical"—Miss Edger and Mr. Winter

PART II.

Fantasia on Irish Airs—Madame Winter
Song, "Come, oh Sleep," Violincello Accompaniment —Miss Edger
Glee, "I see them on their Winding Way"—Glee Singers
Song, "Come into the Garden, Maud"—Mr. Winter
Vocal Valse, Arditi—Madame Moller
Duet, "Sainted Mother" (Maritana)—Madame Winter and Miss Edger
Song, "Come back to Erin"—Mrs. Rayner
Duet, "The Sailor Sighs"—Mr. and Madame Winter
Farewell—Mrs. Colclough.

Tickets, 2s. 6d.
Doors open at 7.30; to commence at 8 o'clock.
Tickets for the unexpired course of lectures can be exchanged for tickets for the Entertainment, on application to Mrs. Colclough.

Top: Advertisement for Mrs Colclough's farewell entertainment, New Zealand Herald, *25 September 1872, p. 1.*

National Library of New Zealand Papers Past website

IN BANKRUPTCY.

RE MARY ANN COLCLOUGH.

Notice is hereby given in pursuance of the Bankruptcy Acts at present in force in New Zealand, that at the first meeting of Creditors held in the estate of the above named Mary Ann Colclough, Thomas Macffarlane, of Auckland, Provisional Trustee in Bankruptcy, was elected trustee of the said estate, and that a Public Sitting in Bankruptcy of the Supreme Court, will be held at the Court-house, Auckland, on THURSDAY, the 4th day of June next, at 11 o'clock in the forenoon, for the said Mary Ann Colclough to pass her final examination, and unless the Court otherwise direct, to make application for her final discharge under the said Acts.
Dated this 18th day of May, 1874.
STEPHEN E. HUGHES,
Bankrupt's Solicitor.

Middle: Notice of Mary Ann Colclough's bankruptcy, New Zealand Herald, *19 May 1874, p. 1.*

National Library of New Zealand Papers Past website

DEATHS.

HOLMES.—On 11th inst., at Cashmere, from an accident, William Holmes, late of Raphoe, County Donegal, Ireland, aged 38 years.
COLCLOUGH.—On March 7th, at Picton, Mary Anson Colclough, widow of the late T. C. Colclough, of West Tamaki, Auckland, late of Galeenstown Castle, County Dublin, Ireland, aged 49.

Left: Death notice, Press, *13 March 1885, p. 2.*

National Library of New Zealand Papers Past website

by Mrs Colclough's respectful request for kindness and leniency, and convinced of the genuineness of her explanation that, having just shifted to the district she needed to buy furniture and a few small items, he agreed to the two-month deferment, after which, they agreed, she would make monthly payments on the day she received her salary.

Respectability and reputation were always foremost for Mary Ann. On one occasion, through no fault of her own, she failed to appear in the Church of England Sunday school to give a reading as arranged, because the section of the book was torn. Anxious that her non-appearance not be construed as a lack of dedication, she wrote to the local newspaper to explain and apologise: 'I am ready at all times, so far as my duties will permit, to help any good cause, and should be sorry to think the public should think I would shirk an engagement after having made it.' Both her respectability and reputation were soon to be tested.[25]

Adept though Mary Ann was at making ends meet, as each month went by and she still did not receive her salary from the board of education, her situation became dire. In the first four months of her employment at Kauwaeranga School, she received only £12/10s from the board. Three months after her arrangement with Saunders, she wrote to thank him for his kindness and long patience, apologetically explaining that she had not yet received her due payment from the board, and promising to settle the greater part of her account as soon as her salary was paid. On 22 November she forwarded £5 from what the board had sent her that month, an action that left her only £10 to live on. Despite a monthly note expressing her gratitude for his patience, her apologies for not being able to pay him, and how shameful she considered the board's treatment of her, she was never able to send Saunders anything more beyond that initial payment.

There is no doubt that Mary Ann had every intention of repaying her debts as soon as she was in a position to do so. Having sought advice from her minister and other friends, she developed a plan. At her request, Mr E.T. Herbert, who owned a drapery and millinery business in Grahamstown and who was one of her creditors, circulated a document she had written to everyone to whom she owed money. In it, she outlined how she would honour her debts. After drawing a monthly sum for her immediate needs to provide for her family, she proposed binding the remainder of her salary to her friend Mr Renshaw, who would then distribute that sum among her creditors until they were paid up to 20 shillings in the pound. As treasurer for a number of local organisations, including the Thames Hospital Committee and the Shortland Volunteer Fire Brigade, Councillor Renshaw was more than suitable for this role. Although this arrangement would mean Mary Ann would continue to be in straitened circumstances for years, she had agreed to it on the advice of her minister and other friends. The problem was that only a few of her creditors were prepared to sign the agreement.

On 7 March 1874, Saunders received word that Mary Ann was about to file for insolvency, and he immediately went to see her to ask what her intentions were towards her debt to him. She explained that if the Bankruptcy Court declared her insolvent, she would make arrangements to pay him because he had been so good and kind to her. In fact, everyone she had dealings with in the Thames had been understanding and sympathetic to her case; it was her creditors in Auckland who were demanding payment. However, Saunders had his own business and family interests to protect, and he informed Mary Ann that he and others from the Thames had placed the matter in the hands of a solicitor. On hearing this, Mary Ann pleaded with him to withdraw the action. Only that morning she had received a letter in the post confirming she was entitled to an annual salary of £240. She was due to receive £50 in back pay as early as that same day. She assured Saunders that as soon as the chairman of the school committee, Alexander Dewar, delivered the money to her, she would pay him.

But the £50 was not forthcoming. Three days later, she received a cheque for £12 and at the end of March she received another £14. Mary Ann did not tell Saunders she had received these amounts; instead she told him she had received no money and offered to pay off her entire debt at the rate of one pound a month if that would be acceptable. But it was too little too late. On 14 March, Wilson and Company, a bakery in Parnell, took legal action against Mary Ann for an outstanding debt of £11/5s. Joseph Saunders followed suit on 2 April, lodging a complaint at the Thames District Court for £25/10/6d. Six days later, George Hulme registered a complaint for £4/2/7d. In all three cases, the judge determined in favour of the plaintiff, and court costs added another £3/4s to Mary Ann's debts.[26]

Even though she was still receiving a fraction of her salary entitlement, Mary Ann could have afforded to pay out the one pound a month to Saunders. The fact that she deliberately misrepresented her circumstances to Saunders is evidence of the extreme stress she was under. Faced with no other options, she had been selling off furniture and personal items to make ends meet. Turning to what she knew best, as a means to earn some additional income, she placed an advertisement in the *Thames Advertiser* early in April announcing her intention to begin 'classes for the instruction of young ladies' immediately after the Easter vacation. These were to be held each day between four and six o'clock at a cost of

£1/1s per term, payable in advance. In particular, she wished to cater for young ladies who were studying to be teachers and whose home duties did not allow them to attend school. The 'Thames Tattle' columnist in the local newspaper picked up on the news, remarking: 'I think the sooner the Kauwaeranga [sic] School Committee make a fresh start with their "white elephant" the better; her crochets and complaints are becoming quite a nuisance; before she "intends to start" another class let her bestow a little of her surplus energy on those a, b, c's and go go's she has got already. Five pounds a week ought to be enough for her to devote *all* her *time* and *attention* to the State's scholars.'[27]

Someone from the school committee drew the situation to the attention of the board of education, which at its next fortnightly meeting 'expressed its opinion that it did not consider that teachers, of large schools especially, should engage in teaching private classes, their time being fully required for the public schools and for instructing the pupil-teachers, who add so much to their average attendance and consequent salary.'[28]

By now, Mary Ann's financial problems were overwhelming, and less than a week after the board's pronouncement, with liabilities to the value of £235, no assets and no way to meet the demands of her creditors, Mary Ann had no option but to file a declaration of insolvency. On 14 May her creditors met, and a few days later Mary Ann's solicitor filed a declaration of bankruptcy, after which the following notice appeared in the public notices section of the *Herald*:

IN BANKRUPTCY

RE MARY ANN COLCLOUGH

Notice is hereby given in pursuance of the Bankruptcy Acts at present in force in New Zealand, that at the first meeting of Creditors held in the estate of the above named Mary Ann Colclough, Thomas Macffarlane, of Auckland, Provisional Trustee in Bankruptcy, was elected trustee of the said estate, and that a Public Sitting in Bankruptcy of the Supreme Court, will be held at the court-house, Auckland, on THURSDAY, the 4th day of June next, at 11 o'clock in the forenoon, for the said Mary Ann Colclough to pass her final examination, and unless the Court otherwise direct, to make application for her final discharge under the said Acts.

Dated this 15th day of May, 1874.

STEPHEN E. HUGHES,

Bankrupt's Solicitor[29]

Financial concerns had plagued Mary Ann since her marriage, but this public declaration of bankruptcy was humiliating for someone who had lived independently for many years. She had sold almost all of her personal possessions, including her beloved piano, although she managed to keep some of her sheet music. As befitting her middle-class social etiquette, she remained silent, however, as to the true causes of her personal circumstances. Besides, the day-to-day work at the school had to proceed, and the board gave permission for the school to advertise a new position, that of work-mistress to teach needlework. The advertisement attracted 10 applications, and the school committee professed itself particularly impressed with the standard of the examples of plain and fancy needlework submitted; after a close vote, Mrs O'Connell was appointed.[30]

Despite the new appointment, the financial pressures on both the school and the board of education were beginning to tell. For example, within a few weeks of Mrs O'Connell's appointment, the school committee, at Mary Ann's behest, applied to the board of education for the new work-mistress to be paid more than the regulation rate because of the large number of pupils under her tutelage. The board refused the application. Their reaction was the same when they learned that both the girls' and boys' schools had installed clocks in their schoolrooms so as to ensure that school hours were strictly kept. The board said it would not pay for the clocks because to do so would set an unwelcome precedent. The schools duly removed the clocks and returned them to Mr Wilkes, the supplier, who obligingly did not charge for their use. Undaunted, Mary Ann, Miss Boon, Mrs O'Connell and the three pupil-teachers, Misses Lovatt, Keven and Wells, along with the pupils, joined together to purchase a replacement clock. Although they could not raise enough money to pay for the handsome eight-day clock originally supplied by Mr Wilkes, another local businessman from Grahamstown, Mr J. Shappere, sold them a very good alternative at cost.

In a small settlement such as Kauaeranga, circulation of stories about the circumstances that had led to the headmistress of the girls' school being declared bankrupt were inevitable, and voices of dissent began to be heard within the school committee as to the wisdom of retaining Mrs Colclough's services. The committee sent the board a letter on this matter. The board responded by ordering the secretary to inform the school committee that it 'had no desire to trench on the powers conferred upon them by the Act, and leave the case in question to their decision'. Mary Ann kept her silence until the day of her bankruptcy proceedings. But on Friday 12 June, appearing before Sir G.A. Arney, she explained her difficulties clearly and to the satisfaction of the court.

The report of the trustee was read and showed that on 7 November 1873 her liabilities were £230 and her assets £30. Between then and 7 April 1874, she had received £130 in income from her school teacher's salary and had spent £130. Her solicitor, Mr Hughes, applied for her final discharge, and this was granted. Any creditors to her estate who had not already proved their debts had 14 days to do so before Thomas Macffarlane, her trustee, would be obliged to declare a first and final dividend.[31]

Surprisingly, beyond reporting the facts of the case, there was very little editorial comment on Mary Ann's public fall from grace. The exception was the *Auckland Star*, which, thankfully for Mary Ann and her close circles, took a very sympathetic line. Explaining that her debts had been building up for some time prior to her appointment at Tuakau and were largely a result of illness and other misfortunes, the editor stressed that her income had been used for 'the common necessaries of life'. The editor then proceeded to take her creditors to task, chastising them for not allowing her reasonable time to recover her position and pay off her debts. Instead, they had pushed her to extremities, and this had resulted in her appearance at the Bankruptcy Court.[32]

Despite her high public profile over the years, Mary Ann had always been a very private individual. For those closest to her, it was distressing to think that members of the public might impugn her character in some way because of her financial difficulties. Polly Plum had written many times of the plight of widows in debt, and now Mary Ann was the one being written about, but the bare facts reported in the newspapers obscured the great hardships she had personally endured over many years. In his letter to the *Thames Star* mentioned above, Mary Ann's 'Friend', finding the whole situation most unfair, detailed the human story behind the newspaper accounts:

> *There is a case of great hardship amongst us just now, of which I feel the public should know something. Mrs Colclough, the teacher of Kauaeranga Girl's [sic] School, has been for many years in this province, having landed in Auckland in December, 1857. Her coming here was most disastrous, as she lost her only protector, a brother who came from England with her, on the voyage. Her talents as a teacher held her in good stead, and things went smoothly till her marriage. This was followed by heavy losses on the part of her husband, whose health suffered severely from these trials, and Mrs Colclough again took up the burden of breadwinner, and has from that period, as wife and widow, been the sole stay of the family ...*[33]

149

Mary Ann's friend went on to relate the circumstances that had led to Mrs Colclough's current situation. Explaining that although Mrs Colclough had occasionally written not only for Mr Varty, a bookseller and stationer operating in Queen Street (Auckland) in the early 1860s and the publisher of 'Varty's Literary Circular', but also for the proprietors of the Melbourne newspaper the *Weekly Argus*, she was not really known beyond Auckland literary circles until after her husband died, which was when she began contributing articles to the *Cross* under her *nom de plume* Polly Plum. As someone who had always been mindful of women's social and political disadvantages and had experienced more than her share of these first-hand, she was predisposed to embrace Mill's *The Subjection of Women*, which had proven to fully convert her to the cause of women's rights. Wherever one stood in relation to the truth or falsity of Mrs Colclough's views, it could not be denied that she was earnestly and sincerely devoted to a cause she believed to be that of truth and right, and her personal conviction in this regard could not be doubted:

> [I]t is as the untiring helper of the lost, the wretched, and the miserable, that Mrs. Colclough is most respected in her 'own city', Auckland. Through her instrumentality great and needed changes were made in the women's department of Mount Eden Stockade, and the door of well-doing opened to any poor wretch, willing to do well, so long as she was able to help them. She found, as most philanthropists do, that without a long private purse, continuous work in this field of labor was impossible, and she reluctantly abandoned it and accepted employment under the Board of Education in the Waikato; choosing to go a long distance to break effectually the links that would bind her to 'prison work' if she remained within reach. 'Teaching and gaol work cannot go on together,' she said, and, for her children's sake, she had to abandon the latter. Up to this time, to use her own words 'I have been often in trouble and distress of mind, frequently short of money, and, during my period of prison work, much straightened [sic] and almost dependent on the kindness of the friends of the cause for support. But I was always respected and treated with kindness and confidence, and I managed to get along.'[34]

And for years Mary Ann had indeed managed to get along. She had faced debt while living in Auckland, but her creditors had always shown respect and every possible consideration. But this time was different. Not reported in the newspapers was the reality that 'delays in officialism' meant she had received a mere fraction of the salary she was entitled to. Although the board had decided at the end of February 1874 that her salary would be settled at £230 per annum, this decision had not brought her financial security. Salary arrangements between the board and its teachers carried a high degree of uncertainty, in part because the arrangements were based on the system of average attendances of pupils, but also because the education system in general was in a very unsettled state at this time.

According to the friend in his letter to the *Thames Star*, the turning point in Mary Ann's financial downfall came when Saunders threatened legal action and raised the spectre of imprisonment if she failed to settle her outstanding debt to him. Saunders may also have spoken unkindly and unfavourably of her to her other creditors, 'thus bringing an avalanche down on the unfortunate lady she was powerless to meet' and effectively giving her no other option but to sign for insolvency. This action, which not only compromised her reputation but also her position with the school committee and consequently her opportunity to repay her debts, left not one person better off after the facts were presented to the Bankruptcy Court. The judge made no order on her salary, the creditors subsequently did not get paid, and Mary Ann suffered an irredeemable loss in public standing. The cruellest part of the whole proceedings was that her salary for the months of May and June was 'sequestered by the Trustee in Bankruptcy *without a judge's order*', and Mary Ann was allowed from this amount only the meagre sum of £5/19s to support herself and her family for the next two months.[35]

With the legality and fairness of some of these actions certainly in question, Mary Ann, weary, worn, humiliated and beaten down, wrote a long letter to the *Thames Advertiser* to counter some of the rumours and misinformation being circulated.

To the Editor of the THAMES ADVERTISER

Sir, – The animosity and anger of those who lose their money is natural, but to state untruths under a nom-de-plume is almost too bad; therefore, allow me to make a few contradictions. I scheduled a debt to a dressmaker as £4 10s. and it turns out I owe her but £2 10s – the only debt due to a dressmaker, and that is the balance of an account due before I came to the Thames. I did not solicit credit of a grocer, nor do I owe any money for groceries to a poor or crippled man. The only grocer to whom I owe money has property, houses, &c.; and though his case, and the case of many others, is hard, and they ought to be paid; by forcing me to extremities they have put it out of my power to pay them. A draper, who pressed and is then paid half his debt or nearly half, is malicious to attribute dishonesty if immediately afterwards, he presses, issues warrants, and obliges his debtor to file. I did not borrow money and go to Auckland and file. I did borrow money, and look on it as a debt of honor, to be some day repaid. But I did not file until some weeks afterwards when two warrants were out, which I was powerless to avert. I then signed here and forwarded the document to town. The existence of those two warrants the judge and opposing counsels thought due and sufficient grounds for filing – and they were due and sufficient grounds. It was proved in court that I had received about £39 over and above what I had satisfactorily accounted for. And as the Chief Justice said I could not have made a private purse, the sum being not too large for the incidental expenses incurred in the time. Therefore, since my whole means of living have been forcibly seized by the Trustee in Bankruptcy, I am living on private charity. Rent, doctor's advice, &c., cannot be turned into cash, and as there were no superfluities in the liabilities to turn into money, I am penniless. As to the bankruptcy being fraudulent, I will put it to any man of sense whether I was likely to jeopardise, and most likely lose a good position, credit, and character for the sake of £80 or £90 worth of necessaries? It was evident that nothing but dread of imprisonment would drive me to a course so injurious to my own interests. I am sorry, and have far more reason to be sorry than anyone else. After seventeen years in this colony, during which I never entered a debtors' Court, it is very hard to meet with such a blow to my social position and credit. But I have brought it on myself, not wilfully, but perhaps carelessly, by incurring liabilities it would take me some time to pay off. I admit it is hard on those to whom I owe money, specially hard on those who treated me with forbearance and courtesy. But I have myself suffered heavy losses when I did not press, because my debtors turned bankrupt on pressure from other creditors, and I am now, and have ever been far more impecunious than anyone to whom I owe money. I do not consider the fact that my creditors are all well-to-do any reason why they should lose their money, but it is a reason why they will feel the loss less. I did not ask the Trustee in Bankruptcy to arrange my affairs, and by the advice of my solicitor I refused to sanction an arrangement he was anxious to make and that was impracticable. Because of this he has forcibly seized all my earnings, and left me to starve, were it not for the bounty of private friends; and it is of this I complain, and not of the action of my creditors. It was a course that l would not take if I wanted to get money from a teacher or clergyman whose chance of payment rests entirely on the maintenance of their position and character, but it is legal, and if one lays oneself open to it one must put up with it. I have got one of 'men's rights' this time, with a particular drop of gall mixed in it, I suppose, because I am a woman in *the shape of my withheld salary. Men seem to thrive on bankruptcy – fail for thousands. For a couple of hundred pounds' worth of necessaries I am to be punished by two months' penury. As to the 'widow,' I am willing to be treated as a man, as I have all the responsibilities of a man, but I don't think poor widows were meant, or they would have no 'houses' for the lawyers to 'devour.' In conclusion, sir, I think they ought to be satisfied with having destroyed my position and credit, and that it is neither manly, or businesslike, or right, to maliciously prosecute me by the loss of all my means of living – my earnings, my daily bread. I shall not trouble you again. – Yours, &c.,*

MARY A. COLCLOUGH [36]

Her letter elicited a response from Joseph Saunders, in which he expressed his genuine respect for Mrs Colclough and explained why he had taken the matter to court. His letter showed how Mary Ann's financial difficulties had arisen, in part, from her not receiving due payment from the board of education since she had been appointed to the position at Kauaeranga Girls' School in August the previous year. He affirmed that she had duly kept in touch with him by letter at regular intervals, enclosing small payments and explaining that the board had been paying considerably below the rate of salary negotiated.[37]

At first, Kauaeranga's school committee appeared to support Mary Ann. At the board of education meeting on 2 July, the committee asked the board to meet the outstanding debt of £10/4/2d that Mrs Colclough owed Mr J.H. Jefferson, a bookseller in Pollen Street. But the board ruled, with regret, that they had no power to intervene in the matter. By the following month, the school committee appeared to have turned full circle, having written to the board requesting permission to advertise for Mrs Colclough's successor on the basis that retaining her services would be injurious to the school. Mary Ann also wrote to the board objecting to the action the school committee proposed. She pointed out that such an action would ruin her prospects at the Thames and elsewhere. She also detailed events relating to her bankruptcy that vindicated her character.

The board, in its turn, asked the school committee to provide more specific reasons for their proposed action and to make clear in what way Mrs Colclough's actions were injurious to the school, especially given that the increasing school roll seemed to belie the school committee's claims in this respect. The committee responded with a telegram to the board requesting confirmation of Mrs Colclough's dismissal. The board called for a special meeting of its members on 21 August, the outcome of which was that the board could not tender confirmation

until an investigation, as required under Clause 22 of the Education Act 1872, had
been undertaken and the board had been furnished with minutes of evidence of
the investigation. However, during the meeting, the board also resolved:

> *That without questioning Mrs Colclough's competency as a Teacher or
> her conduct at the Kaueranga [sic] School while under her charge, yet
> in consideration of the fact that she had intimated to the Committee her
> intention of resigning and in consideration also of the unsatisfactory
> relations existing between Mrs Colclough and the Committee, the Board
> are of the opinion that the connection between Mrs Colclough and the
> Kaueranga [sic] School should terminate and that a month's salary in lieu of
> notice should be given to that Lady.*[38]

Faced with no alternative, Mary Ann submitted her resignation.
Advertisements appeared in the *Thames Advertiser* and in the *Cross* for the
position of head teacher at the Kauaeranga Girls' School. On the same day,
the *Thames Advertiser*, noting that many exaggerated reports regarding Mrs
Colclough's dismissal were likely to gain currency, published a private letter
Mary Ann had sent to the editor clarifying the circumstances of her dismissal:

> *To the Editor: – Sir, – Fearing that a garbled statement of facts may get
> into the paper, which would only wound and injure me and do no one any
> good, allow me to inform you that I had official notice yesterday 'that the
> Board are of opinion that I should leave Kauwaeranga [sic] School (getting
> monetary compensation – of course) because of the unsatisfactory relations
> between me and the Committee'. No charge is made against me or could be
> proved, for it is necessary first to see me in a position to pay my debts before
> it is decided that I never mean to do it. Out of Kauwaeranga [sic] School
> for some time this would be impossible. My receipts during a full year were
> £221, and the losses and expenses of the bankruptcy £100, therefore it will
> not ruin the Thames all I can have made out of them, and they might let me
> alone and see if, with better pay and brighter prospects, I am not something
> more honest than many of my neighbours who fail without a thought of
> paying. It will suit me much better to go than to remain, now I have money
> to go, which was what I wanted. The pay during wet weather and all the
> approaches to the school cut up, is not high. Our largest class – the infant
> class – is very, very thin for days together. The little things cannot get out in
> the mud and wet, and our poor pay suffers, so, though I was beginning to
> 'save up', having learnt a lesson from the past, it would take me a good deal
> of time to save much. Excuse my troubling you, but I am sure, knowing all,*

*you will not 'cut me up', especially as I could refute any charge against my
character on the clearest evidence, and consequently the School Committee
could only give the celebrated reason for disliking 'Dr Fell', for that is in
substance what the Board inform me. Yours, &c.,*

MARY A. COLCLOUGH[39]

Accepting that the editor had published the letter as a kindness to her, Mary
Ann still felt obliged to present some additional facts. Her preference would have
been to leave New Zealand rather than try to make arrangements through the
Bankruptcy Court because the latter was 'a terrible and expensive yoke'. With the
assistance of one of her creditors she had tried to come to a private arrangement
to repay her outstanding debts, but this had not met with the cooperation of
the majority of her creditors. She also wanted to publicly offer her thanks to
those who had stood by her: 'Allow me to thank that portion of the public at
any rate who have sent their children to the Kauaeranga Girls' School for the
warm-hearted tenderness, countenance, and support I have received from them
through all my troubles. Between myself, my assistance teachers, and my pupils,
there has been a warm friendship which will be the only tie hard to break in
leaving the Thames.'[40]

The prolonged events divided the community. Correspondent 'Pro bono
Publico' took offence at what he considered Mary Ann's maligning of the people
of the Thames in respect of payment of debts. Such a slander on the community,
in his view, only endorsed the correctness of the opinion of the board of
education. 'Tommy Brig' admonished his dear old friend Polly Plum for her
pride and suggested she abandon her efforts to try to teach the men and make a
man of herself in the process. One matter still little acknowledged publicly was
that Mary Ann's financial issues were largely not of her making, nor was it noted
that the head teacher of Kauaeranga Boys' School, Edmund Cornes, appointed
in April 1874, had been experiencing similar difficulties. Within six months of
his appointment, he wrote to the newspapers to explain he was tendering his
resignation because of inaccuracies in the interpretation of pay scales, a situation
which had resulted in him receiving significantly lower quarterly salary amounts
than he had been led to anticipate.

Understandably, Mary Ann was not present when the Kauaeranga committee
met at the girls' school on 31 August to officially hand over interim charge of the
school to the assistant teacher Miss Boon. Two days later, the *Thames Advertiser*
published news from Melbourne. Miss Turner, who had just been elected to the

pastorate of the Unitarian Church, had invited Mrs Colclough to Melbourne, where she was promised an engagement suitable to her scholarly attainments. After the events of the previous few months, the invitation must surely have heralded hopes for Mary Ann of a welcome new chapter in her life.

CHAPTER SEVEN

Educating the Women of Melbourne

A good muster of friends from Auckland gathered to farewell Mary Ann and her children as they boarded the *Hero* at the Auckland dock on 25 September 1874. Bound for Melbourne via Sydney and Newcastle under the steerage of Captain T. Logan, the Colclough family were among the 21 passengers who would be accommodated in the cabin; another 30 had booked to travel below in steerage. Now 38 years of age and travelling with Lulu, who was nearly 12 years old and William, who was 10, Mary Ann would have been facing a sea journey very different from the one she had undertaken with her brother 17 years earlier.

Several newspapers carried news of the Colclough family's departure. According to the *Otago Witness*, word was that Mrs Colclough intended to settle permanently in Melbourne. The *Auckland Star* informed its readership that 'Mrs Colclough, better known by her literary *nom de plume* of "Polly Plum" whose lay sermons and moral stories once graced the pages of a contemporary, has taken her departure with her little family by the *Hero* for Melbourne. Mrs Colclough has had enough of New Zealand, and hopes by mental energy to win a pleasanter livelihood than she did at the Thames, and breathe unmolested in the free atmosphere of Australia.' The *New Zealand Herald* was less supportive: 'We really do not know that Auckland has sustained any serious loss in the absence of this lady, or that Melbourne has won a grand prize in her acquisition.'[1]

Squally weather and strong gales persisted for much of the eight-day journey across the Tasman. For Lulu and William, the company of four other girls and one young boy travelling with their parents must have been a relief and distraction for them, and no doubt for the adults as well. By the time Mary Ann and the children arrived in Melbourne, the city had mushroomed into a major metropolis. Built largely on the wealth of the goldrushes of the 1850s, Melbourne was now Australia's largest city. It was also a city of contrasts. Dispossessed of their lands and forced away from urban areas, the indigenous population was being relegated to Aboriginal reserves, while in Melbourne itself a small but powerful group of prominent colonial families formed the elite of the city's society. Through intermarriage, as well as links by way of legal, economic, professional and philanthropic networks, these families formed the cultural and social vanguards of civilised colonial life. In addition, the declining influence of large landowners and mercantile classes was being offset by the rapidly growing urban middle and working classes capitalising on the state of Victoria's economic booms. [2]

For Mary Ann, the invitation from Martha Turner she had received in the Thames several weeks earlier was fortunate in more ways than one. Not only had her immediate difficulties in the Thames been remedied, but she now had the support and friendship of a woman sympathetic to her ideas. Although Mary Ann and Martha had very different backgrounds, they held each other in high respect. Three years older than Mary Ann, London-born Martha had arrived in Melbourne in 1870 to visit her brother, Henry Gyles Turner. As a lay preacher of the Melbourne Unitarian congregation, Henry had been called on to preach on several occasions. However, he was, by his own admission, not particularly suited to that calling. His sister had come to his assistance, and in October 1873 a special meeting of the congregation elected Martha as its third regular minister. Described as a cultured and thoughtful lady, Martha was also of a plain, undemonstrative demeanour and lucid intelligence that set her in good stead with her exacting congregation.

Most of Melbourne's population at the time of Mary Ann's arrival in the city was concentrated in the inner suburbs of Carlton, Collingwood, Fitzroy, Richmond, Prahran, and North and South Melbourne. She and the children took up residence at 16 Nicholson Street, Fitzroy. Since the 1850s, this area on the southern part of the Collingwood Flat through to Abbotsford had been a refuge of sorts for many social groups. The small wooden houses, clustered together along the lanes, alleys and narrow back streets, were let by the room. For widows, deserted wives, the unemployed – often with families to support – the elderly and the lonely, the area offered cheap housing that was close to casual employment as well as charitable help. How Mary Ann financed her living costs in Melbourne, and her travel to Australia for that matter, is unknown; perhaps she had private sponsorship from supporters in New Zealand and possibly in Victoria.

Mary Ann's reputation – as a woman who had spearheaded debates in New Zealand on many aspects of the 'Woman Question' through her newspaper journalism and public lecturing over the previous five years – seemed to have preceded her to Melbourne, but early indications were that her reception in the city would not be enthusiastic. The editor of the Melbourne *Herald* announced that Mrs Colclough had just arrived 'from the land of advanced notions ... [having] been induced to visit this country by representations that a field is open for a lady lecturer, on subjects which have excited the greatest interest throughout America'. He added: 'There is nothing of Bloomerism about this lady, simply an advocacy of the elevation of Woman to her due sphere in the world; and, at the same time, of the spread of scientific knowledge on matters which are still commonly trusted according to the benighted notions of the dark ages.'[3]

Mary Ann's was not the first outspoken voice on women's issues in Melbourne. Notable was Henrietta Dugdale, who had been speaking forcefully on women's suffrage since 1869. Described as 'a pugnacious pioneer of the Woman Movement in Victoria', Henrietta was a firm believer in evolutionary progress and advocated disciplined control of human nature through reason and the co-operation of men and women. She considered women's emancipation the key solution to the brutality and darkness of the present age, which manifested itself through male ignorance, vanity, liquor and the illiterate working classes. Women needed to throw off their chains, discard their apathy and learn self-respect. Among the reforms she espoused were women's suffrage, equitable distribution of wealth, the introduction of the eight-hour day, dress reform and political representation for women. Forceful and assertive, she was also at times melodramatic and emotional. As she became increasingly vocal in the early 1880s after taking on the presidency of the first Victorian Women's Suffrage Society, she shocked many conservatives with her views on birth control and her insistence on applying the surgeon's knife to rapists.[4]

Given Mary Ann and Henrietta's shared public advocacy of women's rights, it is likely that they were introduced to each other, possibly by mutual contacts, one of whom would have been George Higinbotham. In 1883 Henrietta dedicated her booklet *A Few Hours in a Far Off Age* to George, 'in earnest admiration for the brave attacks made by that gentleman upon what has been, during all known ages, the greatest obstacle to human advancement, the most irrational, fiercest and most powerful of our world's monsters – the only devil MALE IGNORANCE'. A graduate of Trinity College in Dublin, George Higinbotham arrived in Melbourne in 1853 and embarked on a career that combined journalism with law. At the age of 30 he became editor of the Melbourne *Argus* and gained a reputation for his scrupulous attention to detail.[5]

Elected to the Victorian Legislative Assembly in 1861 and serving as attorney-general from 1863–68, George was described in later years as the leading radical in Victoria. Later, as chief justice of the Supreme Court of Victoria, he was a strong advocate of educational reform, democracy and giving equal voice to the underprivileged, among whom he counted women. In 1869 George had proposed a Married Women's Property Bill that was more generous in its provisions than the English version of the Bill that had inspired it. Four years later, he was ridiculed by the press for advocating that the vote be extended to female ratepayers. He argued passionately for the introduction of a Permissive Bill that, if enacted, would give localities the right to restrict liquor sales and the issuance of liquor licenses if they so wished. Like Mary Ann, George saw reform of laws governing alcohol sales and distribution as a necessary basis for all social and political reform.[6]

An important venue for discussion on the Woman Question in Melbourne during the early 1870s was the Eclectic Association of Victoria, which called on its members to present papers on various topics in line with its commitment to 'unrestricted temperate investigation and discussion of any subject whatsoever of general social interest and importance'. Association records show that selected members delivered several papers during 1870 on women's rights. Titles included 'The Subjection of Women', 'The True Position of Women' and 'Rights of Women'. In 1873 a Miss Armstrong presented a paper on 'Social Conditions of Women'.[7]

Mary Ann's first public lecture in Melbourne was well advertised, with the notifications providing descriptions of Mary Ann as 'a recently arrived advocate' and a 'fair lecturer [who has] gained some celebrity in New Zealand'. The *Age*, another Melbourne newspaper, mistakenly reported that she was a recent arrival from America via New Zealand. The novelty of a lady lecturer on the subject of women's rights was such that the Melbourne *Herald* devoted an editorial to her on the evening she was due to deliver her lecture. The editor appeared ready to receive her with an open mind to any 'reasonable' views, but anyone conversant with Mary Ann's ideas would have known that his view of the reforms needed for women was markedly different from Mary Ann's.[8] His comments in the editorial provide an indication of the conservatism Mary Ann was about to encounter:

> *A lady who rejoices in the nom de theatre of 'Polly Plum', will this evening lecture upon the subject of 'Women, as wives and mothers'. Polly Plum has successfully addressed the New Zealand public upon this delicate and*

important topic. It may, therefore, be assumed that Polly Plum's views of women, in their most interesting aspects, are of a genial kind – such as appeal to the sympathies and approbation of women themselves, without in any way clashing with the hard-grained prejudices of their tyrants and slaves. On the other hand it is suggested that Polly Plum's philosophy must grasp some novel notions in respect to women as wives and mothers. The old hum drum stock platitudes of the loveliness of the marital and maternal conditions would scarcely constitute a recreative or amusing lecture. Polly Plum must have some theory. She can never manage to get along without some speculative ideas upon the subject of her discourse. We own that we shall be prepared to support her in any reasonable views she may advance in the cause of reform of this matter. If she can tell us how to cure the scold, and render neat the slattern; how we can check the gossip, and make thrifty the extravagant: then we shall applaud Polly Plum to the echo. Likewise, if she can teach us the secret of instilling into mothers' minds the conviction that other people really don't care much for anybody's manageries but their own, and that the proper place for dirty little brats is the nursery or the playground – we shall pronounce Polly Plum, a plum indeed. There is ample room for reform in the field which this lady has undertaken to cultivate. Few wives, and still fewer mothers are ruled by common sense in the execution of their duties; little conceiving how much they sacrifice by their thoughtlessness, and reflecting as little that by punctitious attentions to the little details of social life, in their bearing upon wives and mothers, so much real happiness and comfort may be secured. We earnestly hope that Polly Plum's teaching will be of that clear and practical kind, which appeals not only to the intelligence of the pupil, but to his sympathies and affections also.[9]

Obviously this editor, many of his readership, and the 60 to 70 who turned up at the Athenæum for the lecture on the Tuesday evening were in for a surprise. Built at the rear of the Mechanics Institute adjacent to the town hall, the Athenæum in Collins Street was a fine hall with seating for up to 1000 people. Aware that there would be many in the audience who believed it was not appropriate for a lady to take to the public platform, Mary Ann set the tone from the outset by apologising for the lack of a chairman, explaining this was not an oversight, it was simply that she had not been able to find a gentleman with sufficient courage to take the chair at a meeting on woman's rights.

Realising that she was unknown to almost everyone present, Mary Ann began by introducing herself and informing the audience that she acquired the sobriquet Polly Plum when she contributed a series of papers to an American journal under that name. By way of her credentials to speak in public, she explained that she was a member of the Ladies' Vigilance Society of England and also a friend of the Vigilant Society of America, which had been formed to monitor all legislation affecting the weak, particularly the laws relating to women's rights and property. Her main reason for coming to Melbourne was to put before the public the necessity for legal and social reform as regards men and women. She impressed on the audience that she objected to the term 'women's rights': neither she nor the Ladies' Vigilant Society claimed any special rights for women; rather, they simply sought those rights for women that were afforded to men so that each sex could enjoy them equally and without distinction.

Introductions over, Mary Ann started out by presenting her views on the current position of women. For those in the audience with more conservative leanings, her opening comments would not have been too threatening. She argued that it would be premature at the present time to press the issue of women having full equality with men because women had not been educated or fitted to take up a more responsible position in the world than they currently held. She also distinguished between women's position and treatment in primitive societies and their position and treatment in more civilised societies. In the former, men had no argument apart from force and treated women as slaves and beasts of burden. In the latter, men could develop a sense of the intrinsic worth of women and treat them accordingly. Mary Ann embarked on more controversial ground, however, when she argued that in Christian societies, where the duties and obligations of women were a matter of doctrine, it was a great error to bind all women to be ruled all their lives by a set of doctrines in which they did not believe. Binding others to religious convictions they did not subscribe to made, she said, for a situation of oppression and tyranny. Her point was that while there was nothing against women vowing obedience to their husband's rule if they wished to, there were many arguments against enforcing a law of obedience among all wives.

By the time she presented her analysis of the present marriage ceremony, a good many in the audience were probably squirming in their seats. In short, she declared the marriage ceremony wrong from beginning to end: 'With this ring I thee wed' amounted to sorcery; 'With this body I thee worship' was nothing less than idolatry; 'With all my worldly goods I thee endow' was simply a lie. Many of the present criticisms of women's frivolity were due to social and legal sanctions against women's full engagement in public life. Not being allowed to earn money, women resorted to spending it. Their time, Mary Ann argued, would be better spent as doctors at a sick bed or as lawyers than spending their time at balls and other extravagant pursuits. Critical of the ill-treatment women frequently received at the hands of their husbands, she also drew attention to the false shame that prevented many women from earning their living as domestic servants.

Mary Ann probably warmed back a few in the audience when she turned her attention to women's position as mothers. Here, she insisted on the importance of women's maternal functions, duties and responsibilities, and reminded her listeners of how influential these were to a nation's wellbeing. Indeed, raising women's status both as wives and mothers would be a boon to the nation's prosperity and to the world at large as well as to women themselves. However, mothers needed to be educated properly if they were to impart a worthwhile education to their children. Girls, in particular, needed to be educated to ensure they were properly prepared for their roles as wives and mothers or as single women.

Drawing on all her experience as a lecturer, Mary Ann spoke in an earnest and impressive manner, and even though the audience might have felt uncomfortable at times, its members were attentive throughout and often interrupted with applause. In contrast to the approach she had used during her previous lectures, Mary Ann dedicated a considerable part of her address to readings from the work of John Stuart Mill, De Tocqueville, Tennyson and other authors. One reviewer commented that 'her arguments were fairly weighed, and she did not spare her own sex'. On concluding her address, she offered to take any questions or objections from the audience, but not one was forthcoming. Although disappointed with the relatively low attendance, she closed with an assurance that if she received sufficient encouragement, she would lecture on similar subjects in the near future. She also invited any who were interested in the cause of women and felt inclined to assist in the movement to contact her personally. A reviewer from the *Argus* noted, 'She was allowed to retire without any person present apparently having the courage to propose a vote of thanks to the lecturer.'[10]

Various reports of Mary Ann's first Melbourne lecture appeared in the local newspapers, and the general tone could be described best as bemused disregard. The *Australasian* gave a brief comment but did not engage with the content of the lecture. The editor of the *Daily Telegraph* opened an editorial with the comment that 'our new "woman's rights" advocate' was unlikely to find success in Melbourne. Dismissing the erroneous claim that Mrs Colclough was an American agitator, he noted that she had 'won all her honours as "Polly Plum" in the quiet, unsensational, and highly proper city of Auckland'. However, as some portions of her lecture made clear, there was no doubt that she did belong to the sisterhood. Her reference to a reform of the language of the marriage service was, according to the editor, 'capable of a sinister interpretation'. Less contentious was her argument for the physical and mental development of women, the former all the more necessary given the way household chores had become less labour intensive and physically demanding, and the latter already being addressed without, it was noted, Mrs Colclough's assistance.[11] His challenge was of the kind that invited Mary Ann to take up her pen:

> *Sir, – Will you allow me a few words on your leader of the 29th? I assure*
> *you that I have neither the egotism or [sic] impertinence to suppose that*
> *my individual agency is necessary, or even important, in the task of raising*
> *the standard and enlarging the sphere of women in Victoria; but it is so*
> *necessary that in this matter women should come forward and speak for*
> *themselves, and help themselves, that any woman who comes forward and*
> *demonstrates the capacity of women must assist in some degree; and if, in*
> *addition to speaking faithfully what she believes to be truth, she 'takes of*
> *anything her hands find to do, and does it with all her might', she cannot*
> *fail to be of use, even to the largest and most powerful empires in the world.*
> *Many causes led to my enjoying the reputation I did in my dear old home*
> *(Auckland); you are right in calling it 'unsensational and highly proper'.*
> *I must add this – that had I confined myself to mere platform orations, I*
> *should have met with but little sympathy there. I assure you that during my*
> *stay in Victoria, be it long or short, I will try, however imperfectly I may*
> *succeed, to help my sex in every possible way, and not merely preach to them*
> *from the public platform. As to my opinion of the marriage service and the*
> *broad basis of my religious faith, allow me to say that, whilst I do not pledge*
> *myself to what is called orthodoxy in its entirety, I know of no more beautiful*
> *religion or example than that of Christ, and until I find better, if that be*
> *possible, I shall continue to call myself a Christian.*
>
> MARY A. COLCLOUGH[12]

Among those who responded to Mary Ann's invitation to communicate over the cause of women was a correspondent to the *Daily Telegraph* who signed him or herself 'A.H'. In a communication that was not of the kind Mary Ann had hoped for, A.H. pronounced that the advocates of such principles 'do much mischief, and unsettle their weaker sisters, who desire to act well their part in this life'. Pointing to medical and anatomical evidence, A.H. held that the proposition that men and women were equal was 'absurd' and the claim that women were not inferior 'equally erroneous'. It was precisely this kind of 'pernicious teachings' that led to women becoming 'wives of the period: they become unsettled, dissatisfied, their homes are neglected, their husbands are wretched, and their children uncared for'.[13]

It was the Melbourne *Age* which mistakenly reported that Mrs Colclough had arrived in Victoria from America via New Zealand, and although the newspaper's contemporaries corrected this error, the editor continued to draw attention to Mary Ann's 'Yankee notions':

> *Victoria is indebted to America for a good many curious importations, and, either for better or worse, an approximation to the political and social character of the great Republic … Perhaps it is our colonial perversity and conceit that lead us to compliment ourselves on the extreme tardiness of our social reforms, as compared with those of American communities; but we nevertheless do so compliment ourselves, despite the scorn of the social radicals of Massachusetts and New York, and the peevish complaints of Mrs Colclough at the Melbourne Athenæum. This lady, moved, we presume, by the purest feminine compassion for the downtrodden wives and mothers of Victoria, and bearing a commission as an apostle of a trans-Pacific Vigilant Society, has been graciously pleased to come all the way from America to tell the benighted Melbourne public that a legal and social reform in the condition of our women is an absolute and immediate necessity.*[14]

Not that there was great cause for concern, the editor continued: '… the excitement of the audience did not at any period become dangerous … [and] declarations of the speaker on behalf of oppressed wives were placidly received'. He put these reactions down to the fact that 'the generation of sympathetic electricity is difficult in a large room containing only an incoherent group of sixty people, and not to any want of graphic power in the lecturer'. That Mrs Colclough would have to review her intention to stay and lecture for about four months on account of the seeming lack of support for her cause was, for the editor, the last straw: '… our wives are quite competent to take care of themselves, and defend their persons and properties against their matrimonial enemies, without the help of any Yankee society of sentinels or imported female generalissimi'. With that, he congratulated the women of Melbourne for their good sense in letting their visitor know she and her American Vigilant Society were not needed. Moreover, if the provinces were equally as sensible, there would be no need for Mrs Colclough to write libellous letters about the apathy of the Victorians in the noble cause of women's rights, leaving her free to 'return with all possible speed to the open arms of the sympathising society, and renew her Amazonian vigils and wars under other skies'.[15]

The reception from the local press was hardly an auspicious one, and after her years of experience with detractors in the New Zealand newspapers, Mary Ann must have realised she had a long and rocky road ahead if she was to have any success in advocating the cause of women to Melburnians. But there were some positive signs. A.H.'s letter attracted several replies from persons with a genuine interest in the cause of women. Anna D. McKenny wrote that women's work was naturally that of an adviser and a real helpmate to man, not the instrument of his will. She looked forward to the day, hopefully before too many generations had passed, when women would truly be so and the likes of A.H. could no longer complain because divided homes would be replaced by homes 'made happy with the bond of equality'.[16]

Writing from Toorak, 'B.A.H.' likewise observed, 'Anyone that has either heard or read that lady's lecture must surely understand, even with the small modicum of brain "A.H." admits belongs to the weaker sex, that she asks nothing unreasonable – merely that woman may be freed from her subjection and conventional degradation'. This correspondent then proceeded to expose the weaknesses in each of A.H's arguments before offering sympathy to Mrs Colclough 'in her uphill work, as well as my appreciation of the temperate yet forcible way in which she puts forward her views'.[17]

'E.S.F.' had been unable to attend the lecture, but wrote that any woman who takes up such a thankless task as Mrs Colclough had done deserved praise. At the risk of being considered 'a horribly degenerate member of my sex' for saying that he thought women indeed suffered a great deal of injustice and wrong at the hands of men, he believed that 'a married woman's position is often the reverse of enviable, with a husband neglectful, or drunken and brutal, but an unmarried woman is in many respects often worse off' due to restrictions on women's fields of employment.[18]

Mary Ann took heart at those friends to the cause who had taken up her defence against A.H. She explained her policy of declining all controversy with anonymous opponents and her preparedness to send a courteous reply to any lady or gentleman who provided a name and address, regardless of how severely they criticised her opinions. Showing she was more than prepared to up the ante, she also advised that 'the apparent apathy about my first lecture was partly due to a discreet hesitation to side with me until my opinions were understood, and that next time I shall not only have a chairman, but I hope and believe a friend or two to support me on the platform, one of whom, a lady, will either propose or second the vote of thanks'.[19]

In publishing correspondence triggered by Mary Ann's lecture, the *Daily Telegraph*, at least, was ensuring both a level of publicity and a forum for public debate on the position of women. There were other indications that what Mary Ann stood for was starting to enter a wider consciousness. Inadvertently, the mayor-elect of Melbourne entered the fray that was the discussion on women's rights. The *Gippsland Times* seized the opportunity to talk up the episode originally reported in the *Daily Telegraph*: 'Whether he is frightened by Mrs Colclough – "Polly Plum" – or is made bold by the absence of Lady Bowen (the *Telegraph* suggests) … he has made an inroad upon Woman's Cause in one of its tenderest points. He will have none of "the sex" at his inaugural dinner. There shall be cakes and ale at the Mayoral banquet, but Mr Gatehouse will not permit the presence at it of any member of the "shrieking sisterhood"'.[20]

Some of the ladies of Melbourne, many of whom cared little about higher education and even less about gaining the right to vote, nevertheless prized an invitation to the inaugural mayoral dinner. Finding themselves deprived of this opportunity, they considered the mayor-elect to have 'signalled his advent to the highest civic position by an impolitic outrage', according to the *Gippsland Times*. What's more, he had been thoroughly shown up by Nehemiah Guthridge, mayor of Sale, a town situated in the Gippsland region of Victoria. Guthridge had marked his retirement by making a donation to the Ladies' Benevolent Society: 'Instead of giving a banquet, and pandering (as "Polly Plum" might say) to the depraved appetites of the tyrants by whom Woman is coerced, Mr Guthridge prefers to recognise Woman as the dispenser of that "rare benevolence which is the minister of God"'.[21]

Mayoral rivalries aside, the debates triggered by Mary Ann's first lecture took on a life of their own to the extent that the *Daily Telegraph* ran the header 'Woman's Work' in its correspondence section for more than two weeks in response to readers' letters. Many of the usual lines of opposition to raising women's status were aired. 'A Country Sister' of Maldon asked Polly Plum if she would have husbands transformed into nursing mothers, or have cooks, laundresses and housemaids made of them:

> For if we are to abdicate, and march to the magisterial bench, cultivate our oratory in Parliament, and harangue a congregation in Collins street, we must have some substitute at home to look after the babies – but maybe

she does not intend us to have any. And then the question comes, who is to do the mending, the darning, the shirt-buttoning? Will 'Polly Plum' open a school and teach our husbands those essentials of domestic economy? If so, I will send my husband, and the next vacancy put up as M.P.[22]

Country Sister did acknowledge, however, that 'Unfortunately there are many of the gentler sex who have to fight the battle of life and earn their daily bread, and to those who have the brains there are doors of usefulness, honour, and I may say eminence, open in abundance, without becoming that horrible thing – a masculine woman'.[23]

'Self Help' was one such woman. Having read the letter by her country sister, she asked:

Will a 'Country Sister' kindly point out to me the 'doors of usefulness, honour, and eminence open in abundance' to self-helpful women? I find it very difficult to obtain employment in the over-crowded spheres open to women who must earn their bread, and shall be truly grateful for such information as will show me the wider and more lucrative spheres of employment of which she discourses so eloquently. If those spheres do exist, and she can prove that they do, she will do much more, not only for the women of Victoria, but for all women, than Mrs Colclough or any other reformer.[24]

Country Sister obliged with a response, suggesting careers in teaching, the Telegraph Department and in the civil service. In a lengthy and heartfelt response, Self Help, who had high testimonials as to her educational ability as well as children to support, pointed out that these and many other careers were overcrowded and the pay and conditions generally very inadequate.

While not a supporter of women's rights to the extent advocated by the advanced school in America, 'Benedict' wrote in support of women's entitlement to a more thorough education and to endorse the view that the obedience demanded from a wife to her husband by St Paul was not intended as a relationship of servitude. 'A Man' took A.H.'s letter to task for being 'a fair example of the logic used to depreciate persons who endeavour to remedy flagrant evils', while 'Woman and Wife' asked why A.H. neglected to mention the duty of husbands. While she agreed with the view that marriage laws were mistaken in requiring wives to pay 'servile submission to all the odious whims' of a husbands' 'selfish nature', she did not align herself with the cause of women's rights: '"Women's Rights" is not a pretty expression, nor yet a womanly idea, and for my part (with all due respect to Mrs Colclough) I never feel proud of my sex when they come forward in public to preach, lecture, or shout utterances, not that it matters one iota what my opinion is in the eyes of man, considering I am only a WOMAN AND WIFE.'[25]

'Way-Side Pansy' of Fitzroy, who had the pleasure of attending Mary Ann's lecture and wished there were more ladies like her, addressed her comments to younger women, urging them to commit to the work of temperance reform.[26]

Newspaper columnist 'The Man About Town' attended the lecture not for any personal interest but simply because, as he put it, he liked to hear 'the creatures chatter' and enjoyed 'a good piece of folly now and then'. Although prone to circumlocution, his light-hearted description of Polly Plum provides a glimpse of her physical appearance as well as her mental abilities:

> *She is a lady who has passed from the spring of youth into the summer of*
> *womanhood. The rich glow of the setting sun bathes the brow which, but*
> *a few years back was surrounded by the halo of the luminary as he awoke*
> *the world. In fact, and to speak in commonplace language, Polly Plum is*
> *neither young nor old; taking the position which comes after the soup and*
> *fish at dinner, and which, after all, forms the most delectable and substantial*
> *element of the feast. Polly Plum, in short, is developed, both in mind and*
> *body. In relation to this last fact, I was satisfied by the first glimpse I caught*
> *of Polly Plum; in regard to the mental calibre of Polly Plum I was assured,*
> *long ere her lecture was concluded.*[27]

There can be no doubt of Mary Ann's mental calibre or of her ability to use the daily newspapers to promote her cause. Just before advertising her second public lecture, she wrote a long letter to the *Daily Telegraph*. Picking up on some of the threads in the letters that had appeared over the previous couple of weeks, she stressed that only those who did not know her 'would venture to class me with the blatant sisterhood who would have women ignore and neglect every duty and responsibility of life'. She admitted she had held back, to some extent, after her first lecture, having decided it wise to show a 'discreet hesitation' until people understood her views. The tenor of many of the letters to newspaper editors no doubt suggested to her that she should continue trying to gain the confidence of some of the more conservative of her audience. To this end she wrote:

> *In my opinion 'the path of duty is the path of safety', and a woman who*
> *becomes the wife of a man able and willing to support her takes on herself*
> *the duty of steward of his means, and guardian of his home and children,*
> *and she can by no means be excused from the performance of her plain duty,*

no matter what her aspirations may be after what she may consider higher work. There is no higher work, and in her case there is no other work in which she can conscientiously engage. She chose her lot when she married, and if he faithfully does his share and provides means, she should faithfully do hers as the house mother, and if she does not she will be met with little sympathy from me or from anyone else with an ordinary share of common sense.[28]

In keeping with her long-held views, Mary Ann's concerns were foremost for 'the large army of women who are not supported by their husbands, who are not married, or who are penniless widows with children to provide for'. She could not condone men who continued to support 'cruel laws and customs that shut inexorably the door to all the lucrative professions against women'. In the past, women, reduced by ages of dependence, consented to marriage simply as a means of ensuring they had shelter and bread. But in the current age, marriages were fewer and old maids more plentiful. Intending to address these questions more fully, she encouraged all her opponents to muster strongly and dispute with her face to face in her second public lecture, titled 'Why Don't the Men Propose?'[29]

In the meantime, two cases reported in the morning papers caught her attention. Each, she wrote to the *Telegraph*, showed the deficiencies in the current marriage laws. The first case concerned Mrs Mitchell, who had been married for 21 years. During this time, law and custom barred her from obtaining any means of support apart from what her husband chose to give her. Although he had property valued at £100,000, he left her only £200 to support herself and the children while he went to England for a year. From all accounts, he trumped up a charge to absolve himself of responsibility for his family. While he was apparently living in luxury, his wife had in actuality received only £120.

The case of Mrs Burness was even more deplorable. Her husband was a brute. After experiencing years of physical abuse and having received an inadequate education, she was physically and mentally incapable of providing for her children. Mary Ann's point was unequivocal: 'Laws are made, or ought to be made, for restraining and punishing the strong and bad, and protecting the weak and the guiltless, and I will put it to the common sense of any impartial person whether, in the two cases I have referred to, women have found that the marriage law and masculine supremacy is regulated on that only true and Christian basis.'[30]

Interest in Mary Ann's second lecture was high, and a large audience, a fair proportion of whom were women, gathered at the Athenæum lecture hall in Collins Street. True to her word, Mary Ann found a gentleman in the person of educationalist Mr I. Warren Ball to take the chair. He introduced the speaker as an accredited advocate and agent of a philanthropic society that aimed to ameliorate women's social condition, and which numbered among its members some of the most eminent women of the time. According to the reviewer for the *Argus*, Mrs Colclough 'dwelt principally with the inherent profligacy and shameful immorality of men'. She began her lecture by arguing that the practice of raising boys and girls separately instilled in young boys a sense of superiority over girls, and instilled in young girls a want for display and a false and extreme modesty before the male sex. Educating girls largely for showy accomplishments was detrimental to both sexes and to the relations between men and women. Mary Ann then went on to address men's tendency to keep a veil over prostitution for fear of exposing their own dissoluteness, their dread of the responsibilities that accompanied marriage, and the differences between men's and women's views of the marriage relationship. Much of the blame she laid squarely in the laps of men, who undoubtedly gained from current laws and social customs at women's expense.[31]

Apparently, two or three persons present 'calling themselves men' shouted out insults to Mary Ann during the lecture, but they were obviously a very small minority, as she was met with hearty cheering at the conclusion of her address. Mrs Staines, wife of a somewhat controversial local politician who hailed as a champion of the people but was seen by others as prone to self-promotion, proposed a vote of thanks. Mrs Staines commented that those who thought Mrs Colclough had come to create a domestic revolution were wrong; her object was to gain the hearty support of every thoughtful man and woman in the community for the effort required to raise the moral and social status of women. After a few remarks by teacher and well-known public lecturer Mr T.P. Hill, Mr George W. Rusden, clerk of the Victorian parliament, seconded Mrs Staines' proposition, which was carried unanimously. When returning her thanks, Mary Ann expressed her gratitude for the kindness shown her since her last address.[32]

According to Mary Ann, reports in the press of the views she expressed during her lecture contained a few inaccuracies, and she drew them to the attention of the editor of the *Daily Telegraph*. On the whole, though, she was pleased with the *Telegraph*'s kind report of her lecture. The *Australasian* newspaper, however, questioned whether proposals were becoming rarer, and cited statistics to prove that 'the question Mrs Colclough has taken so much trouble to elucidate appears to have as little foundation as the memorable one by which Charles II reduced some learned philosophers to confusion'.[33]

As the mails from Victoria arrived in New Zealand, the local newspapers picked up on reports of Mary Ann's activities that mocked her depiction as an advanced thinker upon the subject of marriage and stated that her ideas had met with no response or sympathy from the women of Melbourne. According to the editor of the Melbourne *Herald*, Polly Plum had made 'just a trifling sensation from a newspaper point of view and supplied smart journalists with pabulum, but beyond this her mission fell still born'. Admittedly, she did speak many home truths, and it would not be fair to say her lectures weren't worth hearing: the truth of the matter was simply that in Australia women faced none of the causes that made women 'in the old world' of England discontent. In Australia, women still had the scope to follow out their destiny – marriage. But because men still outnumbered women in the colonies, women could pick and choose.[34]

After several weeks away from the public gaze, Mary Ann set her next appearance on much less contentious ground. On the evening of 9 December she delivered a lecture and readings on Charles Dickens' work at the town hall in Prahran. In the intervening weeks, she had been very busy meeting with supporters in efforts to establish a society for women as well as a dedicated women's newspaper and a lecture series. Buoyed by the abundance of earnest friends she had made in the short time she'd been in Melbourne, and hopeful that each of these ventures would come to fruition, she announced that she was prepared to reside in Victoria for as long as her influence and assistance was required, even if that meant staying on for several years.

Mary Ann also said that she was planning to hold a meeting during the following week, directed toward giving the new society a name and to settling all necessary preliminaries. Confident of an opening membership of 30 or 40, she wrote to the editor of the *Herald* to assure him that her mission was far from stillborn. She also took the opportunity to encourage any who wanted to join her as yet unnamed society to contact her at their earliest convenience and not be deterred by false and foolish statements. As testimony to the respectability of her credentials, she advised:

> *I am an Englishwoman, connected with an English society, and was never in America in my life. I am a member of the Church of England, though for years I lived entirely amongst Presbyterians, far from an English Church. I have, in the bush, prescented [sic] for the Presbyterians, been ex officio a member of their church committee, and have taken the Sunday school service when a minister could not attend. I don't know whether all this is to my credit, or the reverse, but it should surely shield me from wild and*

false statements. I do not see how anyone would have been injured by my being an American, so long as I confined my advocacy to reasonable bounds. However, this excuse for 'running me down' is wanting. I am an Englishwoman, and count it my high privilege to be associated in this noble cause with some of the most honourable and honoured of England's men and women. Do not say, Sir, the movement is not needed here – it is needed everywhere where women can suffer, must toil, or are driven to sin. Only a millennial country can say to our cause, 'We need it not here.'

MARY A. COLCLOUGH[35]

In Auckland, Mary Ann had long-established contacts and the support of many influential people in educational, political, literary, philanthropic and religious circles. Although some of these contacts would have facilitated introductions with like-minded people in Melbourne, Mary Ann was largely an unknown and, to a hostile media, an outsider. Accentuating her Englishness and Christian faith were important ways to counter the views of those who had misrepresented her during her very public entry into Melbourne society. In response to her declaration of affinity to England, and assuming a cynical stance, the editor of the Melbourne *Herald* made his own declaration:

Polly Plum is not only not dead, but she speaketh, and to the purpose. The wretches who rejoice in whiskers, smoke cigars, and wheedle lovely women, have not yet conquered the Colclough. Her foot is on her hobby, which with the kind assistance of Melbourne friends, she means to ride to the death. In a letter which was our privilege to receive this morning, she states that instead of abandoning the position, as all thought she had, from her silence, she has only kept quiet in order to better prepare for a sortie on the enemy's camp. Woe unto the be-trousered race, for this lady and her friends are about to establish a Woman's Rights Society, and further, to have a special journalistic organ, of which no doubt Mrs C. will be editress, and the compositors ladies, with contributors in crinoline and wearing bustles.[36]

On 15 December, Mary Anne used the letter columns of the *Argus* to announce the imminent establishment and aims of the Society for Improving the Condition of Women. The society had two principal objects: to assist all legal and social reforms that had for their object the benefit of women, and to originate and carry out any scheme for the same object. The first practical task was to establish a home for self-dependent young women – daily governesses, shop women, needlewomen, young women working in factories and the like – whose incomes did not average over £50 per year. Young women on this level of income who did not have suitable accommodation were often driven to prostitution or to semi-starvation. The plan, therefore, was to provide them with a comfortable home and sufficient food at a low cost, suited to their means.

The home, Mary Ann explained, was to be a real home and not one overburdened with rules and restrictions. Because the intention was to prevent young women from falling by the wayside, residents would need to be of respectable character and conduct, and committed to returning at a reasonable time in the evenings; other institutions were already in place to assist their fallen sisters. In the future, the nascent society hoped that a home might be set up that taught all branches of female employment, similar to one that operated in New York and had received high praise in the *Argus*. Mary Ann also announced at this time that she would, by special request, deliver a lecture the following week on the subject of 'Men's Wrongs', during which she would provide more details of the society's aims. Her lecture would be followed by a meeting at the new home a couple of days later for the purpose of enrolling members. Anyone wanting full details could contact her personally or by letter.[37]

Mr Warren Ball again took the chair for the lecture on men's wrongs, delivered at the Athenæum. Admitting that the topic was one on which it was impossible to speak without showing strong bias, and refuting the imputation that she was the mouthpiece of a large international community of discontented old maids, Mary Ann opened by remarking that the subject was both national and political and had the support of a large number of liberal men. Starting by elucidating the political wrongs of men and the faults that arose from legislation written only by men in their interests, she argued that women should have some role in the housekeeping of the state: 'In all matters of law relating to the social evil, female reformatories, the care of infants, employers and female servants, especially domestic servants, educated women should be allowed to have some voice.' She touched on the subject of the marriage laws, the miseries of genteel poverty, and the poor gentility who were prepared to work. She then elaborated on the new scheme for a needleworkers' home, and ended with her usual invitation to those interested to join the movement.[38]

Although Mary Ann had been in Melbourne for only three months, by the end of 1874 she had made a considerable number of contacts interested in progressing the cause of women. Announcing the establishment of a Society for Improving the Condition of Women signalled a bold new step in creating an organised face to the cause. Likewise, the decision to open a low-cost residential home for young working women showed a renewed confidence. The year had been an extremely demanding and stressful one, but all indications were that 1875 would bring brighter hopes and successes. Nonetheless, the stresses of the year weighed heavy; as Christmas approached, Mary Ann's health failed and she was confined to her bed for several weeks. Rest and recuperation were the order of the day to prepare her for the challenges the new year would inevitably bring.

CHAPTER EIGHT

Model Lodging House
for Women

Mary Ann's bout of ill health was more serious than first anticipated. By early January her strength was returning, but she still faced the likelihood of several more weeks of bedrest. Anxious not to lose the momentum she had achieved thus far in Melbourne, she wrote to the city's *Daily Telegraph* on 5 January to explain that although her confined circumstances prevented her from active work, she wanted to alert the public to her scheme to provide accommodation for women whose weekly incomes were less than one pound. She thought it deplorable that a great many women were earning these paltry wages when there was a high demand for domestic servants who would be well paid and comfortably housed and fed. Domestic service was, in her view, a much better training ground for women's roles as wives and mothers than needlework could ever be. Ultimately, though, it should be up to individual women to choose their sphere of employment.

The details of her scheme were starting to take shape. She intended to charge seven shillings and sixpence per week for board, lodging and washing, and 10 shillings a week for those who wanted a few extra privileges. Aware that establishing the scheme would require immense external help at the outset, she nevertheless felt confident that if sufficient financial aid was forthcoming, she would devote herself vigorously to the work as soon as she was physically able. Mary Ann advised that she would like to include some basic domestic training in the daily routines of the home, as she had done in her private schools. However, because the home's residents would have completed a long day's work, this idea would not be practical. For her, the priority was to make the home 'a real and happy home, and thus remove the young girls from temptation'.[1]

The prolonged period of bedrest no doubt frustrated Mary Ann, but it did give her time to think, and she reminded herself of the importance of keeping her options open. As committed as she was to the work she had started, she needed to secure a regular income and was therefore prepared to return to New Zealand if necessary, although doing so depended on a suitable position becoming available. When she learned that the Invercargill Grammar School was seeking a new mistress in its infant department, she forwarded an application. Several weeks passed before she received news that it had not been successful.[2]

Meanwhile, the editor of the *Ballarat Star* had picked up on Mary Ann's letter about the proposed home and commented that some years back a similar scheme was mooted for all unemployed females as part of a system for registering for work. The editor fully supported the idea and thought 'no more immediately beneficial development of philanthropy can take place in any of our large towns than that proposed by Mrs Colclough'. He added that large numbers of girls were often 'herded together' in the clothing establishments in Melbourne without appropriate supervision and with too much freedom for their own good. He was very supportive of the possibility that they have access to a home that was properly regulated and governed by a matron wherein they could be protected 'against their own liability to danger', as he put it.[3]

Noting the endorsement of his contemporary, the editor of the *Daily Telegraph* agreed that Mrs Colclough's proposition was one that 'ought to find friends', although he could see some potential difficulties in the scheme. In order for the scheme to work the home would have to be self-supporting, because any state or private aid given to such an institution would effectively be a subsidy to the manufacturers, who would likely then lower the wages they paid to their workers. At the rates proposed, the residents themselves would need to maintain the home; even then, ensuring the home paid its way would be a struggle. The editor thought it likely, though, that once the home was established, other groups of women who also found making ends meet difficult, such as seamstresses paid on a daily basis and young women working in shops, would seek out such lodgings. There was no doubt that much work was needed to secure the co-operation of the philanthropic community, and a great deal of tact would be required to manage the institution once it was up and running. The editor of the *Daily Telegraph* felt confident that Mrs Colclough 'happily possesses both qualities', and he wished her every success in her campaign. The editor of the Melbourne *Herald* was less generous but gave a cursory nod to the fact that 'after trying the pulse of Victorians, [Mrs Colclough] has resolved to devote herself to the real disabilities of her sex, and we may be sure that in this she will be successful'.[4]

With her health still preventing her from physically active work, and dependent upon public subscriptions to get the home established, Mary Ann was gratefully obliged to the local newspapers for keeping the scheme alive and in the public eye. The publicity was effective. Someone sent her an account of a similar institution in Boston, run under the auspices of the Young Women's Christian Association since 1866. Assisted by a number of kind-hearted and influential ladies, the Boston institution provided assistance for young women who were out of employment, and provided day-boarders with domestic training in its restaurant. The association housed its enterprise in a 'double house' that could accommodate 78 boarders in addition to the day-boarders at the restaurant. Although the institution received four times that number of applications each year, it still managed to assist hundreds of young women annually. Mary Ann also learned of a similar scheme in New York, where an immense block of boarding houses had been built by A.T. Stewart at a cost of a million dollars, to house poor female labourers and provide them not only with shelter but also proper food.[5]

Buoyed by evidence of the necessity and successful operation of such schemes overseas, Mary Ann formally announced 'An Appeal to the Ladies of Victoria', choosing to do so through the columns of the *Argus*, the most widely circulated and influential of the Melbourne newspapers at the time. Asking those harbouring a prejudice against her because of her opinions to try to lay that feeling aside, she appealed 'to the kind hearted and influential ladies of Victoria' to assist her in this 'purely philanthropic and non-political scheme'.[6]

Despite Mary Ann's enthusiasm, early signs were that others were not convinced of the need or viability of her plan. The day after Mary Ann's announcement, the editor of the *Argus* wrote a lengthy editorial in support of the existing Melbourne Home and cautioned against establishing a rival institution. His representation of Mary Ann and her cause was not flattering:

> *After endeavouring in vain to arouse the women of Victoria to a proper sense of the wrongs under which they groan, and the rights of which they are iniquitously deprived, Mrs Mary A. Colclough has determined to leave her sex in the political and social degradation which it refuses or is unable to recognise, and to devote her attention to a subject more likely to command the sympathy of a dull and unprogressive community like this, viz., the provision of board, lodging, and instruction for young women earning low rates of wages, or altogether out of employment.*[7]

Professing 'not the slightest prejudice against her on account of her opinions', he considered her movement ill advised. The Melbourne Home to which he referred had been founded in 1863 after considerable fundraising by Melbourne's leading philanthropists, foremost amongst whom was Mrs Laura Jane a'Beckett, wife of the distinguished solicitor, Anglican layman and elected member of the Legislative Council, Thomas Turner a'Beckett.[8]

The a'Becketts were a well-known and powerful Melbourne family, active in both political and legal fields and one of the most prominent names in Melbourne philanthropic circles. Laura a'Beckett was active in most of the local charitable enterprises and was a founding member and president for many years of the St Kilda Ladies' Benevolent Society. She had also acted as the representative in Melbourne for the Female Middle Class Emigration Society, although her practical assistance to newly arrived ladies was initially limited to recommending them for governesses' positions should any be advertised.

From as early as 1863, Melburnians had identified accommodation for newly arrived emigrants as an issue. A group of philanthropic women and men had established the Melbourne Female Home in temporary premises in Smith Street, Collingwood, in 1857, but had been forced to close it within a year due to a lack of funds. About four years later, during a public meeting presided over by the Governor of Victoria, Sir Henry Barkly, the ladies who had run this home proposed the establishment of the Melbourne Home for Governesses, Needlewomen, and Servants and all Classes of Respectable Single Females. Governor Barkly drew attention to the problems that might eventuate if the home attempted to accommodate too wide a range of social classes. Although he considered the preferable option to be that of separate institutions for each class of single females, he acknowledged that financing more than one institution would be difficult.

The meeting decided to proceed with the establishment of one home, and to that end called for subscriptions to fund this enterprise. When subscriptions for the home were fewer than anticipated, the instigators of the initiative decided to establish a temporary home in the former Prince of Wales Hotel located on the north side of Flinders Lane between Swanston and Russell Streets. Catering for governesses, needlewomen and servants, the premises also housed a registry office for the employment of servants and married couples. A management committee consisting of 26 women and six men was formed, and it appointed Mrs a'Beckett honorary secretary. Several years and several changes of temporary location later, the committee managed to build a permanent home on the south side of Little Lonsdale Street, between Queen and William Streets.

Despite the home being formally called a home for governesses, needlewomen and servants, the fee of 17 shillings per week paid in advance turned out to be prohibitive for many unless they were already engaged in non-residential employment or supported by their families. Although the home was still maintained by public subscription, the committee was set on it eventually becoming self-supporting by extending its functions to include a training school for servants. The idea was to have those servants who were cooks, laundresses and housemaids demonstrate and teach their duties. The only reason this plan had not been carried through was the expense of building an additional wing and providing extra supervision for a day training school. If a sufficient number of young girls approached the institution seeking such training, the committee was more than prepared to appeal for public prescriptions for this. Perhaps prompted by Mary Ann's announcements of her intended plans, Laura a'Beckett had written to the *Argus* about her committee's plans. In the meantime, she noted, there was no reason why lectures and practical lessons should not be given to other than the servant class until such time as additional funds could be secured for a more permanent facility and arrangement.

Mary Ann was well aware of the Melbourne Servants' Home and considered it an admirable institution doing excellent work. She was also familiar with the Industrial Home, run under the auspices of the Melbourne Ladies' Benevolent Society. The Industrial Home provided temporary accommodation for women and their dependent children in the intervals between employment. It also helped women gain positions. What Mary Ann was proposing would complement rather than compete with these two existing institutions. The class of boarder she wished to provide for would doubtless find the classifications used in each of these two homes objectionable, and they would probably be unable to afford the terms of board charged by the Melbourne Servants' Home, particularly as it required payment in advance. Not wishing to make enemies of the established philanthropic community, she wrote to the *Argus* to clarify these points. 'I still hope,' she concluded, 'that after this explanation, you may look kindly on my project, which, though it emanates from one who is proud to call herself an avowed woman's advocate, is conceived solely with the view to benefit that large class, very poor and underpaid working women'.[9]

Despite intending to do only her best by the women she championed, Mary Ann had stepped on the toes of the established philanthropic elite. In her capacity as honorary secretary of the Melbourne Servants' Home, Laura a'Beckett wrote to the *Argus* producing statistics from a survey completed two years earlier to demonstrate that there was insufficient demand for the type of boarding accommodation that Mary Ann proposed. Although Mrs a'Beckett made no specific reference in her letter to Mary Ann's scheme, and although she did not mention Mary Ann by name, there was no doubt as to what and whom she was referring. Laura insisted that not only was the proportion of girls living in lodgings very small but it was also unlikely that they would be persuaded to live in the Melbourne Home. Her assurance that her committee had no wish 'to break up homes, and to induce girls to live away from their relatives', was an implicit criticism of Mary Ann's proposal. Laura also quietly drew the battle lines in respect of the reliability of established charitable networks and philanthropic circles to keep abreast of the changing needs of the city: 'That excellent society, the Melbourne Ladies' Benevolent Society, has information available to no other society, and so long as it makes no sign, I must think that we have not so many young women homeless than is generally supposed.'[10]

The editor of the *Argus* also used his influence to try to close off further talk of squandering money on another institution for which there was no proven demand. In contrast to the polite social etiquette of Laura a'Beckett, he only thinly veiled what amounted to contempt for Mary Ann:

> *Without wishing to discourage Mrs Colclough in the prosecution of her self-imposed task of ameliorating the condition of her sex throughout the world, we may be permitted to hint that in this particular portion of the globe we have not awaited her advent to ascertain what assistance can fairly and properly be rendered to those members of the community on whom fortune has not smiled … Mrs Colclough may rest assured that if any real necessity had existed for an institution such as she advocates, it would have been provided long before she thought fit to honour Melbourne with her presence.*[11]

This was certainly not the kind of media attention Mary Ann wanted for her project, but she staunchly held on to the fact that she had been assured by 'many friends, benevolent people, religious people, even manufacturers and others' that this type of accommodation was needed, and she questioned whether a survey completed two years earlier, no matter how thoroughly it may have been conducted, was an accurate reflection of the current needs of the community. She also questioned whether the Melbourne Ladies' Benevolent Society was the organisation best placed to know the needs of the class of women she was concerned with because only under exceptional circumstances would the very poorest of working women come to the society's attention.[12]

But the editor of the *Argus* had shifted the terms of the debate. Whether or not there were sufficient numbers of poorly paid working women in need of cheap accommodation, did this group of women actually deserve assistance?

> *Are the 'very poor and underpaid women' of whom Mrs Colclough speaks,*
> *deserving of help? We deliberately say that, under existing circumstances,*
> *they are not. What is it that makes them poor and underpaid? Is it not*
> *a foolish vanity which leads them to prefer starvation wages in a factory*
> *to good pay and a comfortable home in domestic service? … They have a*
> *perfect right, of course, to exercise their discretion in choosing the occupation*
> *they will follow, but as long as they foolishly and obstinately adhere to*
> *a calling which affords them a bare subsistence, while another equally*
> *respectable is open to them in comfort, they cannot with any good grace*
> *appeal to the public for succour.*[13]

The editor's line of reasoning was an all too familiar one for Mary Ann. She had encountered the same issue in Auckland when advocating on behalf of women who had served prison sentences, and when arguing for a reformatory for young girls as an alternative to sending them to prison to share cells with hardened criminals. As had been the case then, she was at odds with conservative public opinion on who was deserving of assistance, let alone who should provide that assistance.

Fortuitously, fuel for Mary Ann's arguments came from an unlikely source. Comment in the recently published report of the annual meeting of subscribers to the Melbourne Home had upset some of the governesses residing at it. They were dismayed to read that the chairman of the committee overseeing the home had said it was time for the institution to 'die a natural death'. The governesses expressed their concerns in a letter to the *Argus*. Most of them had been brought up 'in a totally different sphere of life, well educated and refined, but forced, through loss of parents or fortune, to work for our daily bread, strangers, as many of us are, in the country, too often friendless and homeless'. The Melbourne Home was their saviour. As governesses either seeking employment or needing accommodation during the holidays, the expenses associated with ordinary lodgings were beyond their means. They loved and revered their matron and could not imagine a more desirable quiet and respectable institution than the one they presently called home.[14]

The sentiments the governesses expressed toward the home and their matron were exactly what Mary Ann hoped for with respect to her proposed working women's home. She capitalised on the governesses' letter by suggesting that the relative numbers of governesses, needleworkers and servants residing at the Melbourne Home were clear indication that servants might be used to being classified as inferiors, but 'needlewomen will not submit to these distinctions in their own home'.[15]

However, even if the tide of public opinion had at some stage turned toward her, it was now well and truly ebbing. News of her endeavours had reached other parts of Australia, but that it had done so did not necessarily mean widespread interest in or support for her advocacy for women and for social reform. In Queensland, the editor of the *Queenslander* stated that Mrs Colclough was 'a woman in advance of her age ... bitten with a rage for rescuing the poor and the oppressed ... a burglarious benefactor who bursts in and helps'.[16] In South Australia, the *South Australian Register* reported that 'Polly Plum's maxims are now the general theme of conversation' and summed them up as:

1. *Every man is bad to the core, especially the married ones.*

2. *Married men habitually deceive and ill-use their wives.*

3. *A woman to ensure perfect happiness should never marry.*

4. *Woman, being the superior animal, should assert her position, and get rid of the brute portion of the creation, which at present lords it over her.*

5. *All male children should at once be put out of the way, to save future misery and trouble.*

6. *Men, being cowards, have not the courage to take the chair at a woman's rights meeting, and therefore require to be speedily disposed of.*[17]

A lengthy letter that Mary Ann had written to the *Argus* at the end of January on the issue of servants received more favourable responses. The *Sydney Mail*, for example, considered Mary Ann's ideas of encouraging well-educated young girls who would generally be employed as governesses to become helps and companions worthy of consideration. However, the Melbourne *Weekly Times* considered the idea just one more in a list of failed attempts to impose her views on the women of Melbourne.[18]

Back in New Zealand, the newspapers continued to report Mary Ann's lack of success, but she doggedly continued with her plans and repeatedly wrote to the various Melbourne newspapers challenging their misrepresentations of her intentions. Having scaled down her original plan, all that was needed was £50 to rent and furnish a house, and 'a discreet and sensible matron [who] might succeed in persuading those who could, and would, to enter the higher sphere of domestic service as ladies' maids, nurses, parlourmaids, &c., in well-conducted establishments, where they would be treated with kindness and consideration'.[19]

As correspondent John Sloe pointed out, however, appeals to start new schemes of benevolence had frequently been made to the Melbourne public, and where the promoters were known as persons of independent means, acting from pure philanthropy and having no personal interests to serve, they generally met with a ready response. For the public to support Mrs Colclough's cause, they would need to be assured that such an institution really was needed, and recent newspaper reports had cast doubt on this. Importantly, they would also need to be convinced that Mrs Colclough herself was not an interested party.[20] Mary Ann obliged with a reply:

> *To the Editor of the Argus*
>
> *Sir, – There is one part of Mr Sloe's letter in The Argus that I feel obliged to reply to.*
>
> *I will refer him to anyone in the province of Auckland, N.Z., where I was well known for 17 years, from his Honour the Superintendent, the inspector of police, and the late mayor, down to the poorest fallen girl that walks the streets, as to the integrity of my motives in any work of philanthropy with which I connect myself.*
>
> *I am a stranger here and such assurance seems necessary.*
>
> *Were His Excellency Sir George Bowen here, or the Hon. Julius Vogel, he would not have to go so far for testimony to my respectability, for from the many tokens of respect with which both gentlemen have favoured me, I feel assured they would both kindly bear testimony to my character.*
>
> *I have many letters of thanks for hard services in New Zealand as a philanthropist – I was going to say 'unpaid' service; but work that wins gratitude and does good is not unpaid.*
>
> *I am sorry to trouble you with this, but must beg as a favour that it is inserted. Yours, &c.,*
>
> MARY A. COLCLOUGH[21]

In what appeared to be a deliberate attempt to undermine her personal integrity, the editor of the *Argus* assigned the title 'Interested Benevolence' to Mary Ann's letter. But her personal integrity was impeccable, as anyone who had worked closely with her was well aware. What mattered was that the home be established, for the sake of young, single, poorly paid women, rather than who or what organisation was behind the venture.

Although well recovered from her long illness, Mary Ann admitted to feeling discouraged and disheartened. When she read that Mr Marsh, the Secretary of the Young Men's Christian Association, had raised the issue at a reunion of the Christian Association of Female Workers and expressed criticism of the fact that it took a stranger to Melbourne to propose such a scheme, she wrote to him of her willingness to hand over the venture to the Christian Association of Female Workers if they were able and willing to take up the work.

Just when Mary Ann was ready to relinquish her oversight of the project, several earnest philanthropists who had engaged in mission work among the poor rallied around her. One person donated £10, while other smaller donations meant that £13 cash and almost that again in pledges became available to establish the home. Not losing any time, Mary Ann and her supporters obtained, within a few days and for a very cheap rent, a 'plain, unpretending, and old-fashioned, but very suitable' house at numbers 78 and 80 Gore Street in Fitzroy.[22]

The building had a large day room, two offices, and four large, airy dormitories that could take up to 22 beds or, in cases of emergency, could manage up to 26. The plan was to charge sixpence per bed per night, threepence for a breakfast of tea or coffee with bread and butter or four pence including meat. Throughout the week, residents would be able to buy a supper consisting of meat and vegetables with tea, coffee or soup for threepence, or four pence if bread and butter were included. A Sunday dinner with meat, vegetables and pudding would be available at a charge of sixpence. These charges totalled to one shilling per day or, with Sunday dinner, seven shillings and sixpence per week. Residents would also have to abide by strict rules of conduct, which included being home by ten o'clock at night and always of a quiet demeanour. A servants' registry office would be opened in the building, with its services available for residents at no charge. Employers and non-residents seeking employment would be charged a small fee. It was hoped that the cheap rates, as well as the plain fare and lodgings and the strict rules relating to decorum, would be sufficient to encourage young girls not to leave their parental homes if those homes were loving and safe.

The scheme had elements in common with a former initiative of the Governesses' Benevolent Institution, which Mary Ann had walked past when attending London's Queen's College as a teenager. The Governesses' Benevolent Institution Committee had purchased a house in Harley Street where governesses could stay for short periods while they looked for a new position. That home, run by a committee of ladies, also operated as an office where governesses and prospective employers might register their names.

On 10 March 1875 Mary Ann proudly announced that the Model Lodging House for Women had opened and that she had taken on the role of superintendent of the home. One of her supporters, noted physician and philanthropist Dr John Singleton, had offered his services as treasurer and was available to collect subscriptions. As assurance that any subscriptions received would be used for the purpose for which they were donated, donors could, if they desired, receive tickets valued at either sixpence or threepence up to the value of their donation. They could then give these tickets to any deserving woman of honest decent poverty, and she in turn could use the tickets as payment for board and lodging.

Laudable as the intention to provide cheap accommodation was, Mary Ann and her committee set the charges so low that some commentators doubted the home would ever be viable enough to become self-sufficient. As the editor of the *Daily Telegraph* pointed out, unless the home was comfortably furnished and there were sufficient funds to meet all preliminary expenses, it might not attract sufficient custom to survive beyond a trial period. Despite this reservation, he wished Mrs Colclough well and considered that if the home did receive sufficient support, there was no reason it should not achieve the same results as similar institutions in America. He added that the one thing most in favour of the undertaking was that it had been 'initiated by a lady who appears to be thoroughly in earnest, and to be possessed of energy sufficient to carry herself and her project through all ordinary difficulties'.[23]

Appreciating full well the part played by the daily newspapers in publicising and encouraging practical support for the Model Lodging House, Mary Ann wrote to the *Ballarat Star*, which had expressed support for her plans earlier in the year. She wished to inform the newspaper's readers that the home was now in operation. The move was a strategic one. Mary Ann and others were aware that because many of the young women arriving in Melbourne came from outlying areas and neighbouring colonies and generally had no knowledge of the city, they tended to seek out cheap accommodation in public-houses or in lodgings in the narrow streets and lanes of the city where they were exposed to discomfort and 'temptation'. Mary Ann explained that she and her supporters were prepared to go to the railway station to meet young women arriving in Melbourne intent on taking up an apprenticeship or a service position and to assist them, free of charge, to find suitable employment. The model house, Mary Ann pointed out, was ideally located near routes taken by buses heading for the railway station via Brunswick and Spencer Streets; the Smith Street and the Hobson's Bay buses passed almost by the house's door.[24]

Mary Ann wrote with candour to the Ballarat newspaper of the attempts by some members of the Melbourne press to paint her as a 'pestilent humbug' and a 'pestilent Yankee agitator, and a mere platform declaimer', and of how inconvenient and annoying it must have been for them when they found out she was an Englishwoman of orthodox respectability. As the editor of the *Ballarat Star* rightly observed, she was not one to hide her light under a bushel.[25]

Just days after the Model Lodging House opened, Mary Ann wrote to the *Argus* to draw attention to the plight of 'elegant, refined, educated' ladies in Melbourne who were daily 'reduced to the verge of self-destruction for want of the means to buy bread'. Several cases had come to her attention in recent weeks of women unable to apply to the Melbourne Home because they could not afford to pay the fees in advance. They had talents and abilities, but as long as the market remained overstocked, they would be left, after paying their board, paying for advertisements and replying to advertisements, with their money, strength and courage exhausted. With only one shilling between them and the streets, they found themselves contemplating 'self-destruction' through an overdose of laudanum to avoid having to resort to the ranks of prostitution. Because accommodation in the Model Lodging House was too simple and plain for such refined educated ladies, Mary Ann urged, through her letter, for the committee of the Melbourne Home to find a way to extend aid to such cases.[26]

Once again her good intentions backfired. The *Australasian* reported that 'The philanthropy of the irrepressible Mrs Colclough is very apt to take a highly mischievous form' and referred to her claims as 'sensational nonsense' and 'highly fanciful'. The Melbourne correspondent to the *Otago Witness* described Mary Ann as 'a troublesome old woman' who had resorted to practical philanthropy after failing 'to rouse Melbourne women to a sense of their degraded, oppressed position'. Convinced that no true, pure-minded, genteel lady who had been properly brought up would ever consider options of the kind Mary Ann proposed, the editor of the *Argus* accused her of over-exaggeration and having a 'morbid imagination'. Then, having discounted her as an 'irrepressible busybody' who was displaying her ignorance of Melbourne matters, he drove in his main point: 'We have long since proved – long before Mrs Colclough came to Melbourne – that we are ever ready to lend a helping hand to any really charitable movement, but we must confess that, as a rule, we have very little sympathy with the schemes of "professional" philanthropists.'[27] Undeterred, Mary Ann responded:

Is it any wonder that I and other ladies from the platform and through the press exclaim at all the injustices and want of consideration our sex receive? Our need, our poverty, our protection from ruin is to be left to private enterprise or our own powers of endurance; only men are to be helped in the way of well-doing by the Government and the public. You may be very sure that I have not abandoned the cause of my sex. Articles such as yours of this morning show how needed are advocates of women's rights to ask for them both justice and consideration. In a city plentifully supplied with institutions to put safe homes within the reach of men, such institutions being inaugurated and partly supported by public funds, shall the leading paper declare that no such help shall be given to women? Surely, then, Victoria badly needs women's advocates.[28]

Mary Ann's tenacity struck a chord, and offers of second-hand furniture and books came in. Having always taken a rather cynical stance with respect to her activities, the editor of the *Herald* gave her credit for ability to advertise herself and her home by stirring up debate in the newspapers: 'Though the lady denies that she is a Yankee, certainly by her knowledge of advertising dodges, in getting up an agitation in the papers during the silly season, she has cunningly obtained such publicity that if her "Home" is a necessity, it must be a success.' The inference that Mary Ann was a 'professional' philanthropist would not go away, however. A letter to the Melbourne *Age* signed by 'One Who Believes in Disinterested Philanthropy' asserted that three questions needed to be asked before public charity should be invoked: 'Is a model lodging-house for women required? Has the scheme been properly introduced? Have we confidence in the self-selected manager or matron?'[29]

This continual questioning of her motives led Mary Ann to reflect on the extreme difficulty of getting established in a new town without one's familiar and long-standing networks. Aware through friends from the Thames that reports from the Melbourne press were regularly making their way into New Zealand newspapers, she wrote to the *Thames Star* to correct the erroneous impressions perpetuated in these accounts. Assuring her friends back in the Thames that she had hosts of good friends in Melbourne, she described the set-up of the Model Lodging House and then stated:

In Auckland there would be great confidence in my managing such an institution, for (whatever my faults) my old friends know me well and would trust to a faithful and conscientious carrying out of the principles of the institution to the best of my means and ability. But here some of the newspapers, and noticeably the Argus *which should know better, have tried to write me down a much needed institution with a persistent blindness to its usefulness, and a rancour of expression that leads to the fear that they must be actuated by personal animosity against myself, and that nothing I can do can be right unless I could consent to sit quietly in a corner with my fingers in my eyes, and acknowledge that I deserve disgrace because I chose to lift one voice, even against a multitude of dissentients, on behalf of women who seem to me to get much more the worst of it here than in New Zealand; for wife-beaters, even when their crime amounts almost to murder, get off very easily, whereas an unfortunate vagrant woman gets it very hot in Court as compared with her male associates and employers; and if a letter is sent to some of the papers, calling attention to this, 'it is not inserted'.*[30]

Providing a rare personal insight into her predilections, Mary Ann also joked about compromising her reputation for strong-mindedness by admitting she had a weakness for following ladies' fashions. Apparently no-one in Melbourne wore strings in their bonnets; everyone wore falls and the kick-up style of hat. It was also fashionable for ladies to wear their dresses as tightly drawn around them as was consistent with decency in front and then to 'pile on' the fullness behind. A jacket with sleeves was considered an abomination, while black, loaded with jet, was the most *distingué* wear. Mary Ann's 'weakness' for fashion may have extended to her buying the latest fashions and thus contributing to her debts, or perhaps her limited finances denied her the pleasure of keeping up with the latest trends.

On a more serious note, Mary Ann found time to visit Melbourne gaol and was sobered by what she encountered. Only a few women were in the hospital section on the day of her visit, but one patient became etched on her mind. She was young, no more than about 23 years of age and with a singular beauty. Her white face, beautiful eyes and hair and refined features reminded Mary Ann of a picture she once saw in the Mater Dolorosa. The young woman had been in her bed for nine months, and the medical staff feared she would never rise from it.

After Mary Ann had seen the hospital, prison staff took her upstairs to see the large workroom. Formerly the chapel, the room was now so crowded it could no longer be used for that purpose. Mary Ann was distressed to learn that the inmates were not allowed to leave their work to attend religious services throughout the week, and visits from prison missionaries were not permitted. If prisoners expressed a desire to see the gaol chaplain, they were permitted to do so on Mondays and Thursdays, but otherwise their only spiritual provision was the Sunday service. Mary Ann thought it a special hardship that Protestant missionaries were not permitted to speak to Roman Catholic prisoners. Her visit to the prison brought to her mind all the work she had undertaken with female prisoners at Mount Eden Gaol and reignited her very genuine concern for women prisoners:

> *We want to get at their hearts, and their lives, to demonstrate to them that we love them, and would fain serve them, and though it requires a person to be specially gifted for the work with ease, judgement, common sense, great caution, and little credulity; still these qualities are to be found, and will become developed in prison work; and where the prison officials can depend on the judgement, and prudence of the missionary, I think no obstacle should be placed in the way of their having free access to the prisoners at all times. For prisoners to sit at work round a good lady who is kindly reading to them is surely better than for them to occupy their minds and tongues with old scandals and tales of the past.*[31]

Much as she wanted to, Mary Ann realised she could not commit to being involved with these women. Her time now was majorly devoted to her work as superintendent of the Model Lodging House, and her physical health was still compromised. Another bout of illness prevented her from engaging in public lectures, but by early June she had recovered sufficiently to accept a special invitation to present a paper to the Eclectic Association of Victoria. As had been the case in Auckland, her sphere of friends in Melbourne now included some very influential and high-standing men, among them Justice George Higinbotham, Alfred Deakin and Henry Gyles Turner.

It was most likely Deakin and Turner who introduced Mary Ann to the Eclectic Association. Melbourne-born Alfred Deakin was said to have 'strayed into the study of law at the University of Melbourne', attending evening lectures while working during the day as a school teacher and private tutor. Prominent in the spiritualist movement, he excelled at journalism and was also a keen member of the debating club. Henry Gyles Turner, banker, historian, part of the Melbourne literati and brother of Martha Turner, was the founder president of the Kew Literary Institute and Free Library, co-founder of the *Melbourne Review*, and later a trustee of the Public Library, Museum and National Gallery. Although not sympathetic to broader feminist agendas, Turner was one of the founding members of the Free Discussion Group formed in 1867, which was the forerunner to the Eclectic Association of Victoria. Mary Ann subsequently became a member of the Eclectic Association, and after a long break from the public platform she presented an address titled 'The Employment and Education of Women' on 3 June. With 62 people present, the lecture proved to be one of the best-attended sessions the association hosted during 1875. Mary Ann was the third woman to address the association and one of only six women to present a paper to the association throughout its 27-year existence.[32]

By August, Mary Ann was able to report that the Model Lodging House was operating, after a hesitant start, with a moderate amount of success. The work so far had been extremely demanding and done with little thanks and little assistance. By her own admission, she now knew the house was entirely unsuitable for the class of residents she had wanted to attract; it was not central enough to the city, nor was it large enough or sufficiently appointed. Not wanting to turn away those in need, she had allowed, for the first few months, any woman who had the means to pay to have a bed. She was the first to admit that this decision was unfortunate, as it had attracted a lower class of women, ready to benefit from the cheapest accommodation possible in order to squander their savings on alcohol. These women avoided places like the Immigrants' Home because establishments of this kind required a certain amount of work in return for shelter. The lower-class lodging houses also rejected these women because they feared the women would rob them when they arrived home drunk. Many of these women, street-savvy and hardened by their addictions, had mastered the art of false pretences to acquire more respectable lodgings. From first-hand experience, Mary Ann knew that it had been 'a bitter mistake to listen to their stories and take them, for their habits are so low, so dissolute, and often so filthy, that their presence banishes completely decent inmates'. She hoped the Society for the Promotion of Morality, under the guidance of Dr John Singleton, might be more successful in securing help for these women who still required suitable accommodation.[33]

Six months of experience had also convinced her, however, that she was right in identifying the need for cheap accommodation for young working women of respectable habits. There were sufficient numbers of such women to make a good, centrally located lodging house useful and financially viable. The success of such an establishment relied on it being respectably conducted and having a strict admission policy directed towards ensuring all unsuitable women were excluded. In the meantime, Mary Ann was determined to keep her lodging house open until something more desirable could be put in place. Most nights the house was full to capacity, sometimes with women sleeping on the floor, and even though Mary Ann had been working without assistance for months, the home was still five pounds in debt. Having walked Melbourne until she was footsore in her efforts to raise the small amount needed to cover the debt, Mary Ann was dismayed that so many men who held high positions and took a good share of public money had no sympathy for her cause and would not donate so much as a pound. Eventually, she realised she would never be able to secure the money to establish a more suitably located home and so resigned herself to leaving the task to someone more popular:

> *I am, to a great extent, unconventional and unorthodox, and so, though I appear to be the only woman in Melbourne ready to give time and means towards helping the young and friendless of my sex by providing them with cheap and safe nightly shelter, the highly conventional and professedly orthodox button up their pockets against the good cause, and say to me, in effect, 'Go to, I am holier than thou:' and so, sir, I do sincerely wish some party or parties who have the public respect and confidence would take up this work.*[34]

A level of weariness was evident in her correspondence. Convinced that public opposition to her as an individual was behind the lack of support for her lodging house, and tired of the newspapers misrepresenting her views as well as her personal circumstances, she wrote to the Melbourne *Herald*:

> *I did not derive my ideas from America; I never was in America in my life. The error that I was American emanated from The Age newspaper. I am an Englishwoman, a Londoner, the widow of an old Victorian, a thorough Melbournite, and it was the constant praises my husband used to sound in my ears of his adopted country, the warm-heartedness, its kindness, its liberality of opinion, that led me to come to Victoria. Unhappily I was met with prejudice as undeserved as it was ill considered and through a long and tedious sickness and many subsequent trials in trying to benefit others, I and my orphan children have felt all the bitterness of misrepresentation and the consequent unpopularity.*[35]

Her private face was clearly evident. This was the first time she had claimed a legitimate presence in Melbourne based on being 'the widow of an old Victorian'. Even had that fact been widely known on her arrival, this knowledge would probably have made no difference, however. Powerless to shield her children from undeserved prejudices, Mary Ann was close to admitting defeat.

But just when Mary Ann was feeling most downcast, signs emerged to reassure her that her constant challenges to the Melburnian elite to provide more appropriate support for working women were making a difference. In an effort to increase the usefulness of the Melbourne Home, Mrs Laura a'Beckett announced that the home was now offering cookery classes and certificates of competency to those who completed the entire course. As one of the secretaries of Mrs Perry's Fund for Distressed Governesses, Laura a'Beckett advised that donations to the fund would be received to further the committee's work in this area. The *Argus* fully endorsed both initiatives.[36]

Mary Ann must also have taken heart from the knowledge that not every sector of Melbourne society snubbed her. From mid-August she embarked on a series of public engagements, no doubt prompted by the need to raise much needed funds. On 14 August she delivered a lecture on 'Woman's Rights and Wrongs' for the Melbourne Free Discussion Society at the Trades Hall in Lygon Street. The following week she took part, by invitation, in the Fitzroy Popular Concert, a weekly event held at the local town hall. To the delight of the crowd, she performed 'Mrs Caudle's Lecture' in character. The brainchild of English writer and dramatist Douglas William Jerrold, Mrs Caudle has been suitably described as 'interminably loquacious and militantly gloomy under fancied marital oppression'. Her 'curtain lectures', usually delivered in bed to her husband, 'expatiated at length on her supposed sufferings and denounced the failings of her spouse' and lent themselves superbly to recitals. Trained as Mary Ann was in elocution, her rendition of the archetypal nagging wife would have been unmissable.[37]

Back in the Thames, the *Coromandel Mail* couldn't resist the opportunity to joke at Mary Ann's expense: 'May the powers above be merciful! Is it – can it be true that Polly Plum will allow the curtain at the Fitzroy Hall to be drawn up, and exhibit herself in a nightcap and a full suit of bedclothes? And we should like to ask who will be the Caudle to be lectured to? Polly, we fear thou are becoming naughty in thy old age.'[38]

Mary Ann's revitalised schedule of public engagements was due, in part, to her advertising her availability for lectures, readings and recitations at town and country societies and debating clubs. On 29 August she appeared in the first of a series of sacred recitals at the recently rebuilt Apollo Music Hall, next to the Haymarket Theatre in Burke Street. Although the attendance was small, the programme was varied, with vocal and instrumental selections from Handel, Haydn and Mendelssohn and a reading from Milton's 'Eve's Lament' from Mary

Ann. Midway through the entertainment, she delivered a lecture on 'Sabbath Recreation' in which she argued that the Lord's Day was appointed for rational recreation and that the Sabbath of Mosaic law was not binding upon Christians. Several weeks later she was a vocalist at a concert at the Kew Town Hall.[39]

A month after writing to the *Daily Telegraph* and the *Herald* to explain that her experiment with the lodging house had been fraught with difficulties, Mary Ann wrote to the *Argus* to admit they had had more insight than she when they cautioned that her scheme would be open to great abuse and the house would likely become a shelter for loafers. Through well-meant kindness, she had allowed her philanthropy to overmaster her discretion. By now it was very clear to her that she would need considerably increased funds, a better site, superior appointments and 'altogether a more complete organisation' to make the home what she wanted it to be – a safe haven for poor innocent girls who were temporarily deprived of a home and shelter and in need of a friendly hand. She had been determined to do it of her own means but now was financially crippled.[40]

Describing her venture as 'an utter failure', the editor of the *Argus* gave some credit for her candour in surrendering her task but still denied there was a need for such an institution as Mrs Colclough continued to promote. Not all agreed. Seeing Mary Ann's endeavour as only a partial failure, the editor of the *Herald* continued to express support for Mrs Colclough and for the cause she espoused. He hoped that her exertions and sacrifices to assist her fellow women would not be allowed to pass 'without some sort of recognition at the hands of the people of Melbourne' and then added that 'we hope to see this recognition take some substantial form' before suggesting that the mayoress might take up the matter.[41]

In true fashion, Mary Ann's attention shifted to other groups in the community who needed assistance. She had recently received news from New Zealand that Cyrus Haley, the man who had asked to see her several years back when he was facing an extended prison sentence for multiple charges of arson and attempted murder, had been shot and killed while attempting to escape from prison. Mary Ann had advised him to send his children to relations and friends in England where the circumstances of their parents were not known, thus providing them with the opportunity to grow into respectable citizens. Circumstances such as those the Haley children faced, where neither parent was fit or capable of providing them with a good life, turned her mind to the conditions state paupers in industrial schools faced, and she wrote a long letter to the *Argus* about the need for reform in these areas.[42]

Demand for her public speaking remained steady. In early October Mary Ann delivered a lecture on 'Strong Drink and its Victims' at the Temperance Hall in Emerald Hill (South Melbourne) for the local Total Abstinence Society. The following month she took part in a complimentary entertainment at the Prahran Town Hall to acknowledge the work of Mr R.W. Carey, the manager of the local popular concerts, and on 24 November delivered a lecture on temperance at the Trinity Schoolroom for the Good Templar Speedwell Lodge. She also submitted a formal request to the Sandridge Borough Council for a concession to lease the Sandridge Town Hall for a benefit concert to be held on 6 December. Unfortunately, the council resolved that the usual terms be acceded to. The *Argus* subsequently reported that the complimentary benefit for Mrs Colclough was postponed for a week.[43]

Despite her attempts to raise funds from public engagements, the failure of the lodging house meant Mary Ann had no livelihood and had been reduced to a state of destitution. For the sake of herself and her children, she had no option but to appeal to the generosity of the public for assistance. She needed about £15 or £20 to enable her to return to New Zealand, where she had many friends and better prospects. Uncharacteristically, the editor of the *Argus* wrote sympathetically of her circumstances: 'We have had many quarrels with Mrs Colclough on public grounds, but personally we believe her to be a lady of considerable ability and unquestionable earnestness of purpose, and therefore have no hesitation in making this appeal on her behalf and that of the helpless children. We shall be happy to take charge of subscriptions and to acknowledge them in the usual way.'[44]

The New Zealand newspapers were less generous. Under a new editorship, the *Daily Southern Cross*, for many years a strong supporter of Mary Ann's endeavours, questioned her priorities. Noting that some time back Mrs Colclough had intimated to some of her former acquaintances in Auckland that she would like to return to her position at Tuakau, the editor commented:

> *Had she devoted her attention to teaching, or otherwise earning an honourable living for herself and support for the young children she was left with on her husband's death, when she was here, her financial circumstances would probably have been more satisfactory than they are today. Her first care should have been her duty to her children, as she was left their sole protector, and allowed some one else, who had less responsibility resting upon her, to become the platform advocate of advanced Yankee notions as to the relations which should be maintained between the sexes.*[45]

Once again, provincial rivalries were at play. The *Waikato Times* reported that 'Auckland it seems is threatened with the return of that pestilent man-woman Polly Plum, whose mischievous writings and doctrines did no little harm among weakminded women in this community a few years ago.' Delighting in the fact that the *Cross*, once her champion, was now publicly critical of her actions, the editor of the *Waikato Times* suggested that Mary Ann should be sent to America where she could meet with congenial spirits. The *Wanganui Chronicle* held her destitution as 'a lesson to all strong minded females ... to content themselves with the position in the world assigned them by social customs and their own natural peculiarities of physical organization and mental disposition.'[46] This writer furthermore claimed:

> *Polly Plum was scarcely adequately appreciated when in Auckland, where, as a newspaper contributor, she was pretty well known. Distance apparently lent enchantment to the view, Australia's shores were greener to her than those of New Zealand, and Polly Plum emigrated thereto. As a lecturer she was not a success, and even such topics as woman's rights failed to draw, and the irrepressible Mrs Colclough is fain to appeal to a generous public, and exclaim peccavi. She has found that there are worse places south of the Line than New Zealand, and it is only to be hoped that her experience in other lands will be of practical service to her in the future.*[47]

A writer in the Melbourne *Leader* recounted a practical joke played on a public servant at Mary Ann's expense. The young gentleman had delivered a lecture on behalf of the Australian Natives' Association and the next morning received a scented letter on gilt-edged paper signed Mary Colclough but sent by his fellow office clerks. The letter expressed enthusiastic admiration for the talents of the lecturer, and requested that he at once wait upon her with a view to the formation of a lecturing partnership, and a tour through the Australian colonies, America and Europe. Delighted, the young man arranged two hours' leave on account of urgent private business. On arriving at Mrs Colclough's residence, he was informed that she was ill and could not be disturbed. Insisting he see her immediately on business of the most urgent importance, the servant, awed by his manner, led the way to the room where Mary Ann lay in bed. The writer commented: 'I need not describe the scene that ensued. I only hope that he may never, at any of his political meetings, call forth such angry feelings as he did in his interview "by appointment" with the redresser of woman's wrongs.'[48]

Over the days following the *Argus* editor's endorsement of assistance for

Mary Ann and her children's return passage to New Zealand, a steady number of donations were received and eventually totalled £11/13s. Early in the New Year, Mary Ann wrote to the *Argus* to express her thanks:

> *Sir, – Allow me through the medium of your columns to thank those friends who are kindly endeavouring to facilitate my object to return to New Zealand. So much depends on my doing so if I do go, as soon as possible, that it may not be out of place for me to beg those who will help me, and who have not already done so, to do so as soon as possible. I should have been in New Zealand by now, according to promise, but I found myself utterly unable to accomplish my object by private effort or exertion, so I consented to the painful course of asking help of my friends publicly. In thanking those who have so promptly and kindly responded to the appeal, permit me to add that if it were possible to remain here for another 12 months, and to obtain here the money I can only hope for by returning to New Zealand, I would stay, and at my own cost provide what, much as the belief has cost me, I still believe is a necessity in Melbourne – a cheap respectable nightly shelter for young women. Whilst I admit that for want of funds my scheme failed, the experiment, by bringing many facts to my knowledge, confirmed my belief, and my urgent request to the benevolent ladies of Melbourne is, that they will carry out what I attempted, and I shall feel that all my trials and hardships in Victoria have not been in vain. In this matter I am at issue with* The Argus, *but I do not doubt that a spirit of fairplay will insure admission for this. – Yours, &c.,*
>
> MARY A. COLCLOUGH[49]

As she bid her farewell in the columns of the *Argus*, Mary Ann returned once more to the topic of her first public appearance in Melbourne. Describing mercenary marriage as 'one of the pregnant sources of all the social evils of modern society', she reiterated one final time that the only remedy for such evils was the improvement of women's education and the enlarging of the spheres of women's occupations. Her last public act was to write a letter to the secretary of the Young Women's Association of Christian Workers, encouraging the association to involve itself in 'the task of altering that terrible state of society in which the non-remunerative character of women's industry causes prostitution to be the most lucrative of all women's employments'. To this end, she impressed upon the association the appropriateness of it establishing a home to protect its young and innocent sisters. It was almost as if she was symbolically handing over the reins of the cause to a younger generation.[50]

CHAPTER NINE

A Woman of Neither Means Nor Leisure

With the generous assistance of friends and supporters in Melbourne, Mary Ann and her children left for their return trip to New Zealand on 19 January 1876 aboard the steamer *Otago*. Somewhat disheartened and humbled by her 15-month sojourn in Melbourne, Mary Ann nonetheless looked forward to returning to New Zealand. The 10-day voyage from Melbourne to Lyttelton proved an experience she would remember with fondness. Departing from the Sandridge Railway Pier at 2.30pm, the *Otago* passed the Port Phillip Heads a couple of hours later. The following morning, the steamer passed the Sisters and later that afternoon cleared Wilsons Promontory.

One of the passengers on board the *Otago* was Charles Bright, with whom Mary Ann had several connections. Bright was well known in Australia and New Zealand as a lecturer on subjects connected with religious and social reform, rationalism and spiritualism. Having been a reporter for the Melbourne *Argus* for 20 years as well as a leading contributor to the *Australasian*, the Melbourne *Age*, the *Leader* and other Australian periodicals, he more than knew his way around the newspaper business. Charles Bright was also a member of the committee of the Unitarian Church, and before Martha Turner's appointment to the pastorate had assisted Henry Gyles Turner and several others to deliver Sunday lectures after service. With many friends and interests in common, Mary Ann and Charles engaged in many stimulating intellectual discussions throughout the voyage.

With fine weather and a light westerly wind for most of the trip, the *Otago* arrived at Milford Sound before daylight on 24 January. To the delight of the 109 passengers on board, the shipping agent McMeckan, Blackwood and Co. had included an excursion to Milford as part of the trip, and with 36 hours at their leisure all of those on board alighted and took in the sights. The shipping agent had also arranged fishing and shooting parties. Many among the *Otago's* passengers described Milford Sound and the southwest coast as the most beautiful scenery in the world. At one o'clock the following afternoon, the *Otago* set steam again. Encountering strong southwest winds through Foveaux Strait, the ship arrived in Bluff mid-morning on 26 January. After the usual discharging of passengers and cargo, the *Otago* headed on to Port Chalmers, near Dunedin, arriving there early the next morning. Then it was on to Lyttelton. The *Otago* drew up alongside the wharf there just after nine o'clock on the morning of Saturday 29 January, and the Colclough family disembarked soon after.

In a letter to the *Argus*, Mary Ann wrote enthusiastically of the opportunity to see Milford Sound and thanked the agents for the facilities they provided. She particularly thanked Captain Calder for showing the utmost kindness in giving his passengers every opportunity to see all that was to be seen on such a picturesque voyage. It was, in her words, 'a real pleasure trip' that would never be forgotten. She was also very grateful to the friends who staunchly and kindly stood by her and assisted in her return to New Zealand. She had been determined to come to Christchurch, and although she thought of herself as 'a New Zealand colonist of long standing', this was the first time she had been to Canterbury. Her initial impression was very positive. There seemed to be a universal prosperity, and she was struck with the great hospitality of the people. For the first time in many months, her spirits lifted, and she even wrote to the editor of the *Argus* to offer him her warmest thanks for his role in assisting her passage home.[1]

As news of her return to New Zealand spread, the newspapers in Auckland reported her whereabouts with the usual inaccuracies and prejudices. The *Auckland Star* noted that she had returned 'from her Australian tour in the cause of woman's freedom', while an article in the *Waikato Times* titled 'The Frivolities of Womankind' commented, 'The truth is that women are slaves to the modern Juggernaut, Dress; and Polly Plum, who we see has arrived in Christchurch, would find more useful work in attempting the reform of her own sex in this matter, than in advocating the so-called "rights of women".' On hearing of her arrival in Canterbury, one correspondent wrote to the editor of the *Cross* and bid him 'For goodness sake, sir, do all you can to keep her there, or, at all events, away from Auckland.'[2]

Anxious to obtain work and a steady income as soon as possible, Mary Ann applied for teaching positions as far afield as Wetherstones, a goldmining town near Lawrence in Central Otago. She also advertised her services as a daily governess in either a school or for a private family, giving her contact address as Clontarf House, a private boarding house for gentlemen run by Mrs Creamers in Cashel Street East opposite the Provincial Hotel. Fortuitously, the headmistress position at Rangiora District School just north of Christchurch had become vacant and, at a special meeting convened on 22 March, the school's committee unanimously accepted Mary Ann's application for the position, subject to the approval of the Canterbury Board of Education.

The local newspaper, the *North Canterbury News*, took pleasure in announcing her appointment and noted the numerous testimonials she brought with her, as well as her reputation as a highly respectable and thoroughly efficient teacher. The newspaper also noted that she held a first-class certificate from the Auckland Board of Education and a second-class certificate from the Canterbury Board of Examiners. Picking up on this apparent discrepancy, the editor of the *Cross* commented that it seemed the standard for a teacher's efficiency in Auckland was very much lower than that adopted in Canterbury.[3] Provincial rivalries were sparked, and a few days later the editor found himself eating humble pie:

> We have been requested to state, in reference to a paragraph which
> appeared in the DAILY SOUTHERN CROSS and WEEKLY NEWS, that the
> Auckland certificate which Mrs. Colclough holds, was obtained by the
> Board constituted by the Auckland Education Act, 1857, and not from
> that constituted by the Act of 1872. The fact that Mrs. Colclough holds
> a first-class Auckland certificate, while she obtained but a second-class
> at Canterbury, does not, therefore, show 'that the standard of a teacher's
> efficiency in Auckland is very much lower than that adopted in Canterbury'.
> The standard in Auckland is, we learn, as high as in any other province in
> the colony. In justice to Mrs. Colclough and to the first Auckland Board of
> Education, we would point out that Mrs. Colclough obtained her first-class
> certificate many years ago.[4]

The position of headmistress at the Rangiora school had become vacant due to the resignation of Miss Louisa Kiddell. Although Mary Ann may not have been aware of the circumstances that led to Miss Kiddell's resignation, they were indicative of the precarious nature of the teaching profession for those employed in it during this era. On the basis of an agreement for a two-year teaching position with the Canterbury Board of Education, Louisa Kiddell had travelled from England in 1873. After Louisa completed her two years of service, during which time attendance at the school doubled from 63 to 123, the board informed her that she would now receive a significant reduction in her salary. This, in her view, constituted a violation to her agreement, and on 30 January 1876 she wrote to Minister of Education A.C. Knight to tender her resignation and give the required three-month notice. She also took the matter up with Canterbury's provincial superintendent William Rolleston:

> *You doubtless remember that I, with one or two other School Mistresses, was induced to the service under the Provincial Government for a certain enrolment fixed for two years and which I eventually supposed would be increased after that time if one's services had been satisfactory. I have no reason to imagine that I have failed in the discharge of my duty but I am informed that my salary is to be reduced by one third and as I do not consider such a salary sufficient compensation for the loss of home and friends I have resolved on returning to England immediately and consequently ask you to give me testimony as to my having discharged my duty faithfully (as I am sure I have endeavoured to do) it being necessary to have the evidence of some reliable person in seeking a re-appointment in England.*[5]

The superintendent was sympathetic to her situation and expressed his regret that she had determined to return to England. Acknowledging that she had performed her duties in a conscientious and satisfactory manner and that the government would like to retain her services, he offered to continue her salary at the existing rate for a further three-month period, during which time, he hoped, a suitable position would arise in one of the other public schools. Louisa Kiddell was subsequently offered a teaching position at the Lyttelton Orphanage, which she accepted.

Meanwhile, Mary Ann settled into the recently vacated headmistress's house with the children, now in their early teens. Located between the Waimakariri and Ashley Rivers, Rangiora was 20 miles north of Christchurch. Originally a sawmilling town, it was becoming established as an administrative and commercial centre for the surrounding farms, and its population was growing steadily. Provincial government policy at the time sought to provide schools and teachers in areas where there was a minimum of 25 children of school age. The town already hosted Anglican parish schools for girls and boys. However, as the principal town in the area and given the size of its population, Rangiora had warranted the establishment of a district school.

Opened three years earlier, Rangiora District School consisted of separate boys' and girls' schools located on a four-acre block on King Street South.

Ante-rooms connected the two long, high wooden buildings, while a paling fence bisected the playground. The mistress's house sat next to the gate to the girls' school on Church Street. The school's surroundings were gradually being landscaped with a mixture of pines along the school's north and west boundaries and European deciduous trees along the other sides to form what locals called 'the belt'. The land itself was prone to flooding during winter rains, and this resulted in a lagoon of sorts forming in a gully crossing the grounds. Each time this happened, the road board had to come and drain it.

Many parents at this time were not convinced of the need for education beyond the most basic of lessons that could be provided at home. This attitude, coupled with no compulsion on parents to send their children to school, meant that the number of pupils attending Rangiora District School fluctuated depending on the season and the work needed on neighbouring farms. School hours were fixed, with morning classes from nine o'clock to midday with a short recess at 11 o'clock, and afternoon classes from between one o'clock and three o'clock. As well as her teaching commitments at the school, Mary Ann offered music and dancing lessons from her home on Saturday mornings to supplement her income, which was about half of what she had been entitled to receive when teaching at the Thames.

Despite the decrease in her salary, Mary Ann soon noted the differences between the provincial education systems in Canterbury and Auckland. For years the Auckland Education Board had been impoverished to the detriment of both pupils and teachers and so had been hard pressed to attract well-qualified teachers. In contrast, the schools in Canterbury were admirably appointed and comfortable, the teachers were well and promptly paid, and the general level of qualification of teachers was higher. In fact, contrary to the retraction made by the editor of the *Cross*, a second-class teaching certificate from the Canterbury Board of Education was indeed a guarantee of higher ability and efficiency than a first-class teaching certificate from the Auckland board.

It was not that the educational authorities in Auckland were inferior; rather, it was a combination of circumstances that both attracted and demanded different standards of teaching in each of the provinces. Public education in Auckland, as Mary Ann readily pointed out, was characterised by 'the want of money, poor schools, wretched, miserable buildings, where teachers contract colds, rheumatism, and chronic discontent'. In Canterbury, the education board was committed to training large numbers of teachers, and the provincial government not only paid the pupil-teachers but also paid the head teachers an additional four hours each week for instructing them. Teachers were required to send their pupil-teachers up to the next level of training each year until these young people reached the age of 17, at which time they were ranked as first-, second- or third-class assistants based on their ability. Overall, the situation was, to use modern parlance, one of win-win for head teachers: their duties and responsibilities were lightened, and they gained additional income.[6]

As she settled once again into a new community, Mary Ann joined in the local church and community activities. Early in July, Rangiora's St John's Church held a fundraiser at the Library Institute, and during the evening's entertainment Mary Ann presented a reading from *Nicholas Nickleby* and the always popular Mrs Caudle's curtain lectures. This time, she read 'Mrs Caudle Lectures Caudle on Having Become a Freemason'. Her rendition of Mrs Caudle, the archetype bed-nag who possessed a remarkable talent for turning molehills into mountains, met with cries for an encore from the large audience.

As always, Mary Ann kept a close eye on what was happening nationally and internationally in relation to women's issues – in particular, the education of girls. In October, when reading an Auckland Board of Education report, she learned of a proposal from Miss S. Sophia Stothard to establish a high school for girls that would also be a training school for teachers. Mary Ann's response was a lengthy letter to the *New Zealand Herald* expressing her opposition.

Strongly of the view that if any training school was to be established, it should be done with public money under the auspices of the Auckland Board of Education, Mary Ann drew attention to the relative backwardness of educational provisions in Auckland. Despite the wonderful achievement of her young friend Miss Kate Edger, who had recently attained her bachelor of arts degree, there were many drawbacks and hindrances to women achieving high qualifications in Auckland. Any venture into the establishment of a superior girls' school, let alone a teacher training institution, would likely necessitate advertising for teachers and teacher educators in Canterbury and Otago, or even Australia and England. Granted, Auckland had the advantage of a beautiful climate, 'kindly cordial people ... fair, courteous and excellent educational authorities', and while these might help teachers overlook the troubles caused by bad schools and meddling school committees, in the end, high efficiency and training power would still be very much wanting. Presumably intent on providing an example of what experienced teachers meant for a school, she drew attention to her many years of experience and the higher levels of pupils' achievements at Rangiora School, which she considered remarkable:

I have pupils doing advanced paraphrasing and analysis, just commencing decimal fractions, and with an excellent knowledge of general and New Zealand geography, able to do a map from memory of either the North or the South Island, and any continent, fair historians, and hardly to be puzzled in spelling. Many of these are country girls, some of whom have never been further than Christchurch in their lives. What common school in the Province of Auckland, in a country district especially, can give such an account of the work of a class? The boys do algebra and mathematics, decimals, &c., being nothing. I find the work here splendid – really high class, and little drudgery. A fair share of advanced private teaching whilst in Auckland kept my higher knowledge from rusting, as it would have done had I only had the public schools for a field of work, and I am able to do the work here satisfactorily, and pass my pupils through their examinations either for standard or pupil teacher's certificates.[7]

Wanting the letter to be read, she made a point of signing her name to it. She also asked her old friends in Auckland to forgive her for perhaps stating plain truths too plainly, and insisted that any offence given was unintentional. Surprisingly, there was no flurry of correspondence in the newspapers in response to her letter, but her comments did have some influence. Although making no reference at all to Mary Ann's letter in the *Herald*, the editor of the *Cross* made a passionate plea for more funding for education in Auckland. While complimenting the education board for what they had managed to provide with meagre resources, he pointed out that the superior educational provisions in Canterbury and Otago were largely due to their disproportionate access to their land funds, the money that provincial governments obtained from the sale of Crown land in their respective jurisdictions.[8]

Mary Ann's letter engendered numerous inquiries to the *Herald*. Instead of being published in the newspapers, the inquirers received responses from a recent former employee of the Canterbury Board of Education who was part of the movement to establish the girls' high school and training institution. Deciding to remain anonymous, he identified himself as one 'used to the work of training certificates' and who would 'feign help' other ladies of Auckland wanting to work under government and therefore needing certification. He evidently had access to teachers' records, as he referred directly to 'M.A. Barnes, Blue Book for 1850–51' when citing details of Mary Ann's teaching qualifications. Agreeing that the Auckland Board of Education had done wonders with their 'wretchedly small means', he endorsed much of what Mary Ann had written in her letter. A large number of country schools could be found in Canterbury, and Rangiora District School was considered one of the best, in large part due to the services of its former headmistress, Louisa Kiddell.[9]

Unofficially, there was a hierarchy of schools in Canterbury. The most superior were the borough schools, at which pupils paid one pound per quarter for extra subjects additional to the regular school curriculum, and it was this provision that marked their education as superior to what could be obtained at the best young ladies' private schools. This higher standing was also reflected in the teachers' salaries: whereas a head governess at a private girls' school might receive a salary of £300, the headmistress of a practising school that incorporated the training of pupil-teachers could expect a salary of £350.

When appointing teachers, the Canterbury Board of Education exercised its policy of giving preference to those who had been trained at a recognised training school. All female head teachers of the borough schools were required to hold first-class certificates, and the headmistress of a female training school was further expected to hold high testimonials from a former appointment as principal of a training school. While any teachers who held English certificates would be classified under the Canterbury Board of Education as not needing re-examination, female English first-class teachers had to present themselves for examination in algebra and geometry before they could receive a Canterbury certificate. These two subjects were considered essential, whereas Latin and Greek were deemed desirable but not a necessity. With the exception of algebra and geometry, the level of attainment required for teaching certificates was much lower in Canterbury than in England, and this was why, even though Mary Ann had obtained a third-class English certificate, she gained a second-class appointment with the Canterbury Board of Education, an appointment which, as she had pointed out, was of a higher standing than a first-class Auckland certificate.

Despite Mary Ann's enthusiastic endorsement of the system of education and teacher training in Canterbury, and her 'splendid' experience at Rangiora District School, she had issues with her appointed salary. She wrote to the Rangiora school committee, first reminding them of the increase in numbers attending the girls' school and then requesting an increase in her salary. The committee referred the matter to the board of education along with a recommendation that the board consider the establishment of an infant school.[10]

The matter of equity also came into play with regard to salaries. As 'Rangiora' pointed out in a letter to the Christchurch *Press*, high hopes were held that the newly appointed board of education would address 'the manifest injustice many ladies have suffered' under the old regime:

> *In several cases, in the country districts especially, the mistresses of the girls'*
> *district schools have been expected to assume the whole responsibility, and*
> *discharge the entire duties of the girls' schools for half, or less than half,*
> *the pay received by the masters for the same work in the boys' schools. In*
> *this district, Rangiora, the injustice is very apparent. The girls' school is*
> *numerically as large as the boys', and yet our mistress receives only half what*
> *the master is getting. True, the equality is only of recent date, and due to*
> *the strenuous exertions of our present head mistress; but at any time it was*
> *unfair to pay the mistress only half as much as the master, and under present*
> *circumstances it is most unjust, and I hope amongst the earliest acts of the*
> *new Board, justice will be done in this case.*[11]

The new board was a result of major reorganisation of the education sector throughout the country following the introduction of the Abolition of Provinces Act, which came into effect in November 1876. Under this legislation, central government assumed control of public education. It established a department of education whose role was to oversee the 12 district educational boards that replaced the former provincial boards of education. Board members were chosen from school committees, which were elected, in turn, by householders in each school district. Although many of the changes heralded by this reform of the education system were welcomed, for those working in the field of education the period was a time of both promise and uncertainty.

The provinces may have been replaced by districts, but old loyalties and scars ran deep. Mary Ann's opposition to the proposal of a private teachers' training school in Auckland was a case in point. Sophia Stothard took exception to Mary Ann's stance, which for her amounted to an 'attack on the ladies of Auckland' and was based largely on inaccurate information. Like Mary Ann and their contemporary, Frances Shayle George, Sophia Stothard was committed to the education of girls. Trained in England, she had extensive teaching experience in England and Wales, as well as several years as principal of the Female Training Institution at Bandon in Ireland.

Sophia had come to New Zealand in 1860 with the Church Missionary Society and was posted to a mission station in the Waikato before returning to Auckland, where she offered private classes and acted as a visiting governess for girls. Again, like Mary Ann, she had presented a series of public lectures to ladies, one of which, delivered some years earlier in December 1871, took as its text

'A little real knowledge of science will make a lady a better housekeeper'. Three years earlier she had presented a plan to the Auckland Board of Education for an Auckland Ladies' College and Grammar School for Superior Female Education. The school, as she envisaged it, would teach a comprehensive curriculum, offer up to 30 scholarships and provide a steady supply of female teachers until a separate teacher training institution could be established.

The Auckland board had deferred the proposal amid debates over the use of funds intended for a boys' grammar school. In the interim, Sophia Stothard moved to Christchurch where she had the prospect of being appointed principal of the city's anticipated female training school. In order to gain the necessary Canterbury first-class certificate, she attended university classes in algebra and geometry. She also took a temporary position as headmistress of the girls' section of the West Christchurch Borough School while the female training school was being built, but then returned to Auckland intent again on trying to establish a female teacher training institution there.[12]

The return to teaching did not detract Mary Ann from her interest in following the progress of women more generally. Aware of this, a friend had sent her an issue of a Dunedin newspaper that carried an article about women's choice of employment, and another about the successful establishment of a servants' home. The article on women's employment, published in 'The Ladies' Column', questioned 'whether it is really every wife's duty to attend to all the details of housekeeping before she has a right to use time for work more congenial to her taste?' Why should men, who chose wives who had interests in literature and fine arts, expect them, after marriage, 'to find henceforth their chief pleasure in making bread, pies, jellies, and pickles; in sweeping, dusting, washing, nursing, and sewing'. The other article announced the opening of a new home in Howe Street, near the North Dunedin Presbyterian Church, built at a total cost of around £1200. Largely due to the efforts of the Ladies' Committee of the Dunedin Servants' Home and the procurement of donations from leading local merchants and tradesmen, the home could provide accommodation for 20 general servants.[13]

Having read both articles, Mary Ann wrote to the *Otago Witness* to convey her congratulations to all involved with the servants' home but also to take issue with the sentiments expressed about women's domestic roles:

> *For my own part, while longing to see a larger, more liberal, and enlightened view taken by the law and society at large as to the personal rights and capabilities of women, I regard all the domestic details of woman's*

*undoubted kingdom, 'the home', with profound interest. I do not think any
true woman looks on the details of the home, the nursery, the wardrobe,
and the kitchen with indifference. In a paper about 'Woman's Choice of
Employments', ... it is seriously complained as unreasonable that men
should expect their wives to be domesticated, and speaks of their own free
powers to choose their own employment. But is this so? Are men, as a rule,
any better satisfied with their particular form of drudgery than women are
with domestic work? and can anything, any law, emancipate the mother of
young children from toil, unless she has wealth so as to lift the menial part of
the burden from her shoulders? Nothing. A woman who marries, solemnly
takes on herself the duties of a wife and mother – she accepts the inevitable
domestic burden. Her husband is bound morally to lighten her load of care
and pain by his sympathy, assistance, and a liberal apportionment of his
means. But this is all the best husband can do towards sharing the inevitable
burden, and it is well that young girls entering on life should fairly face this
fact. We are all weak enough and ready enough to find excuses for neglecting
our duties, without being furnished with additional motives for shirking
responsibility in a sentimental depreciation of the work of woman's sphere.
If a man hates baking, let him take care not to open a cook-shop, and if
a woman hates domestic work and all the details of housekeeping, let her
not get married. If she does, and persists in her distaste, she condemns an
unfortunate man to constant discomfort and misery; brings children into the
world to drag through a wretched, disorderly childhood, and to develop into
thriftless men and women; and does her share to perpetuating the immense
'servant difficulty' of the day.*[14]

Mary Ann's words were drawn from personal experience. She had 'escape[d]'
from the drudgery of household work' by her own efforts in paid employment
but she still needed a thorough domestic knowledge to guide and oversee
those she employed to perform various domestic duties. Her main reason for
writing to the *Otago Witness*, though, was in relation to the 'servant difficulty'.
She was still convinced that replacing the 'servant-gal' of the period by a useful,
intelligent, industrious 'help' would be one of the greatest social reforms of
the day. If domestic work was raised in status and if service was accepted as a
conventionally respectable form of employment, the servant difficulty would
cease to exist. In support of her view, she again shared her own experience:

*My children are fast growing up to manhood and womanhood, so my
experience as a housekeeper must be a fairly long one. It is this: After nearly
two years hopeless turmoil with a low class of incapables, certainly only fit*

for the kitchen, and hardly fit for that, I persuaded my husband to allow me to try the plan of taking a poor but respectable girl, treating her as an equal as far as possible. It had its inconveniences, but its many benefits and its undoubted economy (for respectable girls are cheaper, if only because they waste less) far outweighed the drawbacks. Of course, I had no one to abuse, scold, order and lay blame on, nor could I send the girls tripping at a moment's notice, as they came usually from their father's houses to me, their fathers being small farmers, and I being answerable for their safety as if I were their mother. But this seems to me the natural and right way. As a gaol visitor, my knowledge of the awful evils of no control, evenings out, left at a moment's warning, and no place to go to, would appal many who, by a thoughtless and wanton disregard of their duties and responsibilities, leave defenceless girls to their own devices. I have never had a 'servant' since my first trial of respectable 'helps,' and as a rule our domestic machinery has gone smoothly.[15]

Inspired by the work of the Dunedin Ladies' Committee in setting up the Dunedin Servants' Home as a reform institution and a safe shelter, her long letter showed a mellowing of sorts in the way she expressed her views rather than any real change in the views themselves. She was still adamant that a married woman's first duty was to her roles as wife and mother, but her letter revealed a more contemplative and reflective stance in relation to women's choices in how they lived their lives.

In April 1877, six months after Sophia Stothard's letter protesting Mary Ann's accusations about the ladies of Auckland, Frances Shayle George decided to publicly decry Mary Ann's stance in a letter to the editor of the *New Zealand Herald*:

I venture to enquire why Mrs. Colclough should consider herself privileged to attack, as she has done more than once, the teachers and the schools of Auckland, and to indicate the status of female education here. She was herself for a lengthened period a teacher in our provincial district: what did she do for the cause of high class education? What attainments did she contribute to its interests? What finished work did she perform? What accomplished fame, or what distinguished scholars did she leave behind her here to justify her opprobrious epithets, or her uncalled for attacks? To 'question if we have one lady here able to pass a University examination' (I presume she means by this the Oxford and Cambridge University examination) is to insult the ladies of Auckland as a body.[16]

Frances George's lack of esteem for Mary Ann was all too clear. In the past, Mrs George explained, she had, as a matter of principle, generally refrained from publicly expressing her opinion of Mrs Colclough. However, she now felt compelled to describe Mary Ann's actions as 'insufferable impertinence' and 'repugnant' and to condemn her 'eloquent sarcasms' by assigning her to the realms of 'peripatetic philosophers'. Why Frances George waited so long to complain publicly about Mary Ann's criticisms of Auckland teacher training is not known. Mary Ann's response to this personalised outburst has likewise not survived the historical record.[17]

By now Mary Ann had all but retreated from public life. Her teaching responsibilities were very demanding, a situation exacerbated by staffing shortages and conflicts with the school committee. With an average attendance of 119 pupils in the girls' school and only one third-class assistant teacher, she struggled to do justice to her pupils. Her solution was to employ two extra girls to assist her in return for extra tuition. However, one of these two pupil-teachers, Agnes Robinson, left to go to the recently opened Christchurch Normal Training College, and although a young woman named Fanny Stephens replaced her, a serious staffing crisis was in the wings. The boys' school was faring no better. Headmaster Edwin Watkins had recently resigned to take up a position at the training college, and his departure was accompanied by several other resignations. By the time the new master, John George Lawrence Scott, arrived in June 1877, he found himself in charge of 120 boys with assistance from only the former pupil-teacher Edward Jennings, who had recently been promoted to assistant master, and one other pupil-teacher.

The situation at the two schools taxed the school committee, and to add to their concerns, Mary Ann's health began to seriously deteriorate. She had been noticeably overweight for a number of years, and photographs show her looking severely bloated, suggesting that her oedema was worsening. Her heart condition also meant she was prone to extended episodes of exhaustion. But even failing health did not deter her from continuing to take an interest in the causes she had worked so tirelessly for when living in Auckland, in particular the situation of female prisoners at Mount Eden Gaol. A commission of inquiry into the prison had recently completed its work, and Mary Ann eagerly read the commissioners' report. The physical conditions at the prison came in for severe criticism, and the buildings were deemed 'not only unsuitable in construction and faulty in arrangement, but utterly inadequate for even the present number of occupants'. The commissioners attributed most of the fault for the inadequacies to 'the impecunious condition of the late Provincial Government'. The officers in charge were highly commended for their implementation of a reformatory system based on progressive principles. Despite this, the marked absence of efforts for the mental improvement of the prisoners was judged 'a blot on the institution'.[18]

Having read the report carefully, Mary Ann was disappointed, although not surprised, that the commissioners made no specific mention of the state of the female department of the prison. Viewing this omission as indicative of the prison authorities' relative lack of consideration of female prisoners, she wrote: 'Admitted that the women prisoners are usually the worst and most abandoned of their sex, still they are not so much worse than the male prisoners that the latter should monopolise all care and attention.' She had drawn attention to the deficiencies in the female department many times over the years, and it seems that in the five years since she had left Auckland, nothing had changed. Although almost resigned to the fact that 'it is usual, notwithstanding all the talk about chivalry to women, to consider anything for their benefit or comfort as of very little, if of any, importance', she still named it an injustice that the commissioners had not thought it worthwhile to notice how wrong the situation was.[19]

During their inquiry, the commissioners actually had all relevant information in front of them in a report prepared by Edward Mahoney, an architect whom the inquiry had specially commissioned to report on and prepare plans for renovations to Mount Eden Gaol. Mahoney observed:

> *With regard to the female prisoners, they are simply 'huddled' together; there are no cells, and not even a separate room for the sick; so that it may be questioned if proper discipline is possible under such circumstances; certainly no classification is possible. There is a great deal of laundry-work done by the female prisoners for the Hospital, Gaol, and Lunatic Asylum, but the appliances for washing, &c., are sadly deficient, and of the most primitive character. If proper washing and laundry appliances were furnished, this department might be made more remunerative. If the whole of this prison or new department were set aside for females only, by a small expenditure work-rooms, cells, infirmary, and classification could be established, which would meet the wants for some years to come.[20]*

If Mary Ann had known the commissioners had this report at hand during their investigation, she would likely have been far more condemning of them.

The passage of the new Education Act 1877 had brought the issue of religious instruction in schools back into public view, and debates had engaged the readers of the Christchurch *Press* for several months. Under the Act, education was purely secular, which meant there was no obligation on a school to include religious instruction. But at the local level, the Venerable Archdeacon Dudley urged the necessity of continued religious instruction within the school outside regular school hours. Mary Ann agreed. The final decision over the matter with respect to her school, however, lay with its committee, which had jurisdiction over the use of the school's buildings. Eventually, the committee resolved that the schoolrooms could be held for a scripture lesson and prayer between 9.00am and 9.30am, and that the ordinary school hours should be adjusted to 9.40am to noon and 1.00pm to 3.00pm. Although the committee approved the change in timetable, it warned Mary Ann that this arrangement was actually illegal. It did not take long for problems to emerge. The majority of parents supported religious instruction but most children did not arrive at school until after 9.30am. In time, Mary Ann and the committee agreed on a compromise solution wherein classes began at the required time of 9.00am and ministers from the local churches could provide Bible readings and scripture before lunch for several days a week.

By the time the new school year was about to get underway in 1878, the girls' school was on the verge of collapse. The inspector's report for 1877 attested to the seriousness of the situation. Although neither the girls' nor the boys' school had operated to an acceptable standard of efficiency, only 19 per cent of pupils in the girls' school passed the standards in which they were presented compared to 64 per cent of the boys. Some allowance was made for the irregular attendance in the girls' school, but the inspector, Mr Restell, was highly critical of what he considered a waste of teaching power. If this power, he wrote, had been more judiciously shared between the two schools, it would have secured more equitable results. Although not a supporter of segregated schools, Inspector Restell considered the education of the girls had been retarded by sacrificing them to inferior teaching for the sake of separating the sexes. What was needed was 'perfect discipline and efficient supervision'; this, he claimed, could only be achieved within a mixed system. He therefore strongly advocated subdivision of the school into upper, lower and infant levels, with mixed classes at each level in order to make better use of the teaching staff.[21]

The receipt of such a critical report on her areas of responsibility led Mary Ann to write to the school committee urging a second inspection of the school, but her request was eclipsed by the intense public debate on the inspector's recommendation to 'mix' the schools. The main opposition came from the Venerable Archdeacon Dudley, who thought it would be injurious for the girls to be taught alongside the boys. He personally knew of instances in which a great deal of harm had been done within mixed schools. Others who were against the proposal threatened to withdraw their children if the school was combined. Several parents organised a petition and collected over 80 signatures in support of a public meeting to protest against any changes to the school's organisation.

By the time of the subsequent meeting of the school committee, clear divisions were emerging. Several further public meetings to protest against making the school co-educational attracted large attendances. Finally, a resolution that the district school teach the boys and girls separately was passed with a large majority. Despite this resolution, the schools did integrate, and the new infant school opened within weeks with a roll of about 60. The school committee held off advertising for an infant mistress, and for the first few months Mary Ann ran it with the assistance of her pupil-teachers. But once again her health declined, this time to the extent that she was granted leave. Seriously ill, she never returned to her teaching post at Rangiora.

When her health improved sufficiently, Mary Ann decided to return to private teaching. In May 1878 she advertised a new private boarding and day school for young ladies at Ashley House, on Ashley Road in Rangiora. Surrounded by pleasant playgrounds, Ashely House stood on a rise near the railway station. The house itself was commodious, having recently been enlarged and fitted up at considerable expense. Mary Ann's intention for the school was to have it prepare young ladies for scholarships and pupil-teacher examinations. To this end, professors from Christchurch would come to the school to offer tuition in particular subjects, such as music, for which special terms would apply. As principal of the school, Mary Ann would provide full details on application. The school operated for two terms, but was not financially viable. With no option but to return to the public system, she answered an advertisement in January 1879 for the position of headmistress of Upper Heathcote School.

Located at Halswell Road on the banks of the Heathcote River on the outskirts of Christchurch, Upper Heathcote School had opened in 1872. Mary Ann's position as head female teacher afforded her an annual salary of £130 and an additional lodging allowance of £20. Mr William G. Wray as head male teacher had an annual salary of £230. Assistant teacher Mrs Julia Langbridge received £50 per year. At the beginning of the school year, the roll stood at 112. By the end of 1879, it had averaged out across the year at 97 pupils, a welcome increase from the average attendance for the previous year of 82.

The day after Mary Ann took up her new position, the annual general meeting of householders for the district took place in the schoolrooms. One of the matters of concern was the ongoing irregular attendance of pupils. The school committee expressed its earnest hope that parents would refrain from withdrawing the children from school for what the committee members deemed trifling reasons. The committee hoped that awarding prizes to those who passed the inspector's examination would go some way toward addressing this problem. The inspector's report on examinations for the previous year had been encouraging, as the percentage of passes was unusually high; with only one exception, those who had failed their examinations had such low attendance rates that a lack of academic success could only be expected.

The main difficulty the committee identified, however, was the fact that the school budget did not sufficiently allow for incidental expenses. Most of the allowance for these items went on the caretaker's modest salary, leaving insufficient money to pay for the fuel for the three large fireplaces, let alone stationery, ink, pens, small repairs and the school prizes, even though the government grant for the latter was supplemented by subscriptions. The amount allocated to incidentals depended on the average attendance rates, and this circumstance was put to the meeting of householders as another reason for parents to send their children to school more regularly.

Now 43 years of age, Mary Ann had retired from public life, but there were clear indications that Polly Plum was entering the realms of folklore. In the latter months of 1879, parliament debated the Qualification of Electors Bill, and in what one reporter described as a 'legislative blunder', the Minister of Education Mr John Ballance moved that the word 'man' be replaced by 'person', effectively affirming the principle of female franchise. In his coverage, the reporter for the *Manawatu Herald* noted: 'Persons of the class of "Polly Plum" (of Auckland notoriety) have occasionally arisen, agitating in New Zealand the "Women's Rights" idea, but they have been regarded and treated with contempt by both sexes.'[22]

In a similar vein, in October the following year, Mr J.B. Whyte, the Member of the House of Representatives for Cambridge, referred to Polly Plum at a banquet held in his honour. Offering a reason for why he had voted against the interestingly named Deceased Wife's Sister Bill, Whyte said he was against giving women the vote not because he considered them unqualified mentally to exercise it, but because he was sure that if women gained the franchise, they would also have to be allowed to stand as members of parliament, and that 'would result in great inconvenience'. He added: 'If we could ensure that only those possessed of youth, beauty, and modesty would find seats in the House it might be all right, but it would, I fear, be found that the class which would be returned would consist of Dr Mary Walkers, Polly Plums, and other objectionable females of that sort.'[23]

As another teaching year came to a close, changes were afoot at Upper Heathcote School. Julia Langbridge, who taught the infants, tendered her resignation on the grounds that she could not live on her salary. Anxious that she not leave the school, the committee suggested increasing her salary even though she had not passed her teacher's examination. A deputation to the Canterbury Board of Education raised this and several other issues related to the organisation of instruction at the school, but some months passed before the appointment of a pupil-teacher resolved the situation.

When or why Mary Ann left her position at Upper Heathcote School (which had been renamed Spreydon School by July 1880) is unclear. She may have disagreed with the recommendation of the school committee to increase Julia Langbridge's salary given that she was not a qualified teacher. A more likely reason is that she had suffered another bout of ill health. When she did resume teaching at the end of 1880, it was at the lower level of assistant teacher at Papanui School on an annual salary of £100/10s. Taking residence at Ivy Lodge on the North Town Belt of Papanui, Mary Ann joined a teaching staff of five. Senior to her was Mr Edwin Morgan, the headmaster, and Mrs Jane M. Jennings, the headmistress. Miss Derrett, as infant mistress, and two pupil-teachers made up the rest of the teaching staff. During the year, the school's roll had risen from 194 to 235 pupils.

Papanui School came to public attention during 1880 but for all the wrong reasons. Mr Courtney Nedwill, the medical officer for the Christchurch District Local Board of Health, had just completed his rounds of inspection of the government schools in and around Christchurch, and his report was far from complimentary. Some of the schools had too few schoolrooms; in the worst cases, teachers were conducting their classes in passageways. Ventilation was a decided concern, cloakrooms were generally too small, and most were too close to the classrooms and inadequately heated to dry the children's clothes when needed. The greatest concern, though, was that the toilets in nearly all of the schools were either absent or not supplied with water:

> *The urinals are at some schools either not concreted, not flushed with water, or not properly drained. The closets have in no instance received that attention which, judged of from a sanitary point of view, they deserve. At all the schools they are without exception deficient in respect to ventilation, not one of them being ventilated from beneath the seat by a shaft running up above the roof. In some there is no concrete on the floors; in others*

there are leaky pans; while at some of the schools the closets are without
doors, and the very objectionable practice prevails of having two seats in
one compartment. The pans as a rule are not emptied oftener than once
a week, and there is no attempt made at any of them to use earth. At the
Papanui school the disgusting system of cesspits is still in force, and should be
forthwith discontinued.[24]

The chairman of the board of health drew particular attention to the sanitary condition at Papanui, describing it as the worst within the entire district. In January 1881, just as the new school year was about to start, the health board's medical officer reported an outbreak of diphtheria at Papanui that appeared to have spread from the school. Six families had contracted the disease, and there had been two deaths. Children from five of these families were attending Papanui School. He urged that the cesspits at the school be abolished and the urinal concreted over, lest that part of Papanui become 'a hot-bed of disease'. The problems were exacerbated by the regular overflow of the Heathcote River onto the school grounds due to an inadequate culvert at the flourmill dam on the opposite side of Lincoln Road. The whole school, which suffered from overcrowding, needed to be thoroughly disinfected and all of the woodwork thoroughly scrubbed. The chairman of the school committee wrote to the health board seeking advice on the best means of disinfecting the school. The board, in turn, referred the matter to its chairman and also the Inspector of Nuisances, who was authorised to act in such a matter.

The diphtheria outbreak in Papanui continued throughout 1881 and by year's end had claimed six lives. In his 1881 annual report to the local board of health, Mr Nedwill commented that it was no surprise that the disease had retained its hold on the district for so long because the naturally swampy land was saturated with filth and house slops, all of which had found their way into the dirty, stagnant roadside ditches.[25]

Those attending the meeting for the annual school elections, held the week after release of the medical officer's report, heard a mix of good and bad news. The good news was that the board of education had agreed to an additional room for infant classes. The bad news was that the school would not be permitted to reopen until completion of the renovations and cleansing stipulated by the health board. In addition, and much to the school committee's regret, the infant mistress, Miss Derrett, who had been with the school for eight years, had tendered her resignation. Of the four applications received for her replacement, Mary Ann was successful in gaining the appointment.

Although minimal improvements had been made in order for the school to reopen, a deputation from the school met with the board of education early in February to report the need for new toilets and to advise that the interior of the school buildings would have to be altered to accommodate the extra classroom. The deputation left with little assurance that either matter would be attended to with any haste, and indeed the wheels of the education bureaucracy were all too slow to turn. In May another deputation from the school committee met with the board to report that the lighting, ventilation and drainage were still defective, but the board did not commit to any further improvements.

In June, a parent made a serious complaint against Mary Ann. The minutes of the school committee meeting recorded Mr Poninghaus telling the committee that the infant mistress had severely beaten his daughter Charlotte. The committee decided that its chairman, Mr Kruse, should inquire into the facts of the case and report back to the next meeting. Although the outcome of the complaint was not recorded in the minutes of subsequent meetings of the school committee, it seems that it was not upheld, especially given that after Mrs Jennings, the headmistress, resigned, a special meeting of the school committee unanimously appointed Mary Ann over the other four applicants. Committee members obviously held her in high regard.[26]

By now, Mary Ann's children were becoming independent adults. Lulu, an accomplished, elegant young lady, was approaching her twentieth birthday. In May 1882 she attended the Mayor's Ball in the Christchurch Art Gallery, which hosted all the rank, wealth and fashion of Christchurch. Recognised while dancing with Mr Thomas S. Weston, the recent judge of Westland and now Member of the House of Representatives for Inangahua, Lulu was described as a tall, slender girl, wearing pink with crimson chrysanthemums. William, a strapping young 18-year-old, had found employment as an assistant at the Canterbury Museum in January 1879. His first year there turned out to be rather exciting, as he was called to testify in court on a series of robberies at the museum. William was also an active member of the Volunteer Rifle Brigade, and had attained the rank of lieutenant.[27]

Around this time Mary Ann wrote a lengthy 'Letter from Canterbury' to the editor of the Auckland *Evening Star*, in which she gave a snapshot of life in New Zealand. Having just come through what many regarded as a very hard winter, she commented that despite people saying there had been much distress, all her years of living in New Zealand had convinced her that very few people in New Zealand knew what true deprivation was:

The 'poor working man' clamours very loudly and suffers very little. It seems hard to understand on what theory he claims to be the only party in a state who should be exempted from suffering loss in hard times, why labour should not come down in price with everything else I fail to see. There they grown [sic] at taking low wages and certainly 4d per day seems very little and that is all some are getting. But a family could live on that sum at the present price of provisions here. Mutton can be got for 1/6 the fore quarter and I hear that in markets on Saturday night half a sheep may be bought for 2/6, bread is to be got for 4d the 5lb loaf, potatoes of excellent quality are 3/- a bag, butter is 10d a lb, eggs 1/- a dozen, a house may be got for 6/- per week and so I fail to see how anyone who is decently thrifty need 'starve' on low wages. I maintain that food and rent for a family may be got for £1.0.0 per week, plain and scant doubtless but involving nothing like the deprivation that thousands of poor working people suffer in England and to that man or woman who does not take the pure beautiful air, the bright sky and the little cottage to oneself into account in summing up the advantages of New Zealand as against England I have nothing to say.[28]

Sounding more like the Polly Plum of earlier days, she rebuked the emigration agents who led people to hope that coming to New Zealand would mean certain wealth and prosperity as having a lot to answer for. However, those who believed the propaganda were also to blame; after all, '[I]f the labouring class are to enjoy great wealth who is to do the work?' She knew a Cornish woman who had immigrated to New Zealand some months earlier and had done well because she had sense and was willing to work. Taking in washing and sending her daughters out to work in domestic service meant she could keep a home for her sons. This friend had spoken of others on the voyage over who, despite being penniless, helpless and thriftless, talked of keeping a shop, owning a farm and giving their children a sovereign for their birthdays:

Now with all this folly disappointment was inevitable. I have not one bit of patience with them. They waste and squander when they have money and groan and grumble and blame everybody when they have not. Poor gentlefolks who have to keep up that wretched force 'an appearance' in order to earn anything at all and have to stint their table often of necessaries in order to keep up their position are the ones who really suffer and they are often people who really were better off at home and are educated and sensitive.[29]

Mary Ann also wrote in her letter on a topic long close to her heart – the dearth of good reading in the newspapers. Although numerous, the Christchurch newspapers were 'generally very dry'. The *Lyttelton Times* and the *Star* were the most generous in providing news of art, literature and fashion, but the correspondence was not as extensive or as interesting as in Victoria or Auckland: '… newspaper discussion is much checked and curbed and the social questions of the day are not ventilated in the same way'. Matters of particular interest to the ladies were passed over in favour of whole columns on the Ligurian bee, wheat blight, stock breeding and the like. True to her educated, respectable, middle-class English sensibilities, she remarked:

> *I don't lavish at that as the country is agricultural but it is rather ungallant to leave news interesting to ladies quite out in the cold. In Auckland and Melbourne ladies make a great rush for the paper after a grand ball sometimes to see their own names in print sometimes to read of the dresses of the Grandées and celebrities. They don't hurry after the paper here. The ball is dismissed in three lines and two columns are taken up with 'Pig Feeding' or 'Twine Binders'. Just pity us and if ever you get a chance start a real smart paper amongst us.*[30]

She also mentioned the inadequate salaries of teachers and the tendency for those in the teaching profession not to speak out critically about them. She was sympathetic to the masters: despite their salaries being modest in relation to those of men in other professions, they had to be respectably dressed and had many worries and responsibilities. The salaries of the mistresses, however, were 'terrible'.

Knowing that one means of enabling teachers to gain an increase in their salary was through a formal review of their grade as a teacher, Mary Ann wrote to the school committee in August requesting support for her application to the board of education for a review of her teacher's certificate, from grade D2 to grade D1. When the committee put her request to the vote, its members unanimously agreed that they should 'heartily support' the application. The board of education appears not to have been of similar mind, as there is no evidence in its official records of a change in Mary Ann's certificate grade.[31]

While teaching at Rangiora, Mary Ann had spoken proudly of the high level of achievement of her students. Throughout her teaching career, she had done as much as she could to extend her pupils both academically and in what she considered to be important life skills. However, there were those associated with Papanui District School who thought that she was giving some of the children home lessons 'far in advance of their capacity', and their concern was officially brought to her attention. There was an implication that her attempts to extend her pupils were having the opposite effect – that of retarding their progress.[32]

In July 1883 the school inspector's report noted a lack of achievement, described in very severe terms as 'condemnation' of the Standard III class. Part of the issue was Mary Ann's deteriorating health, which had again reached a point where it was affecting her teaching. The headmaster, Thomas May, reported his opinions on this to the school committee, and after considerable discussion the committee unanimously decided to dispense with Mrs Colclough's services. The committee recorded its decision in the minutes of the meeting: 'That in view of Mrs Colclough's state of health, the Inspector's unsatisfactory report upon Standard III and the head Master's report thereon this Committee feels compelled – and with very much regret – to request her to resign her position in the school.' The minutes also recorded the committee's decision that should Mrs Colclough fail or decline to resign her position in the school 'that the Chairman request the board of Education to dispense with her services'.[33]

As had been the case when she left her position at Rangiora District School five years earlier, Mary Ann spent several months recuperating from her latest bout of ill health. When she felt sufficiently recovered, she decided to return to private teaching again. In January 1884 she advertised the reopening of her school at Inglewood on Papanui Road, where she would hold classes in her home between 11 am and 3 pm daily except Saturdays. By the second term she had reduced her teaching days to Mondays and Tuesdays only, an arrangement she continued through to the end of the year.

Perhaps inspired by her memorable stopover at Milford Sound nine years earlier during her return to New Zealand from Melbourne, she decided to take a summer break in Picton. She arrived there on the steamship *Hawea* on 8 January, but just one week later she had an accident in the early hours of the morning in her room. Although she didn't fall, she suffered a sudden wrenching movement and fractured her right arm and right leg. Her arm was set immediately, but severe inflammation of her leg meant it could not be set for several days. Her daughter Lulu travelled to Picton from Christchurch on the *Hawea* to be with her mother, arriving on 19 January. Mary Ann was said to have never recovered from the shock to her nervous system, and on 7 March 1885, at the age of 49, she died. Her death certificate recorded the cause of death as ichorrhemia – a sepsis or severe form of inflammation resulting from infection. She was buried three days later in an unmarked grave at Picton Cemetery.[34]

Brief tributes appeared in some newspapers, acknowledging her as a clever contributor to the Auckland press and a valued contributor to the *Thames Star*. The *New Zealand Herald* noted simply that 'her death will be regretted by many who knew her in the olden times'.[35] The only obituary, of sorts, was from the writer of the 'Random Shots' column in the *Auckland Star*:

> *Poor 'Polly Plum' has gone the way of all flesh – and she has had more than her share of flesh, as well as of impulsive good nature. Like many another philosopher, she preached better than she could practise, and her wit was more useful in satirising, in a thoroughly non-malicious way, the foibles of others than in preserving herself from being fooled. One of her weaknesses was a belief that she had a mission to save her fallen sisterhood, and on one occasion she took into her own house and coddled up two of the choicest specimens of the incorrigible class. Perceiving that with all her wisdom 'Polly' was very gullible, they suffered her with Munchausen stories about the names and characters of their patrons. Of course, they ended in selling her grievously, and then turned round ungraciously and laughed at her gullibility. A glimpse into the private lives of some of our literary heroes has shattered many an idol; 'Polly Plum' was not a literary genius, but she was a clever, pleasant writer, and had a local fame. Personal knowledge of her, however, enhanced rather than detracted from the pleasure afforded by her literary work. She was every inch a true woman, with all a woman's great-hearted sympathies, and a full share of those foibles which accompany an impulsive, passionate nature.*[36]

EPILOGUE

ᎠᏔ

A Chequered Life

A t the age of 34, Mary Ann Colclough referred to her life as 'chequered'. It was an apt description. During her childhood, she experienced security and love as well as 'dread, sorrow, and disappointment'. As an asylum visitor in London in her young adult years, she witnessed helplessness and destitution. At the age of 21, she faced the loneliness and dislocation that accompanied her decision to leave England, heightened by the accidental death of her brother during the passage to New Zealand. Throughout her marriage she experienced the burden of having to assume the role of breadwinner and the loss of face when debt collectors repossessed items to service her husband's debts. At the age of 31, she was left a widow with full financial responsibility for her two preschool children. Although she was well connected and well respected in many circles, her public advocacy of women's rights brought with it public criticism and censure. Accusations of plagiarism and martyrdom, continual misrepresentation and maligning of her political views, and ongoing financial insecurity and eventual bankruptcy all took a toll, and her later years were dogged with ill health.[1]

When introducing her lecture on 'The Subjection of Woman' at Otahuhu in 1871, Reverend John Macky described Mary Ann as exceptional. He spoke publicly of her intelligence and abilities as a teacher of young children, but in deference to social etiquette he did not elaborate on her many private attributes and 'gentle and womanly traits of character', which were not evident in her public persona as an advocate of women. Her words and deeds confirm that she had a big heart and a generous spirit. She was persuasive and sensitive as well as forthright. She was both a pragmatist and an idealist. She was persistent and certainly not easily dissuaded in her commitment to the cause of women. She called a spade a spade and did not suffer fools. Personal integrity was paramount, and she had a strongly developed sense of moral justice. Her advocacy for women did not stop at simply cataloguing women's rights and men's wrongs; she proffered reasoned and well-argued analyses of the causes of social injustices and suggested practical solutions for change. She could also be rather impetuous, throwing herself into some new scheme or project without necessarily thinking through the practicalities and often stepping on others' toes and ruffling feathers. She was canny in her use of the news media, and it could be said that modesty was not one of her strong points. There is also evidence of what would now be considered a class-based arrogance with more than a hint of racism.

There are definite gaps and silences in relation to knowledge of her personal life. It is difficult to gauge her relationship with her husband beyond her fulfilling her wifely duty, and very little is known of her interactions with her children. There is no record of her contact with family back in England after she immigrated to New Zealand. She had many allies and a trusted circle of supporters, but extant sources provide few insights into close personal friendships. Her very public persona as Polly Plum was countered by a very private personal life.

As an educationalist, Mary Ann Colclough made a difference to countless women and their daughters. In the 1860s and 1870s, she was widely known for her innovative teaching methods and her commitment to providing girls with a thorough education to enable them to face the uncertainties of adult life. Whether through kind words of encouragement to women serving prison sentences, accompanying them to court hearings, receiving them in her home upon their release, looking after their children in her own home, or assisting them in gaining employment, she also made a difference to the lives of many individual women who found themselves on the wrong side of the law. Most of the women she helped remain nameless.

A notable exception was Ellen Ellis. Encouraged by the writings of 'Polly Plum', Ellen worked hard to overcome the stigma of the label 'incorrigible dunce' that she bore while growing up. Through a determined programme of self-education, she made her first tentative steps into the public arena by writing letters to the newspapers, under the anonymity of a pen name, to express her views on women's position. Just over a decade later, she was sufficiently confident to step up as a leader in the nascent women's movement in Auckland, organising a series of meetings for women to protest the contagious diseases legislation. In 1882 Ellen also wrote what is now considered to be the first overtly feminist novel published in New Zealand, *Everything is Possible to Will*. We cannot know how many others there were like her or like 'poor Emma', who began demanding her rights after reading Polly Plum's articles and letters and attending Mary Ann Colclough's lectures. However, the tributes accorded to Mary Ann's social reform work when she left Auckland confirm that she made a difference in many individual lives.[2]

Fifteen years after her death and more than 25 years after she left Auckland, she was compared to what were then considered more radical contemporary feminist voices:

> As showing how times change, and women change with them … it may be stated that thirty years ago, when 'Polly Plum' (Mrs Colclough) first took up the crusade for 'women's rights' in Auckland, she was positively boycotted and socially ostracised by many of her sex. Poor Polly did not scruple to aver that women ought to seek a nobler and more useful sphere than 'suckling fools and chronicling small beer', but she was at one crying in the wilderness, and went down to her grave a blighted woman. Today Polly would be 'a hide-bound Conservative', who would be told by the sybil of the National Council of Women that 'drift' was better than stagnation, and not to be afraid of Mrs Grundy![3]

But Mary Ann Colclough never settled for drift. When the newspaper debates on women's rights descended into tiresome reiteration, she put down her pen and took to the public platform. When support was rekindled for the reopening of the Auckland Women's Home, she turned her attention to the needs of discharged female prisoners. When women approached her for assistance in finding domestic servant positions, she set up a private servants' agency. When she saw the need in Melbourne for safe, affordable accommodation for young working women on low incomes, she set up a lodging house for women. An insightful visionary reformer, passionate and totally committed to the cause of women, Mary Ann Colclough was, in word and deed, a firm and earnest woman's advocate.

APPENDIX

Poems

'Cause Celebre': Polly Plum vs Jemmy Jenkins

Written by Diana Damson, 'Cause Celebre' was occasioned by relatively light-hearted newspaper banter between Polly Plum and correspondent Jemmy Jenkins during mid-1869. The flurry of letters published in the *Daily Southern Cross* was triggered by an article titled 'Public Men', in which Polly Plum criticised what she called officialism – the over-abundance of red tape, the propensity for nepotism in politics, and public men who were more inclined to line their own pockets than ensure public resources were used responsibly and for the good of those most in need.

> There was a Plum who once did try
> To leave its pudding and its pie,
> To flutter in the public sight
> And little articles to write.
> There was a boy who took the Plum
> Between his finger and his thumb,
> And said, 'Oh dear, how silly 'tis
> When Plums begin to preach and quiz;
> Stay in your pudding or your pie
> And let us boys the preaching try.'

(Diana Damson, *Daily Southern Cross*, 2 July 1869, p. 4)

Three weeks later, 'Fanny Fast' gave her rendition of the battle of the sexes as represented by Polly Plum and Jemmy Jenkins:

Mr. Jemmy Jenkins wrote
Unto Miss Polly Plum,
And said 'Now don't be frightened, dear,
I am no Fee-fo-fum.

''Tis true, I am a posy card,
But then I am a man,
And you never can come up to me,
So do the best you can.'

Now Polly, she got cheeky,
As any woman would,
And told him mighty curtly
She thought he was 'no good'.

'No good!' says Jemmy, quite alarmed,
'Oh, Polly, say not so.
No good! why that can never be;
Why I'm a man, you know.'

'I don't care if you are,' says Polly,
(Presuming feminine),
'You're a posy old buffer for all that,
And I'll not write you another line.'

Write articles yourself, old boy,
And let the people judge
Which is the writer of the two,
Your plea is now all fudge.

(Fanny Fast, *Daily Southern Cross*, 24 July 1869, p. 6)

Withered Fern Leaves (1)

In an article titled 'A Good Husband', Polly Plum attributed a long list of a husband's failings to the proverbial Mr. John Smith. This poem, written by John Smith, appeared several weeks later.

Of all the social bores one meets in print I now insist,
The worst is she who sets herself up for a moralist.
Of course she is immaculate, and with her virtuous pen
She tries to call attention to us wretched brutes of men.
We're stubborn, heartless, and we lead objectionable lives;
And are a burden and a grief unto our charming wives,
We don't deserve to have such faithful creatures pet and love us.
The female satirist declares they are a cut above us.
I've noticed in the SOUTHERN CROSS with grief and great concern
That we are catching it from a colonial 'Fanny Fern',
Who signs herself as 'Polly Plum' and jerks her mighty pen
To walk into the follies and shortcomings of the men;
She talks about the sorrow of our dear beloved Queen,
Who for so many lingering years all in the dumps has been,
And though the British public think 'tis time she were more jolly,
Her sadness so prolonged is not a problem unto Polly,
Who says Prince Albert was a man you don't see every day,
And, as a husband, always had a fascinating way.
For two-and-twenty years he met his spouse with daily smile,
And in paying her attention his time he would beguile,
And Polly says no wonder that his memory she cherishes
When the best and sweetest husband ever dreamed about thus perishes.
And cruel Polly lashes out at me (my name's John Smith),
And like a doughty Amazon, she wires into me forthwith,
When my infant son was born she says I didn't stay at home,
But to my club so selfishly of an evening I would roam.
She hints I never fed my infant son and heir with pap,
Nor dandied with a father's joy the brat upon my lap,
I kept away from him t'escape that dreadful lingering curse
Embodied in the person of a fussy monthly nurse.
And Polly hints that if I were to leave the hooks tomorrow,
My wife would not evince a corresponding queenly sorrow.
She throws Prince Albert in my teeth, who she says all his life
Was meek, and mild, and never had a shindy with his wife;

But let me now inquire of this colonial fern-leaf Polly
What reason did he ever have to be otherwise than jolly?
Can it be wondered at now that a far from wealthy Prince
Should for a mighty Queen a life of gratitude evince,
Who raised him from obscurity and offered him her hand,
And brought him into notice in that highly-favoured land?
Did ever he come home to dine upon a washing-day
To nothing but cold mutton, or a bread-and-cheese display?
Did he, my clever Polly, ever hungry homeward run
And hear the dismal tidings that the dinner wasn't done?
Or ever have to put up with bad cooks (domestic hags)
Who burnt a joint to cinders and convert it into rags?
Or, when dressing for an evening party, have his feelings hurt
By finding he was dreadful short of buttons to his shirt?
When the infant Alfred squalled at night, does Polly now presume
To say the illustrious German walked him up and down the room?
Had he no private chamber where he'd quietly retire
When Albert Edward woke up and annoyed his sleepy sire?
I've read the 'Memoirs' also, and like Polly waded in,
But nowhere does it ever say that he was short of tin,
And like a poor mechanic who is forced to earn his grub
While his amiable spouse is busy washing at the tub.
We do not read Victoria ever used to gad about
Or if she couldn't have her way began to sulk and pout.
Put me, John Smith, into his shoes, and give me lots of money,
With a great Queen for a consort, I would be as mild as honey.
I'd never wish to go out of an evening to my club,
Or quarrel with my dinner when I had the best of grub.
To play a game of billiards do you think I want to roam,
With a Thurston table, cues, and balls awaiting me at home?
With other females why should I the time wish to beguile,
While lovely maids of honour on the Royal boss would smile!
With heaps of nurses, should I spurn my matrimonial fruits,
Or come home tight, and go to bed all in my regal boots!
Oh, bless you, not a bit of it, my moralising Polly,
I'd be the best of husbands then, so kind and always jolly.
But often you would feel like me, so cross, and have the blues
Were you transferred from ladies' kid to my plebeian shoes.
So, Polly Plum, give over now these hard thrusts at the men,
Nor poke your fun at us, my dear, with your satiric pen,

And let us have no more attempts to write like Fanny Fern,
Your moralising, to my mind, is not so good as 'hern'.
And desiccate, in other words, dry up, my dear, forthwith,
And allow me, Polly, to remain – Yours faithfully,
John Smith

(John Smith, *Daily Southern Cross*, 2 September 1869, p. 5)

Withered Fern Leaves (2)

A week after John Smith's poem 'Withered Fern Leaves' appeared, Jim Browne
published his poetic response to Polly Plum's article under the same title.

Alas! Poor Fanny Fern,
Little did you know
When you gave us something really good
She would walk into your shoe.
My friend John Smith has had his say,
And I'd like to have mine:
I's like to give the reasons why
I make this little rhyme.
First to begin: My name is Jim Browne,
As everybody knows;
And shouldn't name it has she not
Trodden upon my toes.
My other friends, the Joneses,
The Robinsons likewise,
Are as pretty names as any those
That begin with Ps or Ts.
P for Poll – Oh what a name!
I vow 'tis very shocking
That she should put herself right up
For a bug-bear pert blue-stocking.
Yes, they are by Goshen,
Yes, they are by glum;
They are as pretty names, I vow,
As that of Polly Plum.
She writes about her Majesty;
She praises about 'Our Life',

As if she knew the reason why
The Queen was a loving wife.
She never had to dress her kids,
Nor ever turned a mangle;
And therefore when her Prince came home
She couldn't with him wrangle.
She never had to work for life,
In sunshine or in rain;
But the Duke who was out here well knew
That quartz was on the brain.
Her wants are well provided for
By the nation thick and thin;
And while she rules the scepter
John Bull will find the tin.
Her hands were never wrinkled
By washing in a tub,
Nor had she e'er, like our poor wives,
To battle for her grub.
She never let you know her mind,
Or why she e'er looked glum
Whene'er her Prince had greeted her.
Be silent, Polly Plum.
The Queen is but a mortal,
And subject to the ills
That flesh and blood is heir to,
For that's what Nature wills.
Poll, do not aught extenuate
Nor set down aught in malice;
There's a skeleton in every house,
And why not in a palace?
Now, Polly Plum, be ruled by me;
Don't give yourself such airs;
Nor be prying into drawing-rooms,
Nor peeping from the stairs,
To see what you can gather up
'Bout other folk's affairs.
'Twould be indeed no wonder
While we remain mere mutes
That such a thing as Polly Plum
Should call us nasty brutes.

When next you do attempt to mount
Your literary hobby,
I'll introduce you in the street
To a nice detective bobby.
I will, I do assure you,
Or my name is not Jim Browne:
He'll tell you of all the scandal
That's taking place in town.
He'll tell you of all the comings in,
And all the goings out
Of people going to masquerades,
To balls, and plays, and rout.
He'll tell you when Jim Browne goes out
To his club to dine at night:
That when he goes home to his spouse
He goes home very tight.
Your fragments, Poll, are very dry,
Your waifs and strays are musty;
They're like the hinge of a rotten door;
They're worn-out, and rusty.
With Nature you cannot converse
Nor to modest flowers talk
When you take your evening rambles,
Or your silent morning walk.
So now, dear Poll, take my advice,
When next you make a raid
Upon our sex, pray do it nice
On a new velocipede.

(Jim Browne, *Weekly News*, 11 September 1869, p. 15)

Mrs Highflyer to Polly Plum

In an article titled 'The Governess' published in *The Weekly News* on 18 September 1869, Polly Plum quoted 'Mrs. Highflyer', the mistress who thought it beneath her to befriend her governess. Diana Damson responded with this poem.

Dear Polly Plum, when you next write
Your nice sententious bits of prose,
For goodness' sake say something bright,
Something no other body knows.
Don't steal wise sayings, clever Polly,
And stretch them till they're almost folly.
I now forget what great divine
Says, 'Persecution is the Church's
Life,' but I know it is not thine,
The large wise thought which deeply searches,
I wish I could remember, Polly,
But I am not clever – I'm so sorry.
With martyr's blood the Churches seed
Is sown – so nobly says another.
We know it. Polly, there's no need
To scribble such a lot of bother;
The simple words are so much better
Than all the twaddle of your letter.
And as for governesses! Dear me,
Why all the books that tell their woes
Are legion. Come now, Polly, really
Tell us the truth now – don't you 'pose
We know a little of such matters
Without your pulling them to tatters?
Where ignorance, my dear, is bliss,
'Tis folly to be wise, you know;
And where the knowledge really is
There ignorance should blush to show.
Tell us now, Polly, I implore,
Something we didn't know before.
When you can show us how the stars
Unnumbered suns revolve above,
And not one note of discord jars
The music of immortal Love;

How round one central sun they burn
And to his living magnet turn;
When you can tell us how the vast
Assyrian empires rose and fell,
And dive into that mighty past
Which holds us like a burning spell;
Can tell us how the undying light
Was left in Egypt's shrines of night;
When you can show us how to mind
One single lie that rends the State –
Then, Polly, to your pen I'll bend,
And say you've quite a sapient pate
And that it isn't all a folly
To read your axioms, reverend Polly.

(Diana Damson, *Weekly News*, 2 October 1869, p. 15)

Ode to Polly Plum

(By the delirious Hauhau)

'Ode to Polly Plum' appeared in the booklet *Rhymes Without Reason* written by D.S. Cross and published by the *New Zealand Herald*. The booklet was advertised amid public debate in 1871 on the conditions at the Auckland Lunatic Asylum, and elicited some criticism for its insensitivity to inmates at 'the Whau', as the asylum was colloquially known.

I conclude that you're a human,
Polly Plum, Polly Plum,
I suppose that you're a woman,
Polly Plum.
But judging from your talk,
And also from your walk,
I should say that you're a rum'un,
Polly Plum, Polly Plum.

You would like to be a man,
Polly Plum, Polly Plum;

You'll be as like one as you can,
Polly Plum.
You despise the playful fan,
And you frighten by your ban,
Every pretty little flirting Mary Ann,
Polly Plum.

I wish you would skedaddle,
Polly Plum, Polly Plum,
Before your brains you addle,
Polly Plum.
For you lecture and you write;
Irrespective of what's right,
Till I'm weary of your noise and of your twaddle,
Polly Plum.

I've watched you from afar,
Polly Plum, Polly Plum.
Estimated you at par,
Polly Plum.
And I've thought of Mister P.,
And I've blessed my destinee,
That I wasn't born to be that pakeha,
Polly Plum.

Then preserve your senses now,
Polly Plum, Polly Plum;
Don't be making such a row,
Polly Plum.
For if your brain should crack,
You'd become a maniac,
And have to join our party at the Whau;
Polly Plum.

(D.S. Cross, *Rhymes without Reason: Hysterical, farcical, satirical,*
Auckland: Herald Office, 1871)

A Lament from Queen Square, Bloomsbury

By the 'Inimitable'

November fog shuts out the view,
The wind's due east to-day,
The sun's retired from business, and
He sends no genial ray;
And, worst of all, New Zealand lies
Thousands of miles away.

I look at the window here,
Four sparrows I can see:
Three of them hop about the ground,
And one is 'up a tree',
And in this figurative sense
He thus resembles me.

I shiver in my cheerless room
My thoughts to Auckland fly,
And for the land that's far away
I somehow seem to sigh.
Why do I feel so sad, and why
This moisture in the eye!

Oh for a sight of that blue sky
The balmy southern summer,
The heavenly zephyrs too that kiss
The cheek of each new-comer,
The adopted home of Polly Plum
And prison-breaking Plummer.

What's Fleet-street or the Strand to me,
Or e'en Trafalgar Square!
And Oxford-street, where horses fall
And angry cabmen swear,
While country reverends passing by
With pious horror stare.

The weather's vile – I can't go out;
I sigh and look around.
The yellow leaves with every gust
Go whirling o'er the ground,
As to myself the following
Conundrums I propound:

Does Crombie still take photographs
Or hold his head so high,
And when asked for a negative
Give a negative reply?
How are Long Drives, and is it safe
Caledonians to buy?

The City Board – but pr'aps they're called
The City Council now:
Does Tonks to the suggestion of
The stout Macready bow,
And Atkin get his back up and
With Hampton have a row?

Do Smart and Asher sit and have
A quiet bit of chaff?
Does Staines propose some monstrous thing
That makes the Council laugh?
And in the Borough Chamber have
They hung his photograph?

Does Beckham still sit on the bench?
And, to try and make him pleasant,
Has any publican of late
Made him a feathered present?
Or do they fear 'twill be no go,
As 'twas with Benstead's pheasant?

Unto the famous Manukau
The 'buses now who runs?
Do folks go to that lovely spot
In a trap of Hardington's?
And does the Reverend Edger still
Snub pious parson's sons?

Do the Thames volunteers still stick
To Lush (I don't mean whiskey)?
Is getting credit now for clothes,
A thing that's rather risky?
Can swells no more, like those of yore,
Get tick from Posseniskie?

The railway, too, is that begun?
Wake up, ye Auckland creepers,
Say will a line up to the North
Soon open all our peepers?
And do they mean to lay down all
The City Board for sleepers?

Oh! Have they caught Te Kooti yet,
By some new-fangled plan?
Does Nathan, junior, still upon
The Bench delinquents scan?
And prophet-like point to them and
Exclaim 'Thou art the man'?

Is being found in boozy state
A five or ten bob crime?
And have the folks forgotten quite
Poor Thatcher's local rhyme?
And how far from the new town clock
Can one make out the time?

How are my old newspaper friends?
Does bilious Creighton rub
The Auckland folks in leaded lines?
Is Montrose still the 'sub',
While little Utting goes about
For 'pars' to earn his grub?

Who wields the mighty thunderbolts
Up at the *Herald* there?
Has dear Von Sturmer gone back
To the editorial chair?
And does Brett, when a ship comes in,
Unto the wharf repair?

Does 'Polly Plum' still in the Cross
Complain of woman's fetters,
And claim a right to vote, and say
That females are our betters?
And does 'Old Practical' still write
Those ------ long-winded letters?

Do mining managers the poor
Shareholders still keep diddling?
And how's my old friend, Fenton?
Is he quite well, or middling?
And has the gout again appeared
To stop the Judge's fiddling?

Have they lit up the Grafton Road?
I wonder, by-the-by,
If gas illuminates the Thames;
And did they there rely
On utilizing Doctor Sam
To furnish the supply?

These are some of the questions that
So oft occur to me
As I sit in my lonely room,
In Queen-square, Bloomsbury.
Pray answer them, and you'll oblige,
Yours truly, C.R.T.

London, November 16, 1871

(Published in *Weekly News*, 17 February 1872, p. 17)

Dialogue on Woman's Rights

The following, copied from the original hand-written manuscript, is by Mary Ann Colclough's friend and supporter Henry Gyles Turner (see Chapter 8). The dialogue was a popular form of literary narrative. Illegible words are indicated by [...]

1. Gentleman
What think you wife of all the talk, the wrangling and the hubbub,
That stirs up strife in every house in City and in suburb,
About the rights and wrongs and claims of those we kindly call
The 'Gentler sex' though I declare that can embrace them all
For if a tithe of what I'm told and read about is true
Some of the ladies who possess the attribute called 'blue'
Have nothing gentle in their ways or in their clamorous tongues
And overbear all sentiment by rigorous strength of lungs.
I really have been quite nonplussed and lately much distressed
To learn from the Daily Telegraph, Mrs Colclough and the rest
That I'm a sneaking tyrant, a hateful selfish churl
Who aggravates each widow's grief – defrauds each helpless girl
Not of her cash directly, but of her rights divine
For fear her claim of justice should interfere with mine
I cannot rest in such disgrace until you let me know
If my past misbehaviour has seemed to strike you so.

2. Lady
Well twenty years of wedded life should give me right to speak
Unless indeed like Duncan I've 'borne my faculties too meek'
But looking back on that long time I scarcely dare to say
That on any point worth arguing I failed to have my way
And I wouldn't give one button for the woman who delights
In calling for assistance to maintain her proper rights
Mrs Colclough may enquire in wrath why don't the men propose
But the instinct of a woman's heart will tell her that she knows
Such questions can't be well discussed before a heady throng
They're sacred to the two concerned to whom they must belong
And if the truth is sometimes false, if sordid [...] prevail
They are but epochs in the span of life's brief stirring tale.
And when the heart is deeply touched, the souls affection shed
On one unworthy of the trust they're better to be dead
For all the laws that man can make can offer no relief
Can save no heart from breaking with such a load of grief.

3. Gentleman

My dear at any rate your views do credit to your heart
But at our Eclectic meetings they say that that's the part
The least concerned with proper views of philosophic kind
And anything like sentiment's at war with strength of mind
That love's a myth, a silly dream not worth a sober thought
That must be roughly jostled by when life's battles to be fought
But leaving such high questions, do you never once define
That in the field of politics you have no chance to shine
No vote to be caressed for, no influence to wield
No preference to exhibit for the candidate a field
Have you no bold ambition to be Minister of Lands
Or wield the Treasurers' purse, or wear the cambric bands
That deck the Attorney General's official raiment
Or care to take a seat amongst those whose payment
For patriotic services is now creating
A deal of silly argument and useless prating.

4. Lady

Well no, I cannot say I feel at all concerned
That members are without my aid returned
If I to one should wish to give support
You vote for him, or if you don't you ought!
At any rate I've sense enough to know
If I can't make you you'll have grounds to show
Others I am wrong, and as both can't be right
The vote so canvassed should have double weight
As to the 'House' I've no wish to be there
The continuous wrangling, – the contentious air
May do for men whose rougher grain can bear it
But would bile women, should they have to share it
My home's my 'House' I'm always Premier there
And fear no 'Opposition's discontented glare
No 'Votes of Confidence' disguising selfish aims
No undermining of my rightful claims.

5. Gentleman

It seems to me your servitude gives you but little pain
I cannot make you realise the thraldom of the chain
That binds your sex in bondage and holds you as a slave

That tyrant-man oppresses from the cradle to the grave
Why I am told that if a poll of womankind was taken
Half the men would find themselves by their better halves forsaken
Tis said they want to shine alone and not with borrowed light
And would send their husbands packing as the first step to their rights
If the matrimonial trouble was but once knocked on the head
A deluge of strong mindedness o'er all the lands would spread
In Parliament the female talk would drown the Speaker's voice
And in municipal affairs the she-universal choice
Would soon expel from Gatehouse that unregenerate [...]
Who rudely cut the ladies out from his inaugural dinner
And what with female juries and fair pleaders at the Bar
I think Sir Redmond Barry should feel we'd gone too far
He'd bestow on some stout madam his [...] and his wig
And fly a scene which to her mind must be a [...] dig
Now don't you think in all this stir you'd like to have a hand
And help to revolutionize the customs of the land.

6. Lady
I really don't, nor do I see a revolution needed
To gain th'incongruous state of things for which your friends have
    pleaded
The field for woman's work is wide and ever widening still
Her destiny's a noble one, if her mission she fulfil –
To soothe and cheer, to love and help, the one among all men
To make the world seem brighter to all within her ken.
And if her lot is not so blest, – if she must toil for bread
The world's before her when to choose to work both hand or head
If she have power there's nought can stay her progress where she lists
In school or church, on stage or preps her right to work exists
The healing art reward her well, – the lecture platform too
That is if she has ought to say, – at once well said and true
The Civil Service finds her room and Mrs Grundy's sneer
Is the sole barrier feeble minds allow themselves to fear
If lack of intellect or want of call debar from such high flights
It is not just to maunder on about unheeded rights
For if we have not got the stuff of which success is made
We are but shams if we invoke the Laws imperious aid
Far better to accept our lot and by some humbler calling
There to be propped upon a pedestal with hourly fear of falling

And if there are amongst my sex some such exclusive minds
That in their love for Politics give all else to the winds
They had better cross the ocean in the United States
Watch the progress of the movement and enjoy the hot debates
On the woman's suffrage question which has gained the day
And filled the minds of sober men with terror and dismay.

7. Gentleman

In Bunyan's Pilgrims Progress or some such kind of book
I read a touching passage which has a very truthful look
    'That when a woman will she will, you may depend on't
    'And when she won't she won't, so there's an end on't.
This makes one feel quite well assured that all this present noise
That's made about dear woman's rights comes only from the boys
For if her poor defenceless self but took in hand the matter
The sterner sex would yield at once to escape the awful clatter
She'd get whate'er she wanted or she'd know the reason why
It's quite a genuine blessing that she doesn't care to try
Though I for one can't say I'd feel so very much distressed
If you should wish to do my work while I at home might rest
A month of household cares might work in me a wondrous change
While contact with the outer world would teach you something strange
And satisfy you on one point that in the strife for victuals
It may be soon discovered life's not all beer and skittles
Let's take our stand then hand in hand and do our level best
To make each other's work complete for that's the final test
And though you claim but equal rights it always makes me laugh
To hear my friends with one accord call you my better half.

8. Lady

Quite right, and while you feel the truth of what your friends all say
I shall need no assistance from the reformers of the day
I'd like to make just one remark before we stand aside
This gathering of our friends tonight I view with honest pride
For it grows out of woman's work, and some credit it reflects
That the best things on the programme are allotted to my sex
Variety is charming so with men we just embellish
Lest a feminine totality for some should lose its relish
They'll sing and read, recite and play, oh very well – for these
But everyone observes they're but the selling of the […].

9. Gentleman
My dear I see some gentlemen who think this not polite.

10. Lady
No more – the last word another time – that is a woman's right.

(Henry Gyles Turner, 10 December 1874)

Notes

Introduction: Polly Plum and the 'High and Holy' Cause of Women

1   Polly Plum, 'What women want', *New Zealand Herald*, 31 July 1871, p. 3; 'To readers and correspondents', *Daily Southern Cross*, 19 September 1871, p. 2; Charlotte Macdonald, *The Vote, the Pill and the Demon Drink: A history of feminist writing in New Zealand, 1869–1993* (Wellington: Bridget Williams Books, 1993), p. 17.

2   The official name of the Ladies' Vigilant Society was the Vigilance Association for the Defence of Personal Rights, founded in England in 1871.

3   A.H. McLintock, 'Colclough, Mary Ann, "Polly Plum" (1836–1885)', in *An Encyclopaedia of New Zealand*, ed. A.H. McClintock (Wellington: R.W. Owen, Government Printer, vol. 1, 1996), p. 376.

4   In December 1926, Mary Ann Colclough's daughter Mary Louise Wilson wrote to journalist Laura Bunting at the *Dominion* in Wellington to correct the claim made in an article that Dolce Cabot was the first woman to hold a position on the staff of a New Zealand newspaper. Her letter, subsequently published (*Dominion*, 2 January 1926, magazine section, p. 2.), provided details of Mary Ann's early publications, some of which no longer exist. See also Jenny Coleman, 'For the ladies: Knowing women through the pages of the *Weekly News*, 1868–1872', in *Women's Studies Association Conference Papers 2001* (Christchurch: Women's Studies Association NZ, 2002), pp. 41–48; Jenny Coleman, 'Serendipitous scholarship: Identifying the author of *Alone in the World* (1866)', *Turnbull Library Record*, vol. 37, 2004, pp. 59–67.

5   Editorial, *Argus*, 24 March 1875, p. 5; Editorial, *Evening Post*, 13 July 1871, p. 2; Polly Plum, 'To Jemmy Jenkins', *Daily Southern Cross*, 30 June 1869, p. 4.

6   Mary Ann Colclough, 'Thoughts on a few things', *Daily Southern Cross*, 14 August 1872, p. 3.

Chapter One: From Clerkenwell to Auckland

1   'Auckland area passenger vessels 1838–1885' (Auckland Research Centre, Auckland City Library, Auckland); 'Register of births, marriages and deaths of passengers at sea from 1854 to 1859' (Public Records Office, London, BT 158/Piece 1/Folio 74, no. 407); Family sources suggest the circumstances of James Barnes' death were suspicious.

2   Details of the voyage are from 'Shipping intelligence' columns in various newspapers, including 'Maritime record', *New Zealander*, 16 December 1857, p. 2.

3   'Shipping intelligence: Port of Auckland', *Daily Southern Cross*, 15 December 1857, p. 2; *New Zealander*, 16 December 1857, p. 2.

4   Details of family addresses are from the English census records.

5   Recognised internationally for its clock, watch and jewellery trades, Clerkenwell was also a major centre for printing and the associated trades of the manufacture of stationery, bookbinding and engraving.

6   The 1831 census recorded 6385 houses in the parish of Clerkenwell, with another 152 under construction. By 1841 the number of houses had increased to over 7000 and the population stood at 47,634. By 1851 there were over 7500 houses and a population of 64,778, of which more than two thirds were Londoners by birth. Information drawn from Edward J. Wood, ed., *The History of Clerkenwell by the late William J. Pinks* (London: Charles Herbert, 2nd edn, 1881), pp. 13–14.

7   John Stuart Mill was born in Rodney Street, Pentonville, about one block away from where Mary Ann lived as a child.

8   Polly Plum, 'Childhood', *Daily Southern Cross*, 2 September 1869, p. 4.

9   Polly Plum, 'Female education', *Weekly News* (Auckland), 22 May 1869, p. 15.

10 For further information on the establishment of Queen's College, see F.D. Maurice and others, *Introductory Lectures Delivered at Queen's College, London* (London: John W. Packer, 1849); Rosalie Glynn Grylls, *Queen's College 1848–1948* (London: George Routledge & Sons, 1948); Duncan Crow, *The Victorian Woman* (London: George Allen & Unwin, 1971); and Elaine Kaye, *A History of Queen's College, London 1848–1972*, ed. M.A. Tweed (London: Chatto & Windus, 1972).

11 In his satiric depiction of aristocratic society in the 1853 novel *Pendennis* by William Makepeace Thackeray, the lead protagonist refers to sitting upon charity committees, ball committees, emigration committees or Queen's College committees as part of the duties of British states-womanship.

12 A. Becker, 'Journalism as a profession', in *The First College Open to Women: Queen's College, London. Memories and records of work done 1848–1898*, ed. M.A. Tweed (London: Queen's College, 1898), pp. 51–52.

13 Polly Plum, 'Women as wives', *Daily Southern Cross*, 24 February 1871, p. 3.

14 Polly Plum, 'The thieves of society', *Daily Southern Cross*, 19 November 1870, p. 3.

15 The Author of 'The Half-Caste Wife' [Mary Ann Colclough], *Alone in the World: A tale of New Zealand* (Auckland: Mitchell & Seffern, 1866), p. 17.

16 Minutes of the Auckland Board of Education, 22 June 1858, 23 June 1858 (Archives New Zealand, Auckland office); The Commissioner of Education report for 1858 records her teaching certificate as a first-class second-grade one rather than a first-class first-grade one.

17 *Daily Southern Cross*, 14 May 1861, p. 2. The method of construction of Tintern was significant, and the National Trust of Australia subsequently awarded it an 'A' classification as the best-known example of the iron houses built in Britain during the heyday of nineteenth-century prefabrication; see, in this regard, *Historical Buildings of Victoria*, ed. David Saunders (Melbourne: Jacaranda Press/National Trust of Australia, 1966), p. 144.

18 Edna Soar, *History of the Anglican Church of St. Peter's, Onehunga* (Auckland: Church Army Press, 1948), p. 43.

19 Polly Plum, 'Answers to Jellaby Pater', *New Zealand Herald*, 18 August 1871, p. 3; Mary A. Colclough, 'A letter from Melbourne', *Thames Star*, 13 May 1875, p. 2.

20 Letter from Henry Taylor to Mrs Colclough dated 27 October 1865 (private family collection).

21 Sources indicate that both *The Half Caste Wife* and the early version of *Alone in the World* were first published in the *Australasian*, but an extensive search of this publication failed to locate these fictional works; see Jenny Coleman, 'Serendipitous scholarship: Identifying the author of *Alone in the World* (1866)', *Turnbull Library Record*, no. 37, 2004, pp. 59–67; 'Alone in the world', *Daily Southern Cross*, 19 May 1866, p. 6; and Mary A. Colclough, Letter to the editor, *New Zealand Herald*, 18 November 1876, supplement, p. 1.

22 Review of *Alone in the World*, *Penny Journal*, 19 May 1866, p. 21; Terry Sturm (ed.), *Oxford History of New Zealand Literature in English* (Auckland: Oxford University Press, 2nd edn, 1998), p. 125. The *Penny Journal* was published by Mitchell and Seffern in Wyndham Street, Auckland, to cater to demands for affordable literature of interest to all classes.

23 The Author of 'The Half-Caste Wife' [Mary Ann Colclough], *Alone in the World*, pp. 1, 17.

24 Polly Plum, 'Answers to Jellaby Pater', *New Zealand Herald*, 18 August 1871, p. 3.

25 Polly Plum, 'Explanatory', *New Zealand Herald*, 21 August 1871, p. 3.

26 'Auckland Provincial Hospital 1867 admission and discharge book' (Archives New Zealand, Auckland office).

27 Annual report of the Auckland Provincial Hospital for 1867 (Archives New Zealand, Auckland office); Report of the Auckland Board of Education, 1867, p. 2, in *Journals of the Auckland Provincial Council*, Session XXII, 1867–68, p. 79.

28 A Friend, 'A hard case', *Thames Star*, 30 June 1874, p. 2. The identity of this personal friend is not known.

29 'Mercenary marriages', *Daily Southern Cross*, 23 September 1868, p. 4. *Weekly News* was a weekly version of the *Daily Southern Cross*.

Chapter Two: Entering the Public Sphere

1 'The inky way: A correspondent and an omission', *Dominion*, 2 January 1926, magazine section, p. 2. For further detail on this letter, see Jenny Coleman, 'Serendipitous scholarship: Identifying the author of *Alone in the World* (1866)', *Turnbull Library Record*, vol. 37, 2004, pp. 59–67; 'A friend' and 'A hard case', *Thames Star*, 30 June 1874, p. 2.

2 Polly Plum, 'Pattern women', *Daily Southern Cross*, 29 December 1869, p. 4.

3 See 'The Auckland Presbytery', *Daily Southern Cross*, 4 February 1869, p. 4; The Author of 'The Half-Caste Wife' [Mary Ann Colclough], *Alone in the World: A tale of New Zealand* (Auckland: Mitchell & Seffern, 1866), p. 8.

4   J. Crispe, 'Polly Plum', *Daily Southern Cross*, 2 March 1869, p. 3; A Roman Catholic Layman, 'Religion in common schools – what's in a name?', *Daily Southern Cross*, 2 March 1869, p. 3.

5   Jemmy Jenkins, 'To Polly Plum', *Daily Southern Cross*, 25 June 1869, p. 5; Polly Plum, 'To Jemmy Jenkins', *Daily Southern Cross*, 30 June, 1869, p. 4.

6   Polly Plum, 'Polly Plum's last', *Daily Southern Cross*, 22 July 1869, p. 6.

7   These poems are reprinted in the appendix.

8   'Colonial Fern Leaves' is reprinted in the appendix.

9   Ann D. Wood, 'The "scribbling women" and Fanny Fern: Why women wrote', *American Quarterly*, vol. 23, no. 1, 1971, p. 3.

10 Polly Plum, 'Letter to Mr John Smith', *Daily Southern Cross*, 8 September 1869, p. 5.

11 Polly Plum, Letter to the editor, *Daily Southern Cross*, 13 November 1869, p. 4.

12 Mary A. Colclough, 'Servants', *Argus*, 29 January 1875, p. 6.

13 *The Emigrant's Friend, or Authentic Guide to South Australia, Including Sydney; Port Philip, or Australia Felix; Western Australia, or Swan River Colony; New South Wales; Van Diemen's Land; and New Zealand* (London: J. Allen & D. Francis, 1848), p. 4; Alexander Bathgate, *Colonial Experiences, or Sketches of People and Places in the Province of Otago, New Zealand* (Glasgow: James Maclehose, 1874); and Jenny Coleman, 'Social hierarchies and class sensibilities: A comparative analysis of vocabularies of domestic service in mid-Victorian England and New Zealand, in *Victorian Vocabularies: Refereed proceedings of the 2012 Australasian Victorian Studies Association Conference*, ed. Jessica Gildersleeve (Sydney: Macquarie Lighthouse E-book Publishing, Macquarie University, New South Wales, 2013).

14 The letter from Vogel is cited from an article titled 'Mother's vote: Has it altered the trend of legislation', *New Zealand Free Lance*, 11 November 1936, p. 23. This unauthored article is attributed to Mary Ann Colclough's daughter Mary Wilson (Mrs Hannon Wilson) and is contained in the scrapbook 'From English, Australian and New Zealand papers by Mrs Hannon Wilson' (private family papers). For a discussion of Mary Wilson's journalism, see Jenny Coleman, 'Like mother, like daughter? Women journalists and generational feminism in New Zealand', in *Women's Studies Association Conference Papers 2003* (Palmerston North: Women's Studies Association NZ, 2004), pp. 25–30.

15 Samuel Edger, 'Mr Mill and women', *Daily Southern Cross*, 13 May 1871, p. 3.

16 Polly Plum, 'What women want', *New Zealand Herald*, 31 July 1871, p. 3.

17 Editorial, *Star* (Auckland), 6 January 1871, p. 2; Editorial, *Daily Southern Cross*, 5 October 1870, p. 2; 'The Christian Times', *Daily Southern Cross*, 2 February 1871, p. 3.

18 Polly Plum, 'Polly Plum's reply to "Veritas"', *Weekly News*, 14 May 1870, p. 20.

19 William Hepworth Dixon, *New America* (London: Hurst & Blackett, 1867), p. 346 (see, in particular, Chapter 32, 'Woman at Salt Lake').

20 Polly Plum, 'Lords of the Creation', *Weekly News*, 30 April 1870, p. 21.

21 See 'Notices to correspondents, "Polly Plum" vindicated', *Daily Southern Cross*, 2 July 1870, p. 3.

22 Polly Plum, 'Woman and her master', *Weekly News*, 14 May 1870, p. 21.

23 G.M., 'Polly Plum's mission', *Weekly News*, 28 May 1870, p. 21.

24 'Notice to correspondents, Polly Plum's mission', *Daily Southern Cross*, 1 June 1870, p. 3.

25 Polly Plum, Letter to the editor, *Daily Southern Cross*, 2 June 1870, p. 3.

26 Editorial note, *Daily Southern Cross*, 2 June 1870, p. 3.

27 Polly Plum, 'Woman and her master', *Daily Southern Cross*, 10 June 1870, p. 4.

28 *New Zealand Parliamentary Debates (Hansard)*, vol. 7, 23 June 1870, p. 72.

29 Ibid.

30 The Act extended protection orders for married women's property in cases where a wife was subjected to cruelty by her husband, where a husband was living in open adultery or was guilty of habitual drunkenness, or where a husband habitually failed to provide maintenance for his wife and children unless there was an unavoidable reason for doing so such as sickness (see section 2, The Married Women's Property Protection Act, 1870).

31 R.K., 'Female authorship', *Daily Southern Cross*, 17 June 1870, p. 4; Old Practical, 'Man and wife', *Daily Southern Cross*, 5 July 1870, p. 4. For information on Old Practical's reputation as a correspondent to the press, see letter written by A Country Settler, *Daily Southern Cross*, 16 November 1867, p. 4.

32 A Grandmother, 'Private school examinations', *Daily Southern Cross*, 6 January 1871, p. 3.

33 Polly Plum, 'Examinations in ladies' schools', *Daily Southern Cross*, 23 January 1871, p. 3.

34 Polly Plum, 'A widow in gaol for debt', *Daily Southern Cross*, 18 January 1871, p. 3.

35 Ibid.

36 Polly Plum, 'What can she do?' *Daily Southern Cross*, 24 October 1870, p. 3.

37 Polly Plum, 'A widow in gaol for debt', *Daily Southern Cross*, 18 January 1871, p. 3.

38 Old Practical, 'Polly Plum and Old Practical', *Daily Southern Cross*, 23 January 1871, p. 3.

39 Humble-Bee, 'Widow in gaol', *Daily Southern Cross*, 24 January 1871, p. 3; Polly Plum, 'The widow in gaol', *Daily Southern Cross*, 2 February 1871, p. 3; Polly Plum, 'Women's wrongs', *Daily Southern Cross*, 6 February 1871, p. 6.

40 See Polly Plum, 'The law and the Bible', *Daily Southern Cross*, 27 February 1871, p. 3; Ami, 'Theology for ladies', *Daily Southern Cross*, 1 March 1871, p. 3.

41 See Amicus, 'Law and scripture', *Daily Southern Cross*, 8 March 1871, p. 3; Polly Plum, '"Amicus" on law and scripture', *Daily Southern Cross*, 13 March 1871, p. 3.

42 E. Stephens, 'Woman's rights', *Daily Southern Cross*, 11 May 1871, p. 3; E. Stephens, 'Woman's rights', *Daily Southern Cross*, 4 April 1871, p. 3; Samuel Edger, 'Woman's rights', *Daily Southern Cross*, 8 April 1871, p. 3; E. Earnest, 'Woman's rights', *Daily Southern Cross*, 24 April 1871, p. 3; Editorial, *Daily Southern Cross*, 11 July 1871, p. 2.

43 G., 'Woman's rights', *Daily Southern Cross*, 4 May 1871, p. 3.

Chapter Three: A Modern Female Fanatic

1 'Polly Plum's lecture', *Evening Star* (Auckland), 27 June 1871, p. 2.

2 Editorial, *Evening Post* (Wellington), 3 July 1871, p. 2; 'Polly Plum's lecture', *Evening Star* (Auckland), 27 June 1871, p. 2.

3 'Lecture by Polly Plum', *Daily Southern Cross*, 27 June 1871, p. 2.

4 'Subjection of Woman', *New Zealand Herald*, 27 June 1871, p. 2.

5 Editorial, *New Zealand Herald*, 15 July 1871, p. 3.

6 Mary A. Colclough, 'Mrs. Colclough's lecture', *New Zealand Herald*, 28 June 1871, p. 3.

7 '"Polly Plum" at the Thames', *Weekly News* (Auckland), 8 July 1871, p. 6.

8 Nathaniel Beeswing, Untitled, *Evening Star*, 10 July 1871, p. 2.

9 Editorial, *Evening Post* (Wellington), 13 July 1871, p. 2.

10 Ibid.

11 Polly Plum, 'What women want', *New Zealand Herald*, 31 July 1871, p. 3.

12 See Mary A. Colclough, Letter to the editor, *Wellington Independent*, 18 October 1871, p. 3; see also editorial comment, p. 2.

13 'Lecture on female education', *Evening Star*, 31 July 1871, p. 2.

14 Polly Plum, 'Good housewives', *Daily Southern Cross*, 8 May 1871, p. 3.

15 In the Victorian hierarchy of domestic service, "thorough" referred to the ability to perform the widest range of duties associated with the role.

16 Mary A. Colclough, Letter to the editor, *Daily Southern Cross*, 2 August 1871, p. 2.

17 Editorial, *New Zealand Herald*, 24 July 1871, p. 2.

18 Frances Shayle George, 'Female education', *New Zealand Herald*, 2 March 1872, p. 3; Editorial, *Daily Southern Cross*, 11 October 1870, p. 2.

19 Polly Plum, 'Examinations in ladies' schools', *Daily Southern Cross*, 23 January 1871, p. 3.

20 Editorial, *Daily Southern Cross*, 9 August 1871, p. 4.

21 'Janie Plum', 'The subjection of woman', *New Zealand Herald*, 2 August 1871, p. 3.

22 Maggie Plum, 'Women's rights', *New Zealand Herald*, 5 August 1871, p. 3.

23 Mother, Letter to the editor, *Daily Southern Cross*, 22 September 1871, p. 2.

24 Polly Plum, 'Polly Plum's opponents', *New Zealand Herald*, 14 August 1871, p. 3.

25 Jellaby Pater, 'Questions for Polly Plum', *New Zealand Herald*, 16 August 1871, p. 3.

26 Polly Plum, 'Explanatory', *New Zealand Herald*, 21 August 1871, p. 3.

27 'Charge of being an old maid satisfactorily answered', *Wanganui Herald*, 22 August 1871, p. 2.

28 Francis Foscari, 'Ancient and modern fanaticism', *New Zealand Herald*, 25 August 1871, p. 3.

29 See 'Ode to Polly Plum' in the appendix. This poem was subsequently reprinted in the *Auckland–Waikato Historical Journal*, vol. 62, April 1993, pp. 9–10.

30 Francis Foscari, 'Ancient and modern fanaticism', *New Zealand Herald*, 25 August 1871, p. 3.

31 Polly Plum, 'A plea for the platform', *Daily Southern Cross*, 20 September 1871, p. 3.

32 Polly Plum, '"Old Practical", "Polly Plum" and the host of newspaper correspondents', *Daily Southern Cross*, 2 October 1871, p. 3

Chapter Four: Widening the Sphere of Philanthropy and Social Reform

1 Mary A. Colclough, 'The lunatic asylum', *Daily Southern Cross*, 9 September 1871, p. 3.

2 Ibid.

3 Ibid.

4 'A sad occurrence: Death of Mrs. W. Buckland', *Daily Southern Cross*, 6 September 1871, p. 5.

5 Mary A. Colclough, 'The lunatic asylum', *Daily Southern Cross*, 9 September 1871, p. 3; Editorial, *Daily Southern Cross*, 13 December 1871, p. 2; see also Lynx, Letter to the editor, *Daily Southern Cross*, 14 December 1871, p. 2., who gives credit to Mary Ann Colclough for the proposal.

6 See Report of the Joint Committee on Lunatic Asylums, *Appendices to the Journals of the House of Representatives*, 1871, I, H-10, and Auckland No. 1 Report on the Auckland Provincial Lunatic Asylum: Reports on the Lunatic Asylums in New Zealand, *Appendices to the Journals of the House of Representatives*, 1873, H-23. The conference of ministers was held on 6 August 1871; see 'Appointment of a missionary for hospital and gaol', *Daily Southern Cross*, 13 September 1871, p. 3.

7 C.B., Letter to the editor, *Daily Southern Cross*, 21 September 1871, p. 2; Hope, 'Homeless young girls', *Daily Southern Cross*, 30 September 1871, p. 3; Philanthropos, 'Missionary for the gaol, hospital, &c.', *New Zealand Herald*, 22 September 1871, p. 3.

8 Mary A. Colclough, 'Missionary for hospital and gaol', *Daily Southern Cross*, 23 September 1871, p. 3, and *New Zealand Herald*, 23 September 1871, p. 3.

9 Editorial, *Daily Southern Cross*, 28 September 1871, p. 2.

10 Mary A. Colclough, 'Homeless young girls', *Daily Southern Cross*, 29 September 1871, p. 3.

11 Rescue, 'A plea for the fallen', *Daily Southern Cross*, 3 October 1871, p. 3.

12 Woman, Letter to the editor, *Daily Southern Cross*, 3 October 1871, p. 3.

13 Mary A. Colclough, 'Auckland Women's Home', *Daily Southern Cross*, 4 October 1871, p. 5.

14 B. Thornton Dudley, 'Auckland Women's Home', *Daily Southern Cross*, 2 October 1871, p. 3.

15 Mary A. Colclough, 'Auckland Women's Refuge', *Weekly News*, 7 October 1871, p. 16.

16 Magnum Bonum, 'Prisoners' Aid Society', *Weekly News*, 7 October 1871, p. 16.

17 See Mary A. Colclough, 'Aid for discharged prisoners', *Daily Southern Cross*, 12 October 1871, p. 3.

18 Advertisements columns, *Daily Southern Cross*, 18 October 1871, p. 1.

19 Educational advertisements, *New Zealand Herald*, 21 October 1871, p. 1.

20 Editorial, *New Zealand Herald*, 21 October 1871, p. 2; Editorial, *Daily Southern Cross*, 21 October 1871, p. 2.

21 Comment, *Auckland Star*, 21 October 1871, p. 2; 'Lecture on marriage', *Daily Southern Cross*, 21 October 1871, p. 2.

22 'Mrs. Colclough on marriage', *New Zealand Herald*, 21 October 1871, p. 3.

23 'Lectures: "Love, courtship and marriage"', *New Zealand Herald*, 28 October 1871, p. 2.

24 Mary A. Colclough, 'Mrs. Colclough's classes', *Daily Southern Cross*, 1 November 1871, p. 6.

25 Mary A. Colclough, 'Mrs. Colclough's educational classes', *Daily Southern Cross*, 31 October 1871, p. 3.

26 Ibid.

27 Henry Worthington, Letter to the editor, *Daily Southern Cross*, 6 November 1871, p. 2.

28 Advertisements columns, *Daily Southern Cross*, 8 November 1871, p. 1.

29 'The industrial school', *Daily Southern Cross*, 20 May 1871, p. 5.

30 Mary A. Colclough, 'Industrial school', *Weekly News*, 25 November 1871, p. 5.

31 Mary A. Colclough, 'A scandal to our province: The women's department of the gaol', *Daily Southern Cross*, 6 December 1871, p. 3.

32 Ibid.

33 Mary A. Colclough, 'A prison to spare', *Daily Southern Cross*, 13 December 1871, p. 3. 'The Man About Town', the regular columnist for the *Auckland Star*, subsequently ridiculed her idea (see 'The Man about Town', *Auckland Star*, 13 December 1871, p. 2.).

34 Women could secure some rights over property they owned before their marriage if they arranged for a marriage settlement to be drawn up as part of the marriage contract. See Polly Plum, 'Polly Plum's opponents', *New Zealand Herald*, 14 August 1871, p. 3.

Chapter Five: Without Means, Without Encouragement and Without Help

1 Samaritan, Letter to the editor, *Daily Southern Cross*, 2 January 1872, p. 2.

2 M.A. Colclough, Letter to the editor, *Daily Southern Cross*, 6 January 1872, p. 2.

3 O.S. Ellis, Letter to the editor, *Daily Southern Cross*, 11 January 1872, p. 2.

4 For further details on Ellen Ellis, see Jenny Coleman, '"Philosophers in Petticoats": A feminist analysis of the discursive practices of Mary Taylor, Mary Colclough and Ellen Ellis as contributors to debate on the "woman question" in New Zealand between 1845–1885', PhD thesis, Feminist Studies Department, University of Canterbury, 1996; Jenny Coleman, 'Missionaries, monstrosities or modern female fanatics? (Re)presenting the identities of nineteenth-century advocates of women's rights', *Australasian Victorian Studies Journal*, vol. 9, pp. 40–51; Angela Caughey, *Pioneer Families: The settlers of nineteenth-century New Zealand* (Auckland: David Bateman, 1994).

5   Ellen Ellis, cited in Vera Colebrook, *Ellen: A biography* (Dublin: The Women's Press, 1980), p. 146.

6   *Thames Guardian and Mining Record*, 10 January 1872, p. 2.

7   'Police Court', *Daily Southern Cross*, 1 January 1872, p. 3.

8   Ibid.

9   'Repentance and promised reformation', *Daily Southern Cross*, 15 January 1872, p. 3

10 Mary A. Colclough, Letter to the editor, *Daily Southern Cross*, 17 January 1872, p. 2.

11 Editorial, *New Zealand Herald*, 29 February 1872, p. 2; Frances Shayle George, 'Female education', *New Zealand Herald*, 2 March 1872, p. 3.

12 Mary A. Colclough, 'Female education', *New Zealand Herald*, 5 March 1872, p. 3.

13 Advertisements, *Daily Southern Cross*, 8 March 1872, p. 1.

14 Editorial, *Daily Southern Cross*, 2 March 1872, p. 2.

15 Ibid.

16 For a comparative analysis of domestic service in England and New Zealand in the 1870s, see Jenny Coleman, 'Social hierarchies and class sensibilities: A comparative analysis of vocabularies of domestic service in mid-Victorian England and New Zealand', in *Victorian Vocabularies: Refereed proceedings of the 2012 Australasian Victorian Studies Association Conference*, ed. Jessica Gildersleeve (Sydney: Macquarie Lighthouse E-book Publishing, 2013).

17 'News of the day', *Press* (Christchurch), 16 March 1872, p. 2; 'Auckland', *Otago Witness*, 16 March 1872, p. 2.

18 'Under the verandah', *Weekly News*, 16 March 1872, p. 13; Advertisements, *Auckland Star*, 20 March 1872, p. 3.

19 Mary A. Colclough, 'An almshouse wanted', *Daily Southern Cross*, 18 March 1872, p. 3.

20 Reformatory, Letter to the editor, *Daily Southern Cross*, 7 December 1871, p. 2.

21 'Meeting of the Auckland Alliance for the Suppression of the Liquor Traffic', *Daily Southern Cross*, 21 March 1872, p. 3.

22 Ibid.

23 Ibid.

24 Editorial, *Daily Southern Cross*, 3 April 1872, p. 2.

25 Mary A. Colclough, 'Employment of fallen women', *Daily Southern Cross*, 5 April 1872, p. 2.

26 Ibid.

27 Mary A. Colclough, Letter to the editor, *Daily Southern Cross*, 9 April 1872, p. 3.

28 Mary A. Colclough, Letter to the editor, *Daily Southern Cross*, 6 May 1872, p. 2.

29 Review of lecture, *Daily Southern Cross*, 11 May 1872, p. 2.

30 Review of lecture, *New Zealand Herald*, 11 May 1872, p. 2.

31 Ibid.

32 Sketcher, 'Portraits of the people', *Auckland Star*, 16 May 1872, p. 2.

33 Polly Plum, 'A Polly Plum paper', *Auckland Star*, 17 May 1872, p. 2.

34 Letter to the editor, *New Zealand Herald*, 18 May 1872, p. 5.

35 See Jenny Coleman, 'For the Ladies: Knowing women through the pages of the *Weekly News*, 1868–1872', *Women's Studies Association Conference Papers 2001* (Christchurch: Women's Studies Association NZ, 2002), pp. 41–48.

36 Mary A. Colclough, 'Ladies and newspapers', *Daily Southern Cross*, 20 May 1872, p. 3.

37 See, for example, 'Sad cases', *Daily Southern Cross*, 11 June 1872, p. 3.

38 Editorial, *Daily Southern Cross*, 27 June 1872, p. 2; 'Lecture on self culture', *Daily Southern Cross*, 29 June 1872, p. 3.

39 Editorial, *Daily Southern Cross*, 1 July 1872, p. 2.

40 Ibid.

41 Mary A. Colclough, 'Servants and farmers' wives', *Daily Southern Cross*, 3 July 1872, p. 3.

42 Ibid.

43 'Random notes', *Auckland Star*, 6 July 1872, p. 3.

44 Mary A. Colclough, 'Gaol visiting', *Daily Southern Cross*, 10 July 1872, p. 6.

45 Mary A. Colclough, 'A sad case', *Daily Southern Cross*, 23 August 1872, p. 3.

46 Mary A. Colclough, 'Thoughts on a few things', *Daily Southern Cross*, 14 August 1872, p. 3.

47 Ibid.

48 Advertisements, *Daily Southern Cross*, 24 August 1872, p. 1.

49 'Mrs. Colclough', *Daily Southern Cross*, 14 September 1872, p. 2.

50 Letter reprinted in 'Mrs. Colclough', *Daily Southern Cross*, 14 September 1872, p. 2.

51 Letter reprinted in *Daily Southern Cross*, 16 September 1872, p. 3.

52 See report on meeting, *New Zealand Herald*, 23 September 1872, p. 2.

53 Editorial, *Daily Southern Cross*, 26 September 1872, p. 2.

54 Advertisements, *New Zealand Herald*, 26 September 1872, p. 1.

55 For a review of her public farewell, see 'Choral Hall', *New Zealand Herald*, 27 September 1872, p. 3.

Chapter Six: Controversies and Public Humiliation

1 One objection to the Act was its imposition of a householder tax in order to boost education coffers. A Tuakau Settler, 'Tuakau School matters', *Daily Southern Cross*, 11 March 1873, p. 3.

2 Mary A. Colclough, 'Tuakau School matters', *Daily Southern Cross*, 10 March 1873, p. 3.

3 See 'Auckland and Waikato Railway', *New Zealand Herald*, 15 February 1873, p. 2.

4 Mary A. Colclough, 'Tuakau School matters', *Daily Southern Cross*, 10 March 1873, p. 3.

5 Mary A. Colclough, 'The Bible in schools', *Daily Southern Cross*, 1 March 1873, p. 3.

6 The official name of the society was the Vigilance Association for the Defence of Personal Rights.

7 'Alexandra: Woman's rights, etc', *Daily Southern Cross*, 17 April 1873, p. 2; 'Mrs Colclough's lecture', *Waikato Times*, 17 April 1873, p. 2.

8 Editorial, *Waikato Times*, 19 April 1873, p. 2.

9   Ibid.

10   Mary A. Colclough, Letter to the editor, *Waikato Times*, 19 April 1873, p. 3.

11   Ibid.

12   Mary A. Colclough, 'Female emigration to New Zealand', *The Times* (London), 21 April 1873, p. 6.

13   Ibid.

14   Ibid.

15   Harriet H. Herbert, Letter to the editor, *The Times*, 24 April 1873, p. 12; R.S. Beatson, Letter to the editor, *The Times*, 24 April 1873, p. 12. Some years later, Miss Herbert became a governesses' agent for the Female Middle Class Emigration Society.

16   'Letter in *The Times*', *New Zealand Herald*, 7 July 1873, p. 2.

17   Editorial, *New Zealand Herald*, 14 July 1873, p. 2.

18   Mary A. Colclough, Letter to the editor, *New Zealand Herald*, 21 July 1873, p. 4.

19   Editorial, *New Zealand Herald*, 22 July 1873, p. 2.

20   Editorial, *Evening Post* (Wellington), 25 July 1873, p. 2.

21   Editorial, *Otago Daily Times*, 15 August 1873, p. 2.

22   Tuakau correspondent, *New Zealand Herald*, 17 June 1873, p. 3.

23   A Friend, 'A hard case', *Thames Star*, 30 June 1874, p. 2. The identity of this personal friend is not known. In 1873/74 Grahamstown and Shortland merged to form the township of Thames.

24   Thames Correspondent, *Daily Southern Cross*, 14 August 1873, p. 3.

25   Mary A. Colclough, Letter to the editor, *Thames Advertiser*, 15 October 1873, p. 3.

26   See 'Plaint book 1871–1875', Thames District Court.

27   'Thames Tattle', *Thames Advertiser*, 8 April 1874, p. 3 (italics original).

28   'Board of education', *New Zealand Herald*, 17 April 1874, p. 3.

29   Advertisements, *New Zealand Herald*, 19 May 1874, p. 1.

30   An advertisement for her estate to be sold at the City Auction Mart, including her pianoforte, appeared in the *Thames Star*, 23 June 1874, p. 3.

31   Auckland Board of Education report, *Daily Southern Cross*, 29 May 1874, p. 3.

32   Editorial, *Auckland Star*, 13 June 1874, p. 2.

33   A Friend, 'A hard case', *Thames Star*, 30 June 1874, p. 2.

34   Ibid.

35   Ibid.

36   Mary A. Colclough, 'A hard case', *Thames Advertiser*, 4 July 1874, p. 3.

37   Joseph Saunders' response was published in the *Thames Advertiser*, 9 July 1874, p. 2.

38   'Special meeting, 27 August 1874', Auckland Board of Education Minute Books 1872–.

39   Mary A. Colclough, Letter to the editor, *Thames Advertiser*, 31 August 1874, p. 2. 'I do not love thee, Dr Fell/ The reason why I cannot tell' are lines from a nursery rhyme written in 1680 by satirical English poet Tom Brown.

40   Mary A. Colclough, 'Mrs Colclough's defence', *Thames Advertiser*, 2 September 1874, p. 3.

Chapter Seven: Educating the Women of Melbourne

1   Editorial, *Auckland Star*, 26 September 1874, p. 2; Editorial, *New Zealand Herald*, 21 November 1874, p. 2.

2   Victoria was the first state in Australia to pass (in 1869) an Act for the 'Protection and Management of Aboriginal Natives'. The Victoria Board for the Protection of Aborigines empowered the governor to order the removal of any Aboriginal child to a reformatory or industrial school. By 1877 about half of the Aboriginal population were living on reserves.

3   Editorial, *Herald* (Melbourne), 24 October 1874, p. 2.

4   Janice N. Brownfoot, 'Dugdale, Henrietta Augusta (1827–1918)', from the Australian Dictionary of Biography: http://adb.anu.edu.au/biography/dugdale-henrietta-augusta-3452/text5269

5   Gwyneth Dow, 'Higinbotham, George (1826–1892)', from the Australian Dictionary of Biography: http://adb.anu.edu.au/biography/higinbotham-george-3766/text5939

6   Ibid.

7   Association records are held in the State Library of Victoria, Melbourne. For a list of documents referred to, see the bibliography to this book.

8   See Advertisements, *Age* (Melbourne), 26 October 1874, p. 1, and *Argus* (Melbourne), 27 October 1874, p. 1.

9   Editorial, *Herald* (Melbourne), 27 October 1874, p. 2.

10 'Mrs Colclough at the Athenæum', *Argus*, 28 October 1874, p. 5.

11 Editorial, *Daily Telegraph* (Melbourne), 29 October 1874, p. 3.

12 Mary A. Colclough, 'Women's work', *Daily Telegraph*, 31 October 1874, p. 3.

13 A.H., Letter to the editor, *Daily Telegraph*, 31 October 1874, p. 3.

14 Editorial, *Age*, 31 October 1874, p. 4.

15 Ibid.

16 Anna D. McKenny, Letter to the editor, *Daily Telegraph*, 2 November 1874, p. 3.

17 B.A.H., Letter to the editor, *Daily Telegraph*, 2 November 1874, p. 3.

18 E.S.F., Letter to the editor, *Daily Telegraph*, 3 November 1874, p. 4.

19 Mary A. Colclough, Letter to the editor, *Daily Telegraph*, 3 November 1874, p. 3.

20 Editorial, *Gippsland Times*, 5 November 1874, p. 2.

21 Ibid.

22 A Country Sister, Letter to the editor, *Daily Telegraph*, 6 November 1874, p. 3.

23 Ibid.

24 Self Help, Letter to the editor, *Daily Telegraph*, 9 November 1874, p. 4.

25 Benedict, Letter to the editor, *Daily Telegraph*, 6 November 1874, p. 3; A Man, Letter to the editor, *Daily Telegraph*, 6 November 1874, p. 3; Woman and Wife, Letter to the editor, *Daily Telegraph*, 6 November 1874, p. 3.

26 Way-Side Pansy, Letter to the editor, *Daily Telegraph*, 12 November 1874, p. 3.

27 'The Man About Town', 'Polly Plum's notion', *Herald* (Melbourne), 29 October 1874, p. 3.

28 Mary A. Colclough, Letter to the editor, *Daily Telegraph*, 10 November 1874, p. 3.

29 Ibid. The title of her lecture tapped into a recurring theme in her writing and lectures. She maintained that men were avoiding marriage because they thought women wanted too much from their husbands in the way of finery and position, a stance on women's part brought about, Mary Ann claimed, by girls and young women being raised according to overrated notions of female etiquette.

30 Mary A. Colclough, 'Woman's wrongs', *Daily Telegraph*, 17 November 1874, p. 3.

31 'Mrs Colclough at the Athenæum', *Argus*, 20 November 1874, p. 6.

32 Notices to correspondents, *Daily Telegraph*, 21 November 1874, p. 3; 'Mrs Colclough at the Athenæum', *Argus*, 20 November 1874, p. 6. See also 'Mrs Colclough's lecture', *Daily Telegraph*, 19 November 1874, p. 3.

33 Editorial, *Australasian*, 21 November 1874, p. 658.

34 Editorial, *Herald* (Melbourne), 7 December 1874, p. 2.

35 Mary A. Colclough, 'Women and their mission', *Herald*, 10 December 1874, p. 2.

36 Editorial, *Herald*, 10 December 1874, p. 2.

37 Mary A. Colclough, 'A needlewoman's home: To the editor', *Argus*, 15 December 1874, p. 10. See also Editorial, *Argus*, 31 December 1874, pp. 4–5.

38 'Men's wrongs', *Argus*, 19 December 1874, p. 4.

Chapter Eight: Model Lodging House for Women

1 Mary A. Colclough, 'Needlewoman's home', *Daily Telegraph* (Melbourne), 6 January 1875, p. 3.

2 The position went to the only other applicant, Miss Lucy F. Bain, who had been overseeing the infant department in addition to teaching her own class for some time (see *Southland Times*, 29 January 1875, p. 2, and 1 February 1875, p. 2).

3 Editorial, *Ballarat Star*, 7 January 1875, p. 2.

4 Editorial, *Daily Telegraph*, 8 January 1875, p. 2; 'A real woman's wrong', *Herald* (Melbourne), 11 January 1875, p. 2.

5 Mary A. Colclough, 'An appeal to the ladies of Victoria', *Argus* (Melbourne), 15 January 1875, p. 6.

6 Ibid.

7 Editorial, *Argus*, 16 January 1875, p. 7.

8 Ibid.

9 Mary A. Colclough, 'Working women's home', *Argus*, 19 January 1875, p. 6.

10 L.J. a'Beckett, 'Is a working women's home needed?' *Argus*, 20 January 1875, p. 6.

11 Editorial, *Argus*, 21 January 1875, p. 4.

12 Mary A. Colclough, Letter to the editor, *Argus*, 21 January 1875, p. 6.

13 Editorial, *Argus*, 21 January 1875, p. 4.

14 The governesses at the Melbourne Home, Letter to the editor, *Argus*, 8 February 1875, p. 6.

15 Mary A. Colclough, 'Melbourne Home: Letter to the editor', *Argus*, 10 February 1875, p. 6.

16 Editorial, *Queenslander*, 6 February 1875, p. 4.

17 'Woman's rights', *South Australian Register*, 22 February 1875, p. 7.

18 Mary A. Colclough, 'Servants: To the editor', *Argus*, 29 January 1875, p. 6; the comments in the Sydney *Mail* and the Melbourne *Weekly Times* were subsequently cited in the *Daily Southern Cross* on 22 February 1875, p. 2, and 3 March 1875, p. 2 respectively.

19 Mary A. Colclough, 'Melbourne Home: Letter to the editor', *Argus*, 10 February 1875, p. 6.

20 John Sloe, 'Melbourne Home: Letter to the editor', *Argus*, 11 February 1875, p. 6.

21 Mary A. Colclough, 'Interested benevolence: Letter to the editor', *Argus*, 12 February 1875, p. 6.

22 Mary A. Colclough, 'Lodging-house for women: Letter to the editor', *Daily Telegraph*, 11 March 1875, p. 3.

23 Editorial, *Daily Telegraph*, 12 March 1875, p. 2.

24 Mary A. Colclough, 'Model lodging house for women', *Ballarat Star*, 17 March 1875, p. 2.

25 Ibid.; Editorial, *Ballarat Star*, 19 March 1875, p. 2.

26 Mary A. Colclough, 'Destitute ladies', *Argus*, 22 March 1875, p. 7.

27 Excerpt from the *Australasian* cited in *Thames Star*, 14 April 1875, p. 2.; Melbourne correspondent, *Otago Witness*, 17 April 1875, p. 6.; Editorial, *Argus*, 23 March 1875, p. 4; Editorial, *Argus*, 24 March 1875, p. 5.

28 Mary A. Colclough, Letter to the editor, *Argus*, 24 March 1875, p. 7.

29 'Woman', *Herald* (Melbourne), 29 March 1875, p. 2; One Who Believes in Disinterested Philanthropy, Letter to the editor, *Age* (Melbourne), 29 March 1875, p. 4.

30 Mary A. Colclough, 'A letter from Melbourne', *Thames Star*, 13 May 1875, p. 2.

31 Mary Ann Colclough quoted in Editorial, *Thames Advertiser*, 20 April 1875, p. 4.

32 R. Norris, 'Deakin, Alfred (1856–1919)', in the Australian Dictionary of Biography: adb.anu.edu.au/biography/deakin-alfred-5927. See also 'Eclectic Association of Victoria annual report 1875', and 'Eclectic Association of Victoria twentieth annual report, 1 May 1887', in *Eclectic Association of Victoria, Association and Institution pamphlets* (vol. 47, Melbourne: State Library of Victoria).

33 Mary A. Colclough, Letter to the editor, *Daily Telegraph*, 11 August 1875, p. 4.

34 Mary A. Colclough, Letter to the editor, *Herald*, 12 August 1875, p. 2.

35 Ibid.

36 L.J. a'Beckett, 'A cookery class at the Melbourne Home: Letter to the editor', *Argus*, 9 September 1875, p. 6; Editorial, *Argus*, 10 September 1875, p. 5.

37 M.H. Spielmann, 'The history of "Punch"': www. aolib.com/ reader_23881_117.htm. For a definition of 'curtain lecture', see www.worldwidewords.org/weirdwords/ww-curl.htm

38 Extract from the *Coromandel Mail* reprinted in *Thames Advertiser*, 28 September 1875, p. 3.

39 Amusements, *Argus*, 17 August 1875, p. 8. The advertisement for her services was repeated with variations several times over the following months; 'The town', *Leader* (Melbourne), 4 September 1875, p. 13; 'Amusements', *Argus*, 15 September 1875, p. 8.

40 Mary A. Colclough, Letter to the editor, *Argus*, 30 September 1875, p. 10.

41 Editorial, *Argus*, 1 October 1875, p. 4; 'Mrs Colclough's home', *Herald* (Melbourne), 4 October 1875, p. 2.

42 Mary A. Colclough, 'Industrial schools and state paupers: Letter to the editor', *Argus*, 26 October 1875, p. 9.

43 Amusements, *Record and Emerald Hill and Sandridge Advertiser* (*Record*) (Victoria), 1 October 1875, p. 2; 'Sandridge Borough Council', *Record*, 3 December 1875, p. 3; Amusements, *Argus*, 6 December 1875, p. 8. It is not known whether this benefit concert subsequently took place.

44 Editorial, *Argus*, 22 December 1875, p. 5.

45 Editorial, *Daily Southern Cross*, 12 January 1876, p. 2.

46 Editorial, *Waikato Times*, 15 January 1876, p. 2; 'The fate of a blue stocking', *Wanganui Chronicle*, 29 January 1876, p. 2.

47 'The fate of a blue stocking', ibid., p. 2.

48 Atticus, 'Under the verandah', *Leader* (Melbourne), 19 February 1876, p. 18.

49 Mary A. Colclough, 'Mrs. Colclough's thanks: Letter to the editor', *Argus*, 4 January 1876, p. 7.

50 Mary A. Colclough, 'Letter to Secretary Young Women's Association of Christian Workers', reprinted in *Argus*, 11 January 1876, p. 10.

Chapter Nine: A Woman of Neither Means Nor Leisure

1 Mary A. Colclough, Letter to the editor, *Argus*, 22 February 1876, p. 10.

2 Editorial, *Auckland Star*, 13 March 1876, p. 2; 'The frivolities of womankind', *Waikato Times*, 18 March 1876, p. 2; T.B. Hannaford, Letter to the editor, *Daily Southern Cross*, 18 March 1876, p. 3.

3 The *North Canterbury News* article was cited in an editorial in the *Daily Southern Cross*, 12 April 1876, p. 2.

4 Editorial, *Daily Southern Cross*, 25 April 1876, p. 2.

5 Letter from Louisa Kiddell to the superintendent, 25 April 1876, written from Rangiora (Inwards correspondence to the Provincial Secretary, 1788/1876 Louisa Kiddell, Box CP174b, Archives New Zealand, Christchurch Branch).

6 Mary A. Colclough, Letter to the editor, *New Zealand Herald*, 28 October 1876, p. 6.

7 Ibid.

8 Editorial, *Daily Southern Cross*, 31 October 1876, p. 2.

9 'One Used to the Work of Training for Certificates, and Who Would Feign Help in That Way Other Ladies of Auckland Who Wish to Work Under Government', Letter to the editor, *New Zealand Herald*, 4 November 1876, p. 7. A letter very similar in content to this one had appeared in the *Daily Southern Cross* the previous day.

10 It is not known whether her salary was subsequently adjusted.

11 Rangiora, Letter to the editor, *Press* (Christchurch), 13 November 1876, p. 3.

12 S.S. Stothard, Letter to the editor, *Auckland Star*, 21 November 1876, p. 4.

13 See 'The Servants' Home' and 'Woman's choice of employment', *Otago Witness*, 28 October 1876, pp. 7, 19.

14 Mary A. Colclough, Letter to the editor, *Otago Witness*, 18 November 1876, p. 19.

15 Ibid.

16 Frances Shayle George, Letter to the editor, *New Zealand Herald*, 14 April 1877, p. 1.

17 Ibid.

18 'No. 1, Mr Mahoney to the chair of the gaol commissioners, Auckland, the Hon. F. Whitaker', *Appendices to the Journal of the House of Representatives*, 1877, Session I, H-30, p. 1.

19 M.A.C. (Mary A. Colclough), 'Mrs. Colclough on female prisoners in Auckland: To the editor', *New Zealand Herald*, 6 July 1877, p. 3.

20 Enclosure 1 in 'No. 1, Mr Mahoney to the chair of the gaol commissioners', *Appendices to the Journal of the House of Representatives*, 1877, Session I, H-30, p. 4.

21 Inspector's report, Rangiora District School, *Press*, 28 January 1878, p. 3.

22 'A legislative blunder', *Manawatu Herald*, 11 November 1879, p. 2.

23 'Banquet to J.B. Whyte, Esq., M.H.R., at Cambridge', *Waikato Times*, 9 October 1880, p. 2. Whyte's local newspaper carried a brief article on Dr Mary Walker of Baltimore, who was arrested for wearing man's clothing. Apart from a description of her attire, no other detail was provided. See *Waikato Times*, 4 December 1873, p. 2.

24 'Board of health, medical officer's report', *Star* (Christchurch), 21 December 1880, p. 4.

25 'Report from board of health', *Star*, 18 January 1881, p. 3; *Medical Officer of Health Annual Report for the Year 1881, Christchurch Local Board of Health*, reprinted in *Star*, 28 February 1882, p. 4.

26 Papanui District School Committee minute book, 7 June 1881 (supplied by Colin McGeorge, Education Department, University of Canterbury).

27 Countess Kate, 'Our Christchurch letter', *New Zealand Observer* (Auckland), 13 May 1882, p. 136.

28 Undated letter from Mary A. Colclough to the editor, *Evening Star* (private family collection).

29 Ibid.

30 Ibid.

31 Papanui District School Committee minute book, meeting held 30 August 1882 (supplied by Colin McGeorge, Education Department, University of Canterbury).

32 Papanui District School Committee minute book, meeting held 25 October 1882 (supplied by Colin McGeorge, Education Department, University of Canterbury).

33 Papanui District School Committee minute book, meeting held 27 August 1883, (supplied by Colin McGeorge, Education Department, University of Canterbury).

34 The editor of the *New Zealand Herald* mentioned the shock to her nervous system in his brief comment on her death. See Editorial, *New Zealand Herald*, 10 March 1885, p. 5.

35 Ibid.

36 'Random shots' column, *Auckland Star*, 14 March 1885, p. 4.

Epilogue: A Chequered Life

1   Polly Plum, 'Examinations in ladies' schools', *Daily Southern Cross* (Auckland), 23 January 1871, p. 3; Polly Plum, 'Childhood', *Daily Southern Cross*, 2 September 1869, p. 4.

2   See letter written by Ellen Ellis under the pen name 'A Woman', *New Zealand Herald*, 27 October 1870, p. 3. See also Judith Elphick, 'What's wrong with Emma? The feminist debate in colonial Auckland', *New Zealand Journal of History*, vol. 9, no. 2, 1975, pp. 126–41.

3   'The old and new woman', *Poverty Bay Herald*, 8 May 1899, p. 4.

Bibliography

Primary sources

I   Unpublished official papers

II   Interviews, private correspondence and information from descendants

III   Miscellaneous manuscripts and collections

IV   Published official papers and legislation

V   Contemporary newspapers and periodicals

VI   Contemporary books, pamphlets and articles

Secondary sources

VII Books and articles

VIII Theses, research essays and unpublished papers

IX   Internet sources

PRIMARY SOURCES

I Unpublished official papers

Archives New Zealand, Auckland Branch

Auckland Education Board Minute Books, December 1857–September 1858, 1872–

Auckland Provincial Hospital Casebook, 1859–79: 'Annual report of the Auckland Provincial Hospital, return of deaths, 1867'

Auckland Provincial Hospital Register of Admission and Discharge 1859–69: 'Auckland Provincial Hospital admission and discharge book, 1867'

Thames District Court: 'Plaint book 1871–1875'

Archives New Zealand, Christchurch Branch

Canterbury Education Board Financial Records: Teachers' salary books for 1878, 1879–80, 1881–83, 1884–86

Canterbury Education Board: Minute books for January 1881–December 1885

Inwards Correspondence to the Provincial Secretary, 1788/1876: Louisa Keddell, Box CP174b

Public Records Office, London

English Census, Parish of St James, Clerkenwell, County of Middlesex, for 1841 and 1851

Register of births, marriages and deaths of passengers at sea for 1854–59 (BT 158/Piece 1/ Folio 74 No. 407)

St James, Clerkenwell, County of Middlesex: Register of baptisms for 1785–1812, 1835–38

St James, Clerkenwell, County of Middlesex: Register of burials for 1798–1810, 1813–18, 1834–43

St James, Pentonville, County of Middlesex: Baptisms and burials during 1798–1810

St James, Pentonville, County of Middlesex: Burials during 1829–37, 1828–36, 1837–48, 1848–55

St James, Pentonville, County of Middlesex: Register of baptisms for 1813–22, 1823–31, 1848–64

Public Records Office, Victoria

Prahran rate books for 1856–58, 1859, 1860

Town of Fitzroy rate book for 1874–75

II *Interviews, private correspondence and information from descendants*

'A letter from Canterbury', undated letter from Mary A. Colclough to editor of the *Evening Post* (private family papers)

Certified copy of death certificate, Mary Ann Colclough, 7 March 1885 (supplied by descendants)

Certified copy of death certificate, Thomas Colclough, 29 July 1867 (supplied by descendants)

Family tree of Colclough family (private family papers)

'From English, Australian and New Zealand papers by Mrs Hannon Wilson' (private family papers)

Interviews with Mary Graham (great grand-daughter), Patricia McKenzie (great grand-daughter) and Sue McTaggart (great grand-daughter), Christchurch, August 1998

Letter from Arthur Bennett to Mary Louise Colclough, 8 May 1877 (private family papers)

Letter from Laura Bunting to Mrs (Mary Louise) Wilson, 15 January 1926 (private family papers)

Letter from Henry Taylor, Education Office, to Mrs Colclough, 27 October 1865 (private
    family papers)

Minute books for Papanui District School Committee, miscellaneous dates 1881–83
    (photocopy supplied by Colin McGeorge, Education Department, University of
    Canterbury)

Miscellaneous letters from Leslie Norman to Mary Louise Colclough and to Mrs
    Colclough, 1876–80 (private family papers)

Personnel files, New Zealand Defence Force, Captain William Caesar Sarsfield Colclough
    (supplied by descendants)

Register of birth, Mary Louise Colclough, 1 November 1862 (supplied by descendants)

Register of death, Mary Ann Colclough, 7 March 1885 (supplied by descendants)

Register of death, Thomas Colclough, 29 July 1867 (supplied by descendants)

Register of marriage, Mary A. Barnes and Thomas Caesar Colclough, 9 May 1861
    (supplied by descendants)

Register of marriage, Mary Louise Colclough and George Hannon Wilson, 3 January 1887,
    Wellington (supplied by descendants)

III Miscellaneous manuscripts and collections

Auckland Research Centre, Auckland City Library
'Auckland Area Passenger Vessels, 1838–1885'
'Comber Index Shipping to New Zealand, 1839–1889'

Documentary Research Centre, Canterbury Museum
A.E. Preece photograph albums

Queen's College Archives, London
Address books
Applications for certificates
Curriculum for 1848–93
Fees books
Index of certificates
Register of certificates for 1847–53
Register of examinations for 1848–53
Register of non-compounders for 1851–56
Registers of non-compounders for 1851–57
Queen's College note books for 1851–52, 1853–56

State Library of Victoria, Melbourne
'Eclectic Association of Victoria Twentieth Annual Report, 1 May 1887'
'Eclectic Association of Victoria Valedictory Report, 5 April 1894'
'Eclectic Association of Victoria, Association and Institution Pamphlets', vol. 47
'Eclectic Association of Victoria, Association and Institution Annual Report 1875'

Turner, Henry Gyles: Miscellanea Literature II, no. 16: 'Dialogue on Woman's Rights, 10
December 1874' (m1656, Box 459/2)

Victoria University of Wellington Library, Wellington
The pamphlet collection of Sir Robert Stout, vol. 84: *Freethought: A Monthly Journal of
Free Thought, Spiritualism, Mesmerism, Clairvoyance and Occult Sciences*, vol. 1, no. 2,
March 1880.

IV *Published official papers and legislation*
Acts and Proceedings of the Auckland Provincial Council

Archives New Zealand, Auckland Branch
Annual report of the Auckland Provincial Hospital for 1867
Annual reports of the commissioners of education for the province of Auckland for 1858,
1859
Auckland Provincial Hospital 1867 admission and discharge book

Appendices to the Journals of the House of Representatives
Annual reports from Minister of Education for 1878, 1879, 1880, 1882, 1883
'Auckland No. 1 Report on the Auckland Provincial Lunatic Asylum, 1873: Reports on the
lunatic asylums in New Zealand'
'No. 1, Mr Mahoney to the Chair of the Gaol Commissioners, Auckland, the Hon. F.
Whitaker, 1877'
'Report of the Auckland Gaol Commissioners and Correspondence Thereon, 1877'
'Report of the Joint Committee on Lunatic Asylums, 1871'

Archives New Zealand, Christchurch Branch
Board of Education, District of Canterbury: Annual reports for November 1876 and
March 1877, 1878, 1879
Education Board of the District of North Canterbury: Annual reports for 1881, 1882

Auckland Research Centre, Auckland City Library
Commissioners of Education: Annual reports for 1859, 1860

Journals of the Auckland Provincial Council
Commissioners of Education for the Province of Auckland: Annual reports for 1865, 1866,
1867–68
'Report of the Auckland Board of Education, 1862'
'Report of the Auckland Board of Education, 1867'
'Report of the Auckland Board of Education, 1875'
'Report of the Inspector of Common Schools, 1869'
Reports by the inspector of schools for 1870, 1871, 1872, 1873, 1874

New Zealand Parliament
'New Zealand Parliamentary Debates (Hansard)', vol. 7, 23 June 1870, p. 72

Sir George Grey Special Collection, Auckland Libraries
Auckland Provincial Council: Records for 1853–75, NZMS 595, Session 9, Box 8

Votes and Proceedings of the Auckland Provincial Council
Commissioners of Education for the Province of Auckland: Annual reports for 1860, 1861, 1862

V Contemporary newspapers and periodicals

Newspapers
Age (Melbourne)
Argus (Melbourne)
Auckland Star
Australasian
Ballarat Star
Daily Southern Cross (Auckland)
Daily Telegraph (Melbourne)
Dominion (Wellington)
Evening Post (Wellington)
Evening Star (Auckland)
Gippsland Times
Grey River Argus
Herald (Melbourne)
Leader (Melbourne)
Manawatu Herald
New Zealand Herald
New Zealander
Otago Daily Times
Otago Witness
Poverty Bay Herald
Press (Christchurch)
Record and Emerald Hill and Sandridge Advertiser (Victoria)
Queenslander
South Australian Register
Southland Times
Star (Christchurch)
Thames Advertiser
Thames Guardian and Mining Record
Thames Star
The Times (London)

Waikato Times
Wanganui Chronicle
Weekly Argus (Melbourne)
Weekly News (Auckland)
Wellington Independent

Periodicals
Frederick's Post Office London directory for 1838
Kelly's Post Office London streets and commercial directories
Mitchell & Seffern's directories of the city and suburbs of Auckland for 1866–77
Sands and Kenny's Melbourne directories for 1858, 1859
Sands and McDougall's Melbourne and suburban directories for 1874, 1875, 1876
Stevens and Bartholomew's New Zealand directory for 1866–67
Tanner's Melbourne directory for 1859

VI *Contemporary books, pamphlets and articles*

Bathgate, Alexander, *Colonial Experiences, or Sketches of People and Places in the Province of Otago, New Zealand* (Glasgow: James Maclehose, 1874).

Becker, A., 'Journalism as a profession', in *The First College Open to Women: Queen's College, London. Memories and records of work done, 1848–1898*, ed. M.A. Tweed (London: Queen's College, 1898), 51–52.

Cross, D.S., *Rhymes without Reason: Hysterical, farcical, satirical* (printed for the proprietors of the Herald Office, Auckland, 1871).

Dixon, William Hepworth, *New America* (London: Hurst & Blackett, 1867).

Greg, William Rathbone, 'Why are women redundant?' in *Literary and Social Judgements* (London: N. Trubner & Co., 2nd edn, 1869), 280–316.

Jacobs, Henry, *Colonial Church Histories, New Zealand: Containing the dioceses of Auckland, Christchurch, Dunedin, Nelson, Waipu, Wellington and Melanesia* (London: Society for Promoting Christian Knowledge, 1887).

Maurice, F.D., and others, *Introductory Lectures Delivered at Queen's College, London* (London: John W. Packer, 1849).

Review of 'Alone in the World', *The Penny Journal*, 19 May 1866, 21.

The Author of 'The Half-Caste Wife' [Mary Ann Colclough], *Alone in the World: A tale of New Zealand* (Auckland: Mitchell & Seffern, 1866).

The Emigrant's Friend, or Authentic Guide to South Australia, including Sydney; Port Philip, or Australia Felix; Western Australia, or Swan River colony; New South Wales; Van Dieman's Land; and New Zealand (London: J. Allen & D. Francis, 1848).

Vogel, Sir Julius, *Anno Domini 2000, or, Woman's Destiny* (London: Hutchinson and Co., 1889).

Wood, Edward J., ed., *The History of Clerkenwell by the late William J. Pinks* (London: Charles Herbert, 2nd edn, 1881).

SECONDARY SOURCES

VII *Books and articles*

Anderson, Bonnie S., *Joyous Greetings! The first international women's movement* (New York: Oxford University Press, 2000).

Banks, Olive, *The Biographical Dictionary of British Feminists: Vol. 1, 1800–1930* (New York: New York University Press, 1985).

Biddington, Ralph, 'Eclectic Association: Victoria's first rationalists, 1866–1895', *Australian Rationalist*, vol. 51, no. 2, 2004, 35–44.

Bingham, P., Verlander, N.Q. and Cheal, M.J., 'John Snow, William Farr and the 1849 outbreak of cholera that affected London: A reworking of the data highlights the importance of the water supply', *Public Health*, vol. 118, 2004, 387–94.

Bolt, Christine, *The Women's Movements in the United States and Britain from the 1790s to the 1920s* (Amherst, MA: University of Massachusetts Press, 1993).

Bradbury, Bettina, 'From civil death to separate property: Changes in the legal rights of married women in nineteenth-century New Zealand', *New Zealand Journal of History*, vol. 19, no. 1, 1995, 40–66.

Brett, Henry, *White Wings: Founding of the provinces and old-time shipping* (Christchurch: Capper Press, vol. 2, 1976).

Burstyn, Joan N., *Victorian Education and the Ideal of Womanhood* (London: Croom Helm, 1980).

Butcher, A.G., *The Education System: A concise history of the New Zealand education system* (Auckland: National Printing Co., 1932).

Caughey, Angela, *Pioneer Families: The settlers of nineteenth-century New Zealand* (Auckland: David Bateman, 1994).

Centennial Celebrations: Spreydon School, 1872–1972 (Christchurch: Spreydon School Centennial Committee, 1972).

Colebrook, Vera, *Ellen: A biography* (Dublin: The Women's Press, 1980).

Coleman, Jenny, 'Echoes from the past: Mary Colclough and the "holy" cause of women's rights, 1868–1874', in *Women's Studies Association Conference Papers 1993* (Auckland: Women's Studies Association NZ, 1994), 25–38.

_____ 'For the ladies: Knowing women through the pages of the *Weekly News*, 1868–1872', *Women's Studies Association Conference Papers 2001* (Christchurch: Women's Studies Association NZ, 2002), 41–48.

_____ 'Missionaries, monstrosities or modern female fanatics? (Re)presenting the identities of nineteenth-century advocates of women's rights', *Australasian Victorian Studies Journal*, vol. 9, 2003, 40–51.

_____ Like mother, like daughter? Women journalists and generational feminism in New Zealand', *Women's Studies Association Conference Papers 2003* (Palmerston North: Women's Studies Association NZ, 2004), 25–30.

_____ 'Serendipitous scholarship: Identifying the author of *Alone in the World* (1866)', *The Turnbull Library Record*, vol. 37, 2004, 59–67.

_____ 'Writing for the ladies: Women journalists in the nineteenth and early twentieth century New Zealand', *Communication Journal of New Zealand*, vol. 8, no. 2, 2007, 47–58.

_____ 'Apprehending possibilities: Tracing the emergence of feminist consciousness in nineteenth-century New Zealand', *Women's Studies International Forum*, vol. 31, 2008, 464–73.

_____ 'Social hierarchies and class sensibilities: A comparative analysis of vocabularies of domestic service in mid-Victorian England and New Zealand', in *Victorian Vocabularies: Refereed proceedings of the 2012 Australasian Victorian Studies Association Conference*, ed. Jessica Gildersleeve (Sydney: Macquarie Lighthouse E-book Publishing, 2013), 34–63.

Cosh, Mary, *The Squares of Islington: Part I: Finsbury and Clerkenwell* (London: Islington Archaeology and History Society, 1990).

_____ *An Historical Walk through Barnsbury* (London: Islington Archaeology and History Society, 2nd edn, 2001).

Cott, Nancy F., *The Grounding of Modern Feminism* (New Haven, CT: Yale University Press, 1987).

Crow, Duncan, *The Victorian Woman* (London: George Allen & Unwin, 1971).

Dalziel, Raewyn, *Julius Vogel: Business politician* (Auckland: Auckland University Press, 1986).

Day, Patrick, *The Making of the New Zealand Press: A study of the organisational and political concerns of New Zealand newspaper controllers, 1840–1880* (Wellington: Victoria University Press, 1990).

Drummond, Alison, ed., *The Thames Journals of Vicesimus Lush 1868–82* (Christchurch: Pegasus, 1975).

Elphick, Judith, 'What's wrong with Emma? The feminist debate in colonial Auckland', *New Zealand Journal of History*, vol. 9, no. 2, 1975, 126–41.

Evans, E.A. 'Polly Plum's battle for women', *New Zealand Herald*, 17 September 1975, page unknown.

Evans, Richard, *The Feminists: Women's emancipation movements in Europe, America and Australia, 1840–1920* (London: Croom Helm, 1977).

Grylls, Rosalie Glynn, *Queen's College 1848–1948* (London: George Routledge & Sons, 1948).

Gunby, David, *Rangiora High School 1884–1984: A centennial history* (Christchurch: Caxton, 1984).

Hammerton, A.J., *Emigrant Gentlewomen: Genteel poverty and female emigration, 1830–1914* (London: Croom Helm, 1979).

Hawkins, D.N., *Rangiora Borough School 1873–1973* (Rangiora: Wilson Bros., 1973).

_____ *Rangiora: The passing years and people in a Canterbury country town* (Rangiora: Rangiora Borough Council, 1983).

Hays, R.B., ed., *Thames: The first 100 years* (Thames: Office of the Thames 'Star', 1968).

J.W.B., *The Story of the Governesses Benevolent Institution* (Southwick: Grange Press, 1962).

Kaye, Elaine, *A History of Queen's College, London, 1848–1972* (London: Chatto & Windus, 1972).

Killip, Rosemary, *To Find a Fortune: Women of the Thames goldfield, 1867–1893* (Wellington: Women's Studies, Victoria University of Wellington, 1995).

Levine, Phillipa, *Victorian Feminism 1850–1900* (London: Hutchinson, 1987).

Macdonald, Charlotte, *A Woman of Good Character: Single women as immigrant settlers in nineteenth-century New Zealand* (Wellington: Allen & Unwin, 1990).

_____ *The Vote, the Pill and the Demon Drink: A history of feminist writing in New Zealand, 1869–1993* (Wellington: Bridget Williams Books, 1993).

Mackey, Rev. John, *The Passing of the New Zealand Education Act, 1877: The genesis of a state school system in the nineteenth century* (Ann Arbor, MI: University Microfilms International, 1963).

Malone, Judith, 'Colclough, Mary Ann, 1836–1885', in *The Book of New Zealand Women/ Ko kui ma te kaupapa*, eds Charlotte Macdonald, Merimeri Penfold & Bridget Williams (Wellington: Bridget Williams Books, 1991), 142–45.

_____ 'Colclough, Mary Ann 1836–1885', in *The Dictionary of New Zealand Biography: Vol. 2, 1870–1900*, ed. Claudia Orange (Wellington: Bridget Williams Books/ Department of Internal Affairs, 1993), 92–93.

McLintock, A.H., 'Colclough, Mary Ann, "Polly Plum" (1836–1885)', in *An Encyclopaedia of New Zealand*, ed. A.H. McLintock (Wellington: R.W. Owen, Government Printer, vol. 1, 1996), 376–77.

Norris, R., 'Deakin, Alfred (1856–1919)', in *Australian Dictionary of Biography: Vol. 8: 1891–1939, C1–Gib.*, eds Bede Nairn and Geoffrey Searle (Melbourne: Melbourne University Press, 1981), 248–56.

'Ode to Polly Plum', *Auckland Waikato Historical Journal*, vol. 62, April, 1993, 9–10.

O'Neill, L.P., ed., *Thames Borough Centenary 1873–1973* (Thames: Thames Star, 1973).

Pyle, Andrew, ed., *The Subjection of Women: Contemporary responses to John Stuart Mill* (Bristol: Thoemmes Press, 1995).

Rendall, Jane, *The Origins of Modern Feminism: Women in Britain, France, and the United States, 1780–1860* (New York: Schocken Books, 1984).

Saunders, David, ed., *Historical Buildings of Victoria* (Melbourne: The Jacaranda Press/The National Trust of Australia, 1966).

Scott, Dorothy, *The Halfway House to Infidelity: A history of the Melbourne Unitarian Church 1853–1973* (Melbourne: The Unitarian Fellowship of Australia and the Melbourne Unitarian Peace Memorial Church, 1890).

Searle, Geoffrey, 'Turner, Martha (1839–1915)', in the Australian Dictionary of Biography: adb.anu.edu.au/biography/turner-martha-4762

Soar, Edna, *History of the Anglican Church of St. Peter's, Onehunga* (Auckland: Church Army Press, 1948).

Sturm, Terry, ed., *Oxford History of New Zealand Literature in English* (Auckland: Oxford University Press, 2nd edn, 1998).

Swaine, Shurlee, 'Mrs Hughes and the "deserving poor"', in *Double Time: Women in Victoria – 150 years*, eds Marilyn Lake and Farley Kelly (Melbourne: Penguin, 1985), 126–31.

Tames, Richard, *Clerkenwell and Finsbury Past* (London: Historical Publications, 1999).

Taylor, Barbara, *Eve and the New Jerusalem: Socialism and feminism in the nineteenth century* (New York: Pantheon Books, 1983).

The Heritage of Victoria: The illustrated register of the national estate (South Melbourne: Macmillan/Australian Heritage Commission, 1983).

Ward, Ian, and McGlynn, Clare, 'Women, law and John Stuart Mill', *Women's History Review*, vol. 25, no. 2, 2016, 227–53.

Wilson, Mary Louise, 'Mother's vote: Has it altered the trend of legislation?', *New Zealand Free Lance*, 11 November 1936, 23.

Wood, Ann D., 'The "scribbling women" and Fanny Fern: Why women wrote', *American Quarterly*, vol. 23, no. 1, 1971, 3–24.

VIII *Theses, research essays and unpublished papers*

Coleman, Jenny, '"Philosophers in petticoats": A feminist analysis of the discursive practices of Mary Taylor, Mary Colclough and Ellen Ellis as contributors to the debate on the "woman question" in New Zealand between 1845–1885', PhD thesis, Feminist Studies Department, University of Canterbury, Christchurch, 1996.

_____ 'Our Own Little Stray Strap of a Modern Female Fanatic: Nineteenth century Australian and New Zealand media representations of women's rights advocates', Research paper presented at the Australian Women's Studies Association Conference, University of South Australia, Adelaide, 18 April 1998.

_____ 'Intersections between women's rights and citizenship in Auckland and Melbourne in the 1870s', Research paper presented at the International Federation of Research in Women's History Conference, University of Melbourne, Melbourne, 2 July 1998.

_____ 'Philanthropy of "Quite a Different Stamp": Boundaries and exclusions in the female philanthropic community in mid-1870s Melbourne', Research paper presented at the Communities of Women Historical Perspectives Conference, University of Otago, Dunedin, 1 July 2000.

Elphick, Judith, 'Auckland 1870–1874: A social portrait', Master's thesis, Auckland University, Auckland, 1974.

Farley, Kelly, 'The "Woman Question" in Melbourne 1880–1914', PhD thesis, Faculty of Education, Monash University, Victoria, 1982.

Killip, Rosemary, 'Women's lives on the Thames goldfields 1867–1889', Master's research essay, University of Auckland, Auckland, 1989.

Turner, G.M.D., 'The history of Rangiora', Master's thesis, Canterbury University College, University of New Zealand, Christchurch, 1921.

IX *Internet sources*

Brett, Michael, 'Brett, Henry', from the Dictionary of New Zealand Biography: www.TeAra. govt.nz/en/biographies/2b39/brett-henry

Brownfoot, Janice N., 'Dugdale, Henrietta Augusta (1827–1918)', from the Australian Dictionary of Biography: http://adb.anu.edu.au/biography/dugdale-henrietta-augusta-3452/text5269

Dow, Gwyneth, 'Higinbotham, George (1826–1892)', in the Australian Dictionary of Biography: http://adb.anu.edu.au/biography/higinbotham-george-3766

Fry, Ruth, 'Stothard, Sarah Sophia', in the Dictionary of New Zealand Biography: www. TeAra.govt.nz/en/biographies/1s25/stothard-sarah-sophia

Smith, F.B., 'Southwell, Charles', in the Dictionary of New Zealand Biography: www.TeAra. govt.nz/en/biographies/1s17/southwell-charles

Spielmann, M.H, 'The history of "Punch"': //www. aolib.com/ reader_23881_117.htm

Index

Roman numerals refer to pages of photographs and other images.
M.A.C. is Mary Ann Colclough.